# Spotlight
on
Teaching Band

MENC
The National Association for Music Education

MENC would like to thank the MEA state editors throughout the country,
who facilitate the distribution
of essential information to MENC members in their states.

Copyright © 2001 by MENC: The National Association for Music Education
1806 Robert Fulton Drive
Reston, VA 20191-4348
Printed in the United States of America
ISBN 1-56545-137-6

Contents

The Spotlight series comprises articles that have appeared in magazines of MENC state affiliates over the past several years. The purpose of the series is to broaden the audience for the valuable work that is being done by music educators across the country. Were it not for the dedication of the state editors and article authors, this series would not be possible. MENC would like to thank these individuals for their contributions and to encourage others to share their expertise through MEA and MENC publications.

Introduction

The articles in *Spotlight on Teaching Band* cover a broad range of topics of interest to school band directors. The book begins with a section titled "Developing the Musician." This section covers fundamental issues such as instrument selection, balance and intonation, performance practice, and practice and rehearsal techniques— the building blocks of strong bands and strong musicians.

Authors of articles in the next section, "Repertoire," offer views on criteria to use when choosing music for school bands to perform. In addition, specific suggestions are given concerning music and composers. The articles in the "Cross-Curricular Projects" section explore activities and ideas for helping music educators work with teachers of other subjects to provide students with well-rounded and meaningful learning experiences. The section on "Conducting" offers practical suggestions, and the next section, "Fine-Tuning" provides articles that offer a fresh outlook on a variety of subjects.

The section on "Adjudication and Competition" includes an article that is full of valuable tips for bands that attend adjudicated events. Also included are articles that help band directors communicate to parents the benefits of competition participation and explanations of rating systems. The articles on "Marching and Pep Bands" provide concrete advice, and the section "Promoting the Music Program" includes ideas that will help bands gain public support— a necessity for success in school music.

This book's articles were contributed by music educators nationwide. It is hoped that this text and this series will inspire further sharing among music educators in venues such as MENC journals, network communities, and division and national conferences. Such communication will result in increased fulfillment in the professional lives of music educators and in long-lasting benefits for music students.

Section 1

 # Developing the Musician

Concepts such as instrument selection, warm-ups, sight-reading, rhythm reading, intonation, and musicality lay the foundation for any successful band program. The authors in this section explore ideas and tips on these building blocks.

 Section 1

Developing the Musician

Rehearsal Strategies and Techniques
by Judd Aetzel

My intent in preparing this is to share with you some thoughts, techniques and strategies that I have used in my daily band rehearsals. For the most part, they have been very effective in achieving the quality of sound that I am looking for, and I hope that you will find them useful.

Breathing
Breathing is the backbone of good tone production/intonation. Some major ideas are as follows: "Breathe DOWN ... not, IN," "Take a YAWN breath," "Take in 20 seconds' worth of air," "Take in four measures' worth of air," and "Inflate."

Warm-Ups
I spend a minimum of 10 to 15 minutes each rehearsal warming up, and each exercise is preceded by one of the above listed "breathing" concepts. Warm-ups consist of:

1. Humming unison scales, scale patterns, and chords. This warms up the ears and also gives an opportunity to develop a good blend and balance. Remind the band there are to be no solos. No individual should stick out. They can transfer this to their horn blowing.
2. Brass on mouthpieces. Your brass should be able to accurately play not only the warm-up drills on their mouthpieces, but also any difficult passages from your music.
3. I encourage my flutes to play overtones at their liberty, as the rest of the band is sustaining long tones
4. If at all possible, relate your warm-up routine to the pieces you will be rehearsing that day. It makes little sense to warm up for 10 to 15 minutes in the key of B-flat, and then begin your rehearsal with a tune in A-flat.

5. Consider incorporating the following into your daily warm-up routine: breathing exercises, long tones, slurred intervals, tonguing and rhythm patterns, and tuning to a concert F or B-flat. I have found John Paynter's chordal sheet to be very effective in achieving a beautiful tone, good blend, and balance, as well as an excellent source for tuning.
6. Dynamic Headroom—This is the term I use to describe the ability of the band to crescendo and decrescendo without allowing the tone quality, the balance, the blend, and the intonation to change or be affected. Using a concert F (from John Paynter's sheet), begin a gradual crescendo with two goals in mind:
   a) Keep the quality of sound from changing. Only play as loud as you can keep the sound from changing.
   b) Control the pitch from changing.

Next, work to achieve the same goals as you have the band or individual section or individual player decrescendo.

Reseating Your Band
As often as possible, I try to reseat the band into various configurations. This one technique seems to accomplish the most in terms of:

1. developing uniformity of unison lines
2. developing the students' *musical sensitivity* to each other and the music
3. alerting me to problem areas that otherwise might have been overlooked.

Seating Arrangements
If possible, set your room up before the rehearsal and draw a diagram of the seating on the board.

1. In stacked sections, such as clarinets, rotate the parts so the first players are not always in front.
2. Try seating your solo and soli voices together

for several rehearsals. They will begin to match their tones, develop a good sense of balance, and begin to adjust their pitch to each other.

3. Try grouping your band by voicings. Seat all of the bass, baritone, tenor, alto, and soprano voices together.

4. Even try rotating your entire band. When was the last time your tubas were in the front and your flutes were in the back?

Musical Concepts

Does your *daily* rehearsal contain the following elements of musicality:

- Do you warm up musically?
- Do you conduct the music or direct the beat?
- Do you rehearse a chorale or a chorale-like piece?
- Do you have a predetermined concept of what the music is trying to say? Does your band?
- Do you sight-read often?
- Do you reseat your band?

Warming Up Musically

A general rule is, "Never high, never low … never fast, never slow … never loud, never soft."

1. Breathing aerobics—"Push the air through the floor."

2. Thinking a concert F, fill the instrument with *hot, soggy breath only.*
   a) Fill the instrument with *hot, soggy breath (air).*
   b) Let the *hot, soggy air* evolve into a concert F. Hot, Soggy Air Flow———Tone (concert F)

3. Play a descending F chromatic scale.
   a) The *release* of each tone should extend beyond the *beginning* of the new tone.
   b) Produce tone "between" the notes as well as through each note.
   c) Add articulations.

Conducting Musically

A lot of rehearsal time can be saved if you conduct

1. the breaths
2. the dynamics
3. the phrases
4. the musical intent.

What is the Music "Saying"?

1. Study the score thoroughly for musical content.
2. Listen to recordings.
   a) Study as many recordings of a piece as you can, including orchestral recordings.
   b) Play these recordings for your students.

Sight-Reading

Sight-reading once or twice a week on a consistent basis eventually develops the band beyond note and rhythm players to interpreters of music.

1. Begin with literature several difficulty levels below your performance literature and gradually increase the level of difficulty as your students become more and more confident.

2. Have separate *sight-reading* folders made up. This will save time when handing out music for sight-reading and collecting it.

3. Try to reserve the last 10 minutes of your rehearsal for sight-reading. Sight-reading at the beginning of the rehearsal seems to "throw off" the rest of the rehearsal.

Some General Comments

1. Isolate a section or individual player each day and have the band match the section or player for both tone quality and pitch.
2. Does your band like its music?
3. "Releases" followed by a rest should disappear into the rest.
4. Maintain the quality of sound as the dynamics change. *Expand* your tone on a crescendo.
5. On passages containing a succession of intervals, have the students *play forward* … not up and down.
6. Be *"emotional"* on the podium.
7. Bring in an extra pair of ears—a colleague or clinician—to rehearse your band.
8. Videotape your rehearsals and performances. Are you really conducting the music?
9. Wander through your band as they rehearse; you will hear things differently from what you hear on the podium.
10. Blow "through" the bar line, not to it.
11. Sing the part as you would like it to be played.
12. Don't wait until you stop rehearsing to make comments. Often times you can "coach" the band as it is rehearsing.
13. Does your literature fit your band? If they are struggling to play the notes, most likely they will not have a chance to play the music.
14. *Solo and Ensemble contest* is one of the best ways for your students to gain valuable experience and develop their musicianship. Encourage them to participate. The knowledge and experience gained will carry into your large group.
15. *Section rehearsals*—I try to have one or two section rehearsals two to three weeks prior to a major concert or festival. They are an hour long, and they provide an excellent opportunity to

develop and "fine-tune" the individual section's musicianship.

More General Comments

1. Have the kids shut their eyes as you walk around the band tapping several individuals on the head. Those players then have been selected to play badly out of tune as the band sustains a unison pitch. Following the release of the tone, ask the members who were not tapped, to identify those who were out of tune. It is interesting that every time this is done, someone is identified who was not supposed to be out of tune.

2. Play as many recordings as you can that demonstrate the kind of band sound you want.
3. Encourage your players to play on matched reeds, mouthpieces and instruments. And when purchasing instruments and equipment for your school, try to purchase matched makes and models, if at all possible.

Judd Aetzel is a teacher of band and orchestra at Bothell High School in Washington. This article originally appeared in the May 1999 issue of Washington's Voice. *Reprinted by permission.*

At the Bench
by Daron Anderson

Q: Can we repair it?
A: Yes!
Q: Is it worth it?
A: Well ... ?

Sometimes we technicians have to make difficult decisions as to whether an instrument is worth the time and effort to put it back into playing condition or if it should be donated to Lamps Unlimited. A good technician will never throw a quality instrument in the trash before it is time, and sometimes the better quality instruments have been found in other people's trash! Trust the opinion of your local professional repair technician. Tell the parents of your students to do the same. Most reputable repair shops will provide a free evaluation of an instrument, an estimate of what it will cost to put it in excellent playing condition, and an opinion on whether it is worth the expense. If the parents of your student want to buy their own instrument, tell them to consider some of the following:

- Is there a school instrument available to them? Most school districts provide the larger and most expensive instruments at no cost (including repair and preventive maintenance charges).
- Is the make and model of the instrument common to their local repair facility? There are a large number of cheaply made instruments, for which your local repair shop can't obtain replacement parts, making them "in effect" disposable.
- Sometimes spending the difference of $50 to $100 more to buy a good quality instrument is all it takes to avoid getting something between a musical instrument and a child's toy.

Daron Anderson is the chief repair technician of the Department of Defense Dependents' Schools Europe Musical Instrument Repair Facility in Wiesbaden, Germany. This article originally appeared in the Fall 1999 issue of Europe's EMEA Journal. *Reprinted by permission.*

Building Up Your Program
Richard A. Atwood

Do you ever feel you are not getting the number of students from your feeder school program that you want? Did you ever stop to think that maybe the answer to this question rests with you? Recruiting instrumental students from feeder schools is a big challenge. Your relationship to the feeder school music instructor is the key. Here are some suggestions that might prove successful.

Communicate. Involve your feeder music instructors in your planning activities so that they know what your groups are doing. By sharing your plans with them, you make them a part of the activity and increase your chances of gaining their help.

Invite the feeder school instructors to the band room for coffee and cookies after school is over and discuss ways in which you can be of service to them. It is hard for most teachers to pass up free food.

Visit the schools that feed into your school, and volunteer to help the instructors with their programs by supplying them with musicians to mentor the beginning players. Arrange to play at least one concert for the feeder school P.T.A. Take a small pep or honors band, not the entire group; usually the stages at these schools are not large enough to accommodate a full band. This is a good chance for your chamber ensembles to perform in front of an audience. Take pictures of your students and send them to the instructor at the feeder school they attended. When their classmates see these familiar faces, they may want to join your program also. Photos and programs from your concerts can spark students interest too. Have your students construct posters out of these items and then send them to the feeder schools.

If you cannot get into the feeder schools to recruit, try preparing a videotape of a concert or recording some of the activities of one of your classes. Be sure to include band members whom the feeder students would remember from the year before. Tape your rehearsal, adding your sales pitch at the end. You can get splendid results with this approach.

Invite your feeder school program to take part in your concert program. For bands, ask the upcoming members to participate in one marching show. Having members from both schools sit together and perform music that is written at a comfortable level for everyone is a good way to build enthusiasm. Even in the early part of the season, the feeder school band can stand in a block on the field while the high school band performs its march routine. Call it Band Appreciation Night; it will give the feeder school band the feeling they are part of something.

Attend all of the feeder school concerts and encourage your students to do the same. If parents and students see and recognize you at their performances, they will begin to understand that you do care about the students who will be coming into your program. Demonstrate a spirit of cooperation by exchanging guest conducting appearances with the director at the feeder school.

Establish a big brother and big sister program. Assign a high school band/string member to each feeder school member. The older students could write notes inviting their younger counterparts to high school concerts, etc. A note from a big brother/sister builds the family spirit that instrumental programs need. (Avoid pairing real brothers and sisters.)

The high school director who does not see his or her incoming students until the first day of class is in for a shock. You can be sure that the cheerleading sponsor and the coaches have been recruiting some of the same middle school students your band needs. If you do not promote your program, you will lose them. With good communication between instructors at all grade levels, your program will continue to grow.

Richard Atwood is the director of instrumental music at Killiam Hill Baptist Church and Christian School in Lilburn, Georgia. This article originally appeared in the Spring 1998 issue of Georgia Music News. *Reprinted by permission.*

Three Steps to Better Sight-Reading in Beginning Band

by Kenneth F. Beard

Yes, sight-reading can be improved, and it can be improved in beginning band. In fact, the best time to work on sight-reading is in beginning band. Students can sight-read from the first months of band, and when taught to expect it, they will regard it as a mental challenge to be enjoyed.

To become proficient at sight-reading, a beginning student must develop several tools. First, rhythm recognition and production must be very stable. Second, note recognition and fingering must be instantaneous. Finally, putting both of these together with tone production must be a "no-brainer" activity. In sight-reading, the more musicians have to think about any of the various activities involved, the less success they will achieve.

Before you start sight-reading with your beginning band, you must lay the foundation for a successful experience. To do this, you will develop a routine that will enable the largest number of students to become proficient at sight-reading. This routine will be used with every new piece that you work on at school and will be taught to the students for them to use at home in their daily practice. In essence you will be teaching students *how to practice* and make good use of their time.

There are three steps to learning a piece of music. Step one is to clap, count, and pat your foot (CCP). Ask the students to repeat (verbally) the three actions in step one until every student knows what to do. Develop the first action, patting the foot with a beat, by explaining that music has a strong feeling of a beat and that we quietly pat a foot on the beat and count numbers ("1-2-3-4") when the foot touches the ground. Be very careful to explain that everyone must count aloud: "Don't just listen to others around you count; *you* must count."

Begin with either whole notes or quarter notes and develop familiarity with quarter, half, and whole notes. On whole notes students will clap on one and hold their hands together as they count "1-2-3-4." On half notes students will clap on one, hold hands together on two, clap on three, and hold on four, while counting "1-2-3-4." On quarter notes students clap on one, two, three, and four, while counting "1-2-3-4."

Write different combinations of rhythms on the board and practice clapping them together as a class. You will immediately spot students who do not understand: they will be clapping at the wrong times. It is crucial that every effort be made to help the large majority of students get this first step. It is the first foundation for successful sight-reading.

After practicing examples from the board, begin with a simple exercise from the class method book. Practice step one until the students are easily able to produce the correct rhythm by clapping. If it takes more than two or three times, the exercise is too difficult for the students at this point. Find an easier exercise, or explain it better.

Step two develops note recognition and fingering facility. Using the same simple exercise that you first clapped, have the students finger, name, and pat their foot (FNP). You will have to guide them by singing with them. Be sure to keep a steady beat, and give each note the proper length. If it is a whole note "C," the student will pat their foot four times while they sing "C" and finger "C" for four beats. You will probably do well to remind the students that players of different instruments will be singing different names for the notes. Students will sometimes say that hearing note names for other parts confuses them. They will soon get used to the procedure, however, and if they can correctly finger and name while others are doing so to different names, they will become very secure in the names and fingerings of their own instrument.

It is very beneficial for ear training to have the students sing the correct pitch. Some may criticize this idea as teaching by rote, but it will not result in rote teaching and *will* result in students with a better concept of pitch. As you practice with the students, it is important that you lead by singing the correct pitch. If you are a bass, you may have difficulty with this, because few beginning band students sing in the bass range. Give up your inhibitions and develop a good falsetto! (You may have to "crown" a couple of boys in the process, but insist that they get used to singing pitches. It is important.)

Step three is putting the first two steps together: play, pat your foot, and count in your head (PPC). Explain to your students that while they play, they are to pat their foot and count numbers in their head at the same time. If steps one and two are well established, step three will usually be a breeze, unless the rhythms or notes are tricky.

This routine of steps one, two and three should be used on every piece you study in the beginning band method book. Over time, you will develop a large number of students proficient in the techniques necessary for good sight-reading. The foundation will be laid for many excellent musicians.

Ready to actually sight-read? First make sure that you select an exercise that contains only the notes and rhythms you have studied to this point. Think in terms of a simple exercise that is easy and accessible to your students. Don't try to challenge them with a difficult exercise. Second, paint the picture that sight-reading is fun. The goal that you want to express to the students is to play the new song as perfectly as possible, with few or no mistakes. Make a game out of it: tell them it is like a video game, and if they push the right buttons at the right time, they win by being great sight-readers. Third, teach them to keep going if they make a mistake, and never stop! Finally, tell them that sight-reading is a test to see who can teach themselves a new piece without the teacher. Tell them that they will not be allowed to ask a question or talk to a neighbor, but that they can use the fingering chart if they need to.

After you tell the students which exercise to study, explain that the best sight-readers start immediately, quietly doing steps one and two (to themselves on their fingertips), then finger and blow into their instrument while trying to hear the correct pitches in their head (a sort of mental step three). Don't time this process except to give them enough time to go through it at least once, and maybe twice in the beginning. Tell them to use the time wisely by going over and over the steps until you stop them. Never let them stop studying. After sufficient time is given, you may want to have them finger the example through once while you count, and then ask them to play it. As time goes on, you will give the class less time to study, and you will not practice the example with them. For now, you want to ensure that their first sight-reading experience is fun so make it successful. Be sure to make a big deal of their success, so they will feel the accomplishment. Not everyone can sight-read, and they are on the road to doing it well. Tell them so!

- Step one: clap, count, pat foot (CCP)
- Step two: finger, name, pat foot (FNP)
- Step three: play, pat foot, count in head (PPC)

Practicing these techniques and sequencing the difficulty of either the rhythm or the notes will increase the students' ability to sight-read. Improving rhythmic proficiency and technical facility go hand-in-hand for further progress in sight-reading.

Use rhythm sheets to improve rhythm recognition of whole, half, quarter, and eighth notes. A simple game of clapping rhythm sheets called "Rhythm Master" will encourage students to work on eighth note rhythms. Have a standard rhythm sheet for every student. Start at some point with the whole class clapping the rhythms. As students miss, they are to be honest and drop out of clapping and begin to quietly finger-tip clap along with everyone. Finally, one student will be left. That student is the "Rhythm Master" for the day. If you give some simple award, you will be amazed at how the students will work to become the "Rhythm Master."

Teaching scales will increase facility as well as knowledge of new notes. Use the fingering chart to help students learn the chromatic scale. The ultimate goal is for every student to be a "walking fingering chart." Have your students finger and name the chromatic scale, then play it. As note recognition improves, sight-reading will also.

Fundamentals of sight-reading can be taught, and, when sight-reading is presented in a systematic way, large numbers of students can become successful readers. There is no other aspect of music education that is more important or more enjoyable.

Kenneth F. Beard is band director at Fayette County High School and Fayetteville Elementary School in Fayetteville, Georgia. This article originally appeared in the Spring 1994 issue of Georgia Music News. Reprinted by permission.

Are Elementary Band Members Really Capable of Critiquing Their Own Rehearsals? Why Don't You Give Them a Chance to Show You What They Can Do?

by Renee E. Brandler

Developing the knowledge and process of critique in elementary instrumental music students—should we be expected to do it? Is it really worth it to try to add this aspect of music education to an elementary band program? Is it practical to expect elementary band directors to fit this "extra" component into their teaching? After reading this article, I hope that your answers to all of the above questions will be a unison response of YES!

For those of us who teach elementary instrumental music, sometimes it may seem that simply getting the students to sit down, put their instruments together properly, take out their music (which they hopefully remembered to bring with them to the rehearsal!), and play the first note of the song (preferably the correct note!) often feels like a major accomplishment on any given day of the school year!! And then, when a minor miracle happens and the melody is recognizable, the bass drummer is playing on the correct beat, and less than ten squeaks have occurred in the past 30 seconds, sometimes we may have that superstitious feeling that it is time to "quit while we are ahead." In the typical band director quest to find the magical combination of the right music, a group of hard-working and enthusiastic students, schedules that provide the least amount of conflict, as well as administrative, staff and parent support, it may seem that worrying about the higher-level knowledge and process of critique can wait until middle school or even high school.

What are the goals of our public school instrumental music programs as we approach the year 2000? Is producing terrific concerts that please parents and administrators the most important aspect of our profession? Should we be focusing on ways to use music to improve and enhance student progress in academic areas? Do we feel that music is important enough to simply "stand on its own" as an integral part of every child's aesthetic and emotional growth? Sometimes it seems that we are asked to accomplish and justify so much, that we may find it difficult to decide what to focus on as we teach.

During the past few years, I have decided to address some of the recent standards and core proficiencies added to our profession. Last year, I chose to find ways to incorporate the need to provide our students with the knowledge and process of critique, at the elementary level. I developed a few forms that could be used during band rehearsals, as well as after concert performances, which would encourage students to use peer- and self-critique techniques to analyze their own individual as well as group, performances. After the December holiday concert, all fourth- and fifth-grade band members completed a form which required them to identify differences between the daytime performance versus the evening performance, which was held at another location. Students were asked to describe how they felt at each performance and to identify pieces which they felt were performed the best, from an individual, as well as group perspective. Students were also asked to list any rehearsal or practice strategies that they felt had contributed to the success of the performances. Finally, students were given an opportunity to include any other comments relating to the concerts or the rehearsals prior to the performances. After collecting and reading through these responses, I spent some time at our next lessons and rehearsals discussing the observations and comments which the students had made, and we talked about how we could use this knowledge to improve the quality of our spring rehearsals and concerts. The students seemed to feel that I had shown them respect by asking for their opinions, and they also developed a more positive group dynamic, as we worked together to make some changes in our rehearsal structure. I repeated this process after our spring concert and was happy to learn that many of the students reported feeling more prepared and confident at these later performances, because they were more aware of what an audience might notice or felt that they were better able to adjust to differences in acoustics at the two different locations. Students also were given an opportunity to compare their answers on the spring form with the one given out in December.

Perhaps the most popular aspect of my "critique" experiment has been the "student observer program." During each "advanced" band rehearsal, students were given the opportunity to sit near the conductor and observe part of a rehearsal. While observing, students filled out a multiple choice form, with questions about different aspects of the rehearsal, including: dynamic balance, tempo control, student attention-level and behavior, posture, etc. The multiple choice form was given as a guide, but students were also given space to freely write down any other comments. These responses were then discussed as a group. As this student-observer program continued to generate enthusiasm among the students, and students were constantly volunteering to participate, the general behavior of the band improved. Students seemed to be listening to each other and paying more attention to what was going on around them as they played. Everyone became a part of the process of improving the sound of the group, so students were more willing to concentrate and worked harder to achieve our performance goals.

When I first initiated these ideas, I did have some reservations. I worried that I would be taking away too much time from actually playing the music during rehearsals. I knew that we would not have as much time to repeat sections over and over, if we were to spend time discussing the stu-

dent responses. But after a few months, I was very pleased with the results of my "experiment" and felt that I was teaching music while helping to actually develop true musicians.

I certainly hope that these young students will continue to feel comfortable critiquing their own musical performances, the musical performance of others, as well as anything that they experience in the world around them, whether in the arts or in some other aspect of their lives.

Renee E. Brandler is an elementary instrumental music teacher in the Parsippanny-Troy Hills, New Jersey, Public School System, and director of the Mount Tabor Summer Music Program in Parsippany. This article originally appeared in the November 1998 issue of New Jersey's Tempo. Reprinted by permission.

A New Look at Student Leaders: Band Officers
by Jeffrey L. Buchanan

If a colleague asked you to describe the impact your student officers have on your band program, how would you respond? Are your officers a self-motivated group that serves as a catalyst for continued improvement of your ensemble? Do they exemplify true leadership and are they a positive role model for the other students?

This article will offer some tried-and-true hints on how to transform your student officer group into an energetic dynamo, a team that will have a positive daily effect on your entire program. The ideas contained herein worked for me, and they will work for you, too.

First, I must confess that, for years, I gave my officers little if any responsibility, training or guidance. I was the classic "if you want a job done right, do it yourself" type of person, and I did not see a need to utilize my student leaders.

"Certainly," I told myself with smug assurance, "junior high students cannot be entrusted with any of the important and routine organizational tasks which need to be done in my classroom." I never stopped to consider the obvious contradiction: although I believed my students were mature enough to be challenged musically, I felt they were too immature to alphabetize a stack of emergency-medical forms. As a result, my band officers had one, and only one, function during the course of the school year: to have their picture taken for the school yearbook.

You know the old saying, "Be careful what you wish for, you just might get it"? I expected nothing out of my student leaders, and I consistently got my wish. My reward for this belief is obvious: I sentenced myself to a daily litany of time-consuming tasks such as setting up chairs and music stands, taking attendance, passing out and collecting music, labeling envelopes and collecting fees and permission slips. To no one's surprise, I often lamented how there weren't enough hours in the day.

Two years ago, I had the great fortune of reading Dr. Tim Lautzenheiser's outstanding books, *The Art of Successful Teaching* and *The Joy of Inspired Teaching*. In both books, Tim speaks at length on the issue of student leadership, how to train good leaders and on the issue of exactly what it means to be a good leader. A light went on in my head, and I realized that, for my sake and for my program, I needed to better utilize my officers.

Using Tim's ideas, I made an instant and positive change in my band program, through a different method of Band Officer selection. Instead of letting the students select our officers, I now hold tryout auditions for our leadership positions, and the final appointments are in my hands.

Although, in the past, the students enjoyed the democratic process, elections were often little more than a popularity contest. This method didn't usually provide me with the best student leaders, to say the least. Leaving officer selection in the hands of the resident expert (you) is a far better option.

We do well to consider this: well-trained and well-chosen officers save us time, while weak/poorly trained officers require constant supervision and more of our time. We've all had student leaders who were popular with their peers, yet lazy or unmotivated, and it's difficult to get your band to grow and improve when your leaders are "treading water," isn't it? Worse still are instances in which a student with a negative attitude is voted into office by his or her peers. When your leaders are "paddling in a different direction" than you are, it's nearly impossible to achieve a positive outcome.

Here's how to nurture a great student officer group:

Train Them – Identify Them – Entrust Them

Train Them

My Officer Auditions begin the third week of the school year and run for two weeks. I select my student leaders based on their work during the audition period. To set the proper tone of our "Officer Candidate School" right from the start, on day one we talk at length about what makes a good student leader. The following ideas were gleaned from Dr. Tim's books and my e-mail conversations with him:

- Leadership is a verb: it requires action.[1] Good leaders are "Doers."[2]
- The best student leaders want to contribute to make things better for the entire band and are not doing it just to gain popularity or higher status.
- Good leaders are not always the most outgoing or someone who is in the limelight.
- Being a leader is often a penalty, and it will be a test. Leadership requires more effort than is expected of other students, and you will be scrutinized at every occasion by your peers.[3]
- Leadership provides the opportunity to learn to serve others. Leadership experience is a valuable skill you will be able to use to your advantage in any future profession later in life.[4]
- A trial period or internship is important. Auditions give students a chance to prove that they can do the job without supervision or outside help.
- In leadership, students can see that they *can* make a difference, but the difference is based on what they give, not on what they say.

On day two I introduce the various offices and give brief job descriptions. On day three the students are encouraged to sign up and audition for the office of their choice, and on day four they receive a sheet which has a detailed job description for their desired office, as well as information on what their tryout will entail.

The audition period then runs for approximately two weeks, during which they perform the actual duties of the position. I spend a little bit of time in class training them how to do their jobs, to be sure, but the time spent is repaid tenfold as the year progresses.

Identify Them

Over the course of the two-week audition, less serious candidates fall by the wayside, while other candidates give consistent quality effort and quietly make their positive presence known. Without fail, the "cream always rises to the top," and although I keep accurate notes and scores on their efforts during the audition period, the final officer selection is usually easy to make.

The best part? When the audition period is over, I not only have identified the best person for the job, they are already trained and ready to go. Many of the students who earned positions were "dark horse" surprises to me, and ended up doing outstanding work. It's like Dr. Tim said: "Good leaders are not always the most outgoing or someone who is in the limelight."

Entrust Them

You've trained them well, and you've found the best person for each job. Now, your job as director is to entrust them with regular duties to perform, and then take that "leap of faith" and let them do it. Remember, if a task is repetitive or routine, it's a job for your officers. Your time is far better spent on the musical and educational advancement of your bands. Trust, balanced with guidance (as needed), will help your officers continue to grow and improve.

Another benefit is that when you give your leaders a stake in the daily organization and advancement of their ensemble, you impart in them a sense of ownership. This is perhaps the best way to cultivate a positive group attitude and sense of teamwork in your ensemble.

Today, I'm blessed with a hard-working, self-motivated group of student leaders who handle the routine tasks every bit as efficiently as I ever did. They are often relentless in this pursuit. Imagine having a group of students who actually arrive at school early each day to organize your room and set up your chairs or a kid who wants to take home 150 worksheets and grade them for you by tomorrow.

We all have these sort of students hiding in our ensembles. My band newsletter is now 100 percent produced by a staff of very creative 7th and 8th graders, and the student editor organizes his own meetings with his staff. If somebody forgets to pay a band fee, my treasurers track them down like little tax collectors. If we have an upcoming trip, students call chaperones and type up bus lists for me. In addition to all her regular duties, my band council president, Heather, often stays an hour or so after school to help out with any odd job that needs to be done around the music room.

On the day of a performance, my equipment-crew captain stands there with clipboard in hand and oversees the moving of our entire rehearsal room downstairs to the auditorium stage. When we have a special event, my officers become the *de facto* planning committee. Last year, we hosted Marc Neiman and his "Sounds of Sousa Band" for master classes and an evening concert. In addition to their work in advance of the event, my officers also were a noticeable presence on the day of the concert. They were everywhere, from setup crews and food service, to ushers, tour guides and gofers. There were no sign-up sheets and I spent no time recruiting helpers, for I already had a reliable work crew in place.

If we're not careful, it's really easy to fall into the trap of becoming our own band secretary, librarian, treasurer, and custodian. While those facets of our job are important, I personally want to wear my band-director hat as many minutes and hours of the school day as I can. It's an inescapable truth that every minute we spend wearing our band-secretary hat is one less minute we're teaching our students. So, I delegate nearly all of the secretarial, librarian, treasurer, and custodial routines to my student leaders.

Although some people are born leaders, leadership is a skill which can be learned, and as such,

we need to give our students a forum in which they can develop these skills. They need to learn that it is important to serve others, without expecting any glory or reward in return. This lesson in humility is perhaps the biggest gift we can give our students.

My band council has informal meetings every month or two to discuss how things are going and give ideas for improvement. I give them recognition, and it's sincere, because they know they are a vital cog in the success of our band. We have their picture in the local newspaper, have their names in bold type in our concert programs, and I give them countless thank-yous and daily words of encouragement as the year progresses. Last spring, we all went out to Chi-Chi's for a thank-you lunch. These are little gestures, but the point is, the kids and I know we appreciate each other.

I often think of the many times over the years when I set up those 85 chairs and music stands all by myself; time I could have spent doing other things, time I will never get back. If money is time, my officers now save me a lot during each school year. My new mantra is: "If you want the job done right, delegate, delegate, delegate."

Notes

1. Tim Lautzenheiser. *The Joy of Inspired Teaching* (Chicago: GIA Publications, 1993), 128.

2. Tim Lautzenheiser. *The Art of Successful Teaching: A Blend of Content & Context* (Chicago: GIA Publications, 1992), 145.

3. Ibid., 146–147.

4. Tim Lautzenheiser, *The Joy of Inspired Teaching,* 129–130.

Jeffrey Buchanan is director of bands at Bellevue Junior High School in Bellevue, Ohio. This article originally appeared in the May-June 1997 issue of Ohio's Triad. *Reprinted by permission.*

Middle School Band Skills Assessment: Constructing a Play-Off System for Achievement, Accountability and Success

by Robert Conger

Imagine walking into your room in the morning and having students at your door clamoring to take a terms test or perhaps ... wanting to play their scales for you, not just one scale but all of them! Imagine 50 students or more practicing in the band room over an hour before school waiting for their chance to pass off requirements. Picture students, after being seated in their 'chair order,' wanting to practice and improve instead of starting arguments. All this is possible with the use of a play-off system in your middle school band. Assigning grades to students based on playing tests tends to be subjective rather than objective. Using a play-off system helps make grading objective and allows students to become responsible for their own progress.

In 1989, Paul Wilson brought an early version to me that was structured for the high school student using the Rubank method books. Under his system there were many requirements per rank (as many as 36) which had to be checked off in the proper order. I revised this system for middle school students, making changes to alleviate time constraints for both my students and myself.

The system uses 100 requirements which are in turn divided into 10 ranks of 10 requirements each. Each rank in the system is labeled as a military rank, from Private to Captain. I have used the *Essential Elements* method book by T. C. Rhodes, D. Bierschenk, and T. Lautzenheiser (Milwaukee: Hal Leonard, 1991), but the system can easily be adapted to any worthwhile method of your choice. Although requirements may be played off in any order, each and every requirement in a rank must be played off before the student moves to the next rank. If a mistake is made, the requirement must be replayed (with no mistakes!) at a later time. Mistakes include: bad tone quality, incorrect horn position, bad posture, wrong notes, wrong rhythms, key signature errors, unsteady tempos, hesitations, or outright stopping. It is crucial that the teacher maintain high standards with every student in the interest of objectivity and fairness. This makes it more difficult to pass off the requirements, but establishes a goal of 'perfection' with the student. This is especially effective during concert and festival preparation. The most important quality when listening to requirements is

characteristic tone. This requires good fundamentals of tone production to be taught from the beginning.

The student must check off ten requirements per nine-week grading period to make an 'A.' If a student plays off more than is required for an 'A' during a grading period, the extra requirements can be applied to the next grade. This encourages students to continue to pass off even after they have achieved their grade. Some ambitious students actually achieved their grade for three grading periods during the first nine weeks of the year. You may add 'bonus' points for attendance at concerts, special events or performances, and class participation. These count only toward the student's grade, not chair placement. Bonus points are not carried over from one grading period to the next.

Chair placement is determined entirely by the total number of requirements that have been played successfully. There are no 'challenges,' only the opportunity to continue to progress toward a higher rank (and a higher chair). The student may attempt as many requirements as they like until the first error occurs. At this point, the student's turn ends and the instructor moves on to the next student.

Students may play requirements before or after school on a first come, first served basis depending on the schedule of the instructor. They may also play them during class time. If you have a voice-mail system at your school, you can actually set up mailboxes for each of your classes so that students may call in from home and play requirements over the phone at night or on the weekends.

Beginning band should be allowed sufficient class time to acclimate to the system. Less class time should be spent as students become more familiar with the process. One of the many positive aspects of the system is the modeling that occurs when students play requirements in a classroom environment. Students listen to others play off requirements and begin to "copy" positive elements within their performance. This develops critical listening skills that enable the student to progress at a faster rate.

How to Set up Your Own Play-Off System

It is important to notate exact requirements beforehand and disseminate them to your students as early in the year as possible. This places the responsibility wholly in the hands of the students and allows them to work at their own pace. Although the students will only be allowed to play off on the rank on which they are currently working, this enables them to 'look ahead' in the method book and practice more difficult exercises.

After you select a method book and determine that it will meet your teaching needs, organize your ranks into ten requirements each.

Private

On the first rank (Private), begin with proper instrument assembly and care, followed by producing a good sound on the mouthpiece. For brass players, start with a steady sustained buzz followed by a wide siren for range development. Flutes should be able to produce four tones through the headjoint only (two covered and two uncovered). Clarinets and saxes should be able to produce a sustained F-sharp with the proper embouchure, and double reeds should be able to produce a double crow and a single pitch with the proper embouchure change. Another part of this requirement should be the demonstration of proper posture and hand position. Percussion should demonstrate the proper grip as well. Next you will pick five lines from the beginning method book which demonstrate the ability to say rhythms out loud. Include each new rhythmic concept in the first third of the book. A measure of four quarter notes would be said: *one - two - three - four* (in tempo, of course) and a measure of quarter-quarter-half would be said: *one - two - three - ee*. It is very important that the students say each note with the count on which it begins. For a whole note for instance you would say *one* for four beats. Steady tempo and accuracy is essential. It does not matter which counting system is used, but students should be able to count (say) any rhythm out loud.

The last seven requirements on the first rank will be other lines out of the book arranged in a progressive order from easy to difficult. Again, be sure to include all major concepts when selecting lines from the book such as eighth notes, key signatures, range (particularly as the clarinets cross the break), and accidentals. Also be aware that you will be hearing these lines from all of your students many times, so select the melodies with care.

Private First Class

As you move into Private First Class, begin with three scales (B-flat, E-flat, and one octave chromatic) as the first requirement for winds. Percussionists must play four rudiments by memory. Pick five lines for the 'rhythm' requirement and include eighth-note and dotted-quarter exercises. This rank is the first to include musical terms. Begin with fifteen easy terms such as forte, piano, tempo, beat,

sharp, and so forth. Construct a multiple choice or matching test (or both for when they take it more than once) and require students to score 100 percent to pass. The remainder of the rank will include playing requirements from the book (up to and including dotted quarter notes). Usually this is the point that the clarinets cross the break, so include additional exercises on two or three requirements for clarinets only so that they may demonstrate their mastery of this important skill.

Corporal

The rank of Corporal should complete book one and will include five scales (F, B-flat, E-flat, A-flat, one octave chromatic), counting (pick five lines), and more complex musical terms (repeat sign, ledger line, slur, tie, da capo, dynamics). A new requirement on tuning has the student match pitches (preferably out of tune) with another instrument and determine which is sharp. The playing requirements on this rank should be a bit longer (to build endurance) and include more complex rhythm and rest patterns if possible. Clarinets should have two or three additional exercises to encourage their upper range.

Sergeant

For Sergeant, the scale requirement will include G, C, F, B-flat, E-flat, A-flat, D-flat, extended chromatic plus 9 rudiments for percussion. Tuning requires each student to match (tune) at least two pitches with a like instrument. Percussionists tune tympani to two different notes as well. Counting and playing exercises (now extracted from book two) will begin to include sixteenth notes and syncopation patterns. Terms become more and more complex: crescendo, unison, dal segno, interval, octave, and so forth.

Sergeant First Class includes two-octave scales, two-octave chromatic and ten rudiments for the percussion. Tuning, counting, musical terms and more complex playing exercises continue to be included. Master Sergeant completes the second book and expands the amount of scales, along with the complexity of counting, terms, and playing exercises. As you continue to include more complexities in each succeeding rank (Second Lieutenant and First Lieutenant), be sure you do not ease up when you listen to students attempting to pass off the exercises.

Captain

By the rank of Captain, students should be expected to be able to perform all major scales two octaves, count complex rhythms out loud, pass a complete musical-terms test, sight-read and perform solos and ensembles from the FBA list as well as play some extended exercises with no mistakes.

Adapting the System to Solo/Ensemble and Concert Festival

For the fall semester, the rank system can be used as the sole method of assessment without exception. In the spring, however, we participate in Solo/Ensemble Festival and Concert Festival. To focus student involvement in each festival, the rank system may be adapted to the needs of the student.

To increase student participation in Solo/Ensemble, we give each student the option of either playing off ten requirements or playing off solo and/or ensemble parts three times, with each performance being successively more polished. By the third time, the solo and/or ensemble should be in a highly polished state. In order to demonstrate significant improvement, the students need to practice their performance from play-off to play-off or it is not acceptable. Each student receives one point from the first play-off (notes and rhythms), two points from the second (adding some expression and phrasing), and three points from the third (a highly polished version) which is to be performed with the accompanist. The remaining four points are earned by performing at

the festival for the judge and being rated either superior or excellent. If a student is rated 'good,' the decision whether or not to award points is up to the instructor. Students will become used to getting ten points per grading period, thus this 'adaptation' will fit right into their mindset.

For Concert Festival, instead of diverting attention to playing off requirements from the method book, each student is required to play off their concert festival pieces with no errors. This takes time on the instructor's part, but is definitely worth the extra effort. Students receive 2 points per selection and an additional 4 points for participating in Concert Festival. The same type of procedure could apply for concerts.

Side Effects of the Rank System

This type of systematic learning procedure could be applied to almost any skill-oriented discipline. Students learn at their own rate and are able to progress quickly through material which they consider 'easy.' They continue to play off until they reach a difficult level. This enables all students to succeed whatever their experience or playing level.

Students develop good critical-listening skills by evaluating the play-off attempts of their peers. It is easy for parents to comprehend and to track their child's progress at all times. Pressure is taken off the student because, if they make an error while attempting to play off, they may try again the next

---

Sample Position Requirements

Corporal

1. *Wind instruments:* Demonstrate proper embouchure, posture, hand position and a characteristic tone on your instrument by performing the F, B-flat, E-flat, and A-flat concert scales and arpeggios using the quarter-note/eighth-note rhythm pattern *by memory* at quarter note = 80. Also perform the B-flat concert chromatic scale one octave *by memory*, in even quarter notes.
Percussion: Perform, on the snare drum, the first 6 rudiments from the American Standard Drum Rudiments, by memory (Open–Closed–Open).

2. *Wind instruments:* By matching pitches with another instrument, determine which instrument is "sharp." Then adjust instrument length so that pitches match exactly.
Percussion: Tune the timpani to a specific note using a reference note played on the bells.

3. Count the following exercises by saying the rhythms out loud: #99, #108, #119, #125, #136.

4. Make a score of 100 percent on the Corporal Music Terms Test.

Play the following exercises from *Essential Elements, Book I* with no mistakes:

5. #87 and #89 (clarinets only, also play #101)
6. #104 and #105 (clarinets only, also play #110)
7. #112 and #118 (clarinets only, also play #116)
8. #120 and #124

Note. The referenced exercises are from *Essential Elements, Book I*, by T. C. Rhodes, D. Bierschenk, and T. Lautzenheiser (Milwaukee: Hal Leonard, 1991).

day. Idle practice time is virtually eliminated because each practice session becomes goal oriented.

Record keeping can be maintained on a computer database program and posted each week for the students, parents and administrators to see. Students can quickly become peer tutors for younger students or slower learners. Bickering over who should have been first chair ceases because each student is responsible for his or her own destiny.

Maintaining Records

Using any worthwhile computer database, one can easily maintain records regarding each student's grade. You will need to include the following text fields: name, instrument, grade, period, and rank. In addition you will need the following numerical fields: one field per requirement (a total of ten), bonus points (one field per grading period), goal (changes each grading period—would include how many requirements you need for an 'A'), plus a field that adds up the requirement totals and bonus points to indicate their total grade *(sum)*. The 'goal' for all students will be 10 the first marking period. You will have to change the 'goal' for the next grading period. Just add 10 to the 'sum' of each student's completed requirements.

This must be done by hand as each student will complete a different amount. You will need a separate formula field that indicates the *total* played off per grading period. Use the formula 10 - (goal - sum) = total. (Remember, both the goal and sum will increase during the year.) This will be the grade for the current marking period. Another field can add up 'nonbonus' requirements to do chair placement.

Student Rewards

Each student should earn a reward as they complete a rank. The reward could be a certificate of completion (easily computer generated), or some other positive enticement for future accomplishment. Reinforcing the success of each and every student helps to keep them motivated to conquer the next challenge. The rank system will motivate your students, raise the level of performance and indicate precisely the performance level of each individual for assessment purposes.

Robert Conger teaches at Gotha Middle School in Orlando, Florida. This article originally appeared in the September 1999 issue of Florida Music Director. *Reprinted by permission.*

"Turning On" the SWITCH
by Greg Crameri

Just visualize this for a second: It is the opening day of your middle school, you walk into your band room and seated before you is a ninety-piece concert band ready to begin its first rehearsal. The instrumentation includes 6 tubas, 6 euphoniums, 10 trombones, 8 horns, 4 bassoons and an upper wind section of 25+ clarinets, 6 alto saxes and only 8 flutes. Sorry, but your second of euphoria is now over. Once the rose-colored tint has dissipated you now see the true makeup of the group before you, and, as so many of the music educators will react, all you can do is step back and take in a deep breath. All you can think is, "What am I going to do with 35 flutes, 20 alto saxes, 15 percussion players, a low brass section that consists of maybe two trombones and a complete void in the double reed section?" "How do I approach the performance of quality wind literature, which ideally calls for equal balance, when I am light-years from that with the instrumentation I have?" In my ten years as a middle/high school

educator I have been very fortunate to have had and currently have feeder programs that work very hard to generate balanced sections at the elementary school level. Yet, when the various elementary schools combine at the middle school level, I continue to face the same dilemma. The question now is how to improve the balance by switching students presently playing flute and alto sax to some of the other essential horns. I know that every one of you reading this article has done this in schools over the years. Go with whatever works best for you and know that the tips and strategies that I use may be the same or may not be possible in your present situation. Best of luck getting those 6 tuba players and remember to just keep "turning on" the switch. I implement *Eight Strategies:*

1. Take the Ball and Run

Recruitment of players may be the most difficult aspect to contend with. On the first day of class, while going over the rules and regs of the course, set aside a time to discuss the instrumentation issue. I hand out student-profile sheets and ask the students to fill in their addresses, phone numbers, etc. On that sheet I also have a section that states:

There may be the possibility that I will be able to offer the chance for students to switch to other very important and needed instruments. Instruments will be provided by the school. It's a great opportunity—interested? If so, please check here. There is absolutely no obligation— I am only trying to determine interest.

After reading through this with the students, I usually follow it up with a discussion about what having a balanced group means. I often use the analogy of sports teams. I ask them what a football team would be like with twelve quarterbacks and no offensive lineman or a basketball team with all guards but no center. Usually the students can relate to this and reply that such a team would not be very successful. I follow that up by having the students listen to a recording, usually a fine wind group playing a standard piece like a march. After playing it I ask how it sounded, and usually the response is positive. Then I turn down one of the channels so that only the higher pitched instruments can be heard. Again, I ask how it sounded and the response is generally much different. Once the sheets are collected it is time to determine the students that would adjust well to a switch. It is essential that you communicate with the elementary teachers and elicit their thoughts about each individual's work habits and dedication to the instrument they now have. Remember, the most important factor is not how proficient a musician the student is but the amount of energy, commitment, and effort they will give to this new instrument.

2. "Gradually Ease" as Opposed to "Stop and Learn"

If you have lesson groups that meet weekly, have the prospective switchers start off in groups with their present instrument. Leave a number of lesson periods open in your schedule to afford lesson blocks for new instrument groups. Many times a director will give students horns, show them the embouchure, and then tell them to go home and learn all of the fingerings for the following week. This may work with some students, but for many, especially at middle-school age, this can be a disaster. It may need to be a gradual process that takes most of the year. A guidepost that I set for myself is to have the new instrument groups in place and running full throttle after the holiday vacation in January. Granted, the holiday program, if per-

formed before January, may not be ideal, but I have found that the dividends in the long run far outweigh the possibilities of frustration, stress, and anxiety that may cause students to quit altogether. To help foster the energy and excitement, I recommend meeting with individual students before school, during lunch and study halls and, preferably, after school during late bus hours during the fall semester. Push the individual growth before trying to assemble large groups of students who at this point do not even know how to produce a good sound on the horn.

3. Set High Expectations Right from the Beginning

Set high expectations, not in a performance sense, but in terms of the effort needed to succeed. The explanation I use is this: if they are not already putting the proper effort into the horn they now have, what makes me think that they are going to do more on a new instrument with its unknown challenges? Be up-front right from the beginning. Those students who may be "wishy-washy" about the whole idea may realize that this may not be for them. Time is priceless and none can be wasted if the student is not truly into it. The core 15 to 25 students who wish to continue will be a great cornerstone from which to build.

4. Communication is the Key

I ask the interested students to go home and discuss the idea with their parents. Before doing a thing I first call each parent and talk about the entire process, as well as send a detailed plan of action in the mail. Almost every parent over the years has been very supportive of this change as long as it is presented in an organized and detailed manner, with them knowing that the child's best interests are at heart. I have found that the most important question a parent raises is, "Will I need to rent or purchase this instrument for my child?" Again, I have been fortunate to have a large number of school-owned low brass and double reed instruments over the years, so when the parent is assured that they do not need to purchase the instrument they are usually very agreeable. If the instrument inventory is a problem at your school, discuss a possible solution found later in the strategy "This is a Two-Fold Process." After you are established with the student and parents it is extremely important to keep the parents informed with a periodic call or report (e.g., interim/ progress report). If the teacher demonstrates the interest, the student will feed off the energy and the parents will support it to the hilt. Communication with the elementary faculty is essential, not only in helping establish suitable students, but also in information and resources such as specific embouchure, reading, or technical problems facing certain students. Ask the elementary teachers to jot down a few comments about your incoming class during the spring of the previous year. You may wish to go even further by designing a standard form detailing a general assessment of each student for the teacher to fill out. Having a handle on each student before they begin the new school year can get the ball rolling before the first day of classes. Remember that as a middle school educator you are like the middle man in business—the switching program is doomed to fail in the long run if the elementary/producer and the high school/consumer are cut out of the equation.

5. "Asking" of Means Doing it Oneself

I am a firm believer that if you are going to pursue such an instrument-switch program you must be able to hold your own on each instrument. That does not mean being able to perform all of the listed All-State concertos on every horn. The director should be able to demonstrate proper embouchure, warm-up exercises, and scales and confidently perform in the student's lesson book and ensemble music. I have listed a few goals that switchers should be able to demonstrate during the year and that directors should be able to play right off the bat. For example:

Low Brass:
- Buzzing exercises on the mouthpiece, going up and down in pitch demonstrating proper embouchure and placement with a full understanding of the aperture and the use of faster and slower air movement. A great exercise is to play the *Jeopardy* theme, first tonguing and then slurring all of the pitches using the mouthpiece alone.
- Long-tone and lip-slur exercises reaching to the 4th and 5th partials, using one breath, and without excess pressure being placed on the lips by the mouthpiece.
- At least 4–5 scales with arpeggios, one octave, using proper tonguing technique (stress that the tongue snaps from the back of the teeth and does not come through the teeth).

6. Pool Your Resources

Once students are progressing, you may suggest and they may wish to pursue private instruction.

The faculty within your own district can often be your greatest resource. If you are a professional clarinetist and the high school director is a tubist, you may wish to teach his clarinet section while he or she works with your new low brass players. Another suggestion is to seek out the finest high school players that demonstrate maturity and responsibility. Many school districts mandate community service hours as a curriculum requirement for high school graduation. What better way to utilize those hours while continuing to maintain the strength of the high school program for years to come. I have found that this type of program builds great camaraderie and pride for the music program at all levels. All it takes is communication, a bit of time, and a willingness to work together to promote the whole district-wide music program.

7. This is a Two-Fold Process

As you were reading, many of you may have said, "I don't have all of the instruments at my disposal." The most important factors for a successful switching program are excitement, energy, and interested students. If there are people who are interested, there is always a way to attain the resources needed. I remember in my first year of teaching having a baritone saxophone that was literally held together with duct tape. Low brass instruments were few and pretty beaten up, and double reeds were nonexistent. By the end of my tenure at the school, three years later, I had new tubas, euphoniums, and a baritone saxophone for the students to use. How? Once the interest was there I borrowed anything I could from fellow directors and even lent out several of my own horns (please don't try this at home). At concerts, parents and administrators would comment on the full rich sound of the ensembles. I responded by telling them that the only way for this to continue and for the program to have ample instruments for those interested students was for the school district to make a commitment to buy new horns. Once the interest and numbers rose then the time came to ask for something in return. The route which many directors take is a lease-purchase program with various instrument manufacturers that may be set up through local music dealers. These programs enable the directors to receive all of the instruments up-front with the cost being paid over a certain number of years. Forty-thousand dollars is a huge amount of money, but eight-thousand over a five-year period makes it much more attractive to the administration and school boards when they set up their capitol outlay accounts for the upcoming year. The bottom line is to receive something—a positive effort within a switching program must be established—in turn making it a two-fold process.

8. Miscellaneous Practical Tips

- Play baritone/euphonium during trumpet lesson groups. Allow students to see and hear how it works. Bring extra mouth pieces with you so that students can experiment. Pump it up while having fun and periodically explain the intricacies of the horn. The most logical transitions are from trumpet to baritone and clarinet to bass clarinet, so work these vigorously in regular trumpet and clarinet lesson groups. Last year, I had six students switch just from trumpet to baritone. Each of the six is still excited and progressing very well.

- Do not take the finest clarinet player in the group and switch him or her to baritone saxophone. If the students look to be All-State caliber players, keep them where they are. I am sure there are plenty of alto saxophone players, that could handle baritone sax just fine.

- Express the fact that more opportunities for outside festivals such as regionals are possible on instruments like tuba and bassoon. Do not downplay the other instruments; only promote a realistic fact.

- When switched players begin playing in the ensemble, do not expect miracles. One thing I try never to do is have a new section play by themselves in front of everyone. In most middle school literature, the parts are cross-cued with other parts (for example: euphonium with tenor sax and 3rd trumpet). Have them play it together to help build confidence.

- If bringing in an outside ensemble is a possibility, make it a point to invite professional or college tuba groups or a bassoon trio. This will give exposure to the instrument, pump up the interest, and afford the opportunity for master classes for students to partake.

- Stress chamber music with switchers. Pull out simple duets and double- and triple-up on parts. Most students enjoy duets/trios, and a close bond will be forged amongst the players. If all goes well, program the groups for the beginning or during a concert program. Again, parents and administrators will see the first fold within the switching-over process.

- Reward progress. I do an instrumentalist-of-the-week program within my school. Awards are given to the students at the end of the year as an incentive to work hard. It is important to remember that these switchers are not only learning something new but are also giving of themselves to help with the balance of the ensemble. Keep a special place in your heart for them each week when you select the student for this distinction.

Greg Crameri is band director at Har Bur Middle School in Burlington, Connecticut. This article originally appeared in the Winter 1998 issue of Connecticut's CMEA News. *Reprinted by permission.*

Are They Listening?

by Clarence Crum

Listen! You folks just are not listening! Now let's go back to rehearsal letter G and try that again!"

I am often asked to go listen to band rehearsals to make some suggestions on how to "fix" the sound of the band before a major performance and/or contest. I have heard the first sentence of this article screamed in frustration by numerous band directors during rehearsals too many times.

When I hear that statement, two questions immediately come to mind:

1. What are the students supposed to listen to?
2. Do the students really know how to listen?

As a student, I can remember being in band rehearsals and having directors make that same statement. My mental reply to that statement back then was, "Sure, I'm listening. Why aren't the rest of the people in the band listening?" I'm also sure that the other band members' mental replies to the statement were similar to mine.

A more accurate statement would have been: "trombones, baritones, and tenor sax, you folks all are playing in unison. The baritones' pitch will be the most consistent, so you folks need to listen closely to them. Now let's go back to rehearsal letter G."

This statement solves more of the tuning problem. It has focus. It gives clear instructions on what to listen for to improve the tuning problem.

The above situation is a two-fold problem. At first it sounds like just a communication problem. But the problem goes much deeper than that. The critical problem here is the director's failure to teach his or her students listening skills. Directors get so caught up teaching students how to play/sing, that they do not spend enough time teaching students how to listen.

As I think back to my early days as a musician, no one taught me how to listen. It was assumed that I could hear the same things the band director heard. I was a high school student who had trouble listening to his mother's singular wishes, let alone multiple musical lines or chord structures. I did not have the listening skills of my director.

The *art of listening* is a skill that must be highly developed by all music students. You are not born with great listening skills. They must be developed! The most successful music educators I know spend many hours developing the listening skills of the students in their ensembles.

The equation is simple. The more time a director spends on developing the group's listening skills, the better the group.

We spend 15 minutes during the warm-up portion of our daily 45-minute rehearsal playing exercises to develop listening skills.

Here is a listing of some topics we cover to develop listening skills:

1. diatonic and chromatic intervals
2. major and harmonic minor scales
3. major, minor, diminished, augmented arpeggios
4. building chords, including chords with added 7ths, 9ths, 6ths, and 4ths
5. inversions of chords
6. playing by ear
7. matching pitches played at random
8. dissonances, tone clusters, and polytonality.

During the rest of the rehearsal, I test the listening skills that I have been developing during the "warm-up" segment of the rehearsal. It is not uncommon for me to stop the ensemble at any time during the rehearsal and ask a student questions like:

- What was the quality of the last chord we played?
- Are you playing the root, third, fifth, or seventh of the chord?
- Your part is in unison with what other part in the band?

For larger sections, I might make requests similar to these:

- Raise your hand if you're playing the third of the chord.
- Would all the people playing the third of the chord at measure 15, please play.
- If you have the counter melody beginning at measure 56, please play.
- If you are playing minor arpeggios at measure 212, please play.
- All those playing the augmentation of Theme 1 at measure 37, please play.

Students must have highly developed listening skills. They must understand how and what to listen for in the complex structure of a musical composition. *These skills need to be taught.*

The result will be music students that have the ability to hear what their director hears, plus a band that has a better understanding of music theory fundamentals and compositional structure. End result: a band that sounds great!

So the next time you find yourself stopping the band to say, "You folks need to listen," refocus your statement to help your students develop their listening skills.

Clarence Crum was a music educator for twenty-one years and now serves as principal at Malvern High School in Malvern, Ohio. This article originally appeared in the September/October 1997 issue of Ohio's Triad. *Reprinted by permission.*

The Raving (With Apologies to Poe)
by Phil Fahrlander

Once upon a day so dreary, as I labored weak and weary
O'er many a well-marked measure of a long-neglected score,
While I nodded, nearly napping, suddenly there came a tapping
Gently first, then louder tapping—tapping at my office door.
Gazed then I toward the portal, seeking to perceive what mortal
Intervened this late-day hour, knocking at my office door.
'Twas Caruso, nothing more.

Entered he and sat before me, proceeding promptly to implore me
To assist him with his musical for a quarter hour or more.
Vowing to assist his show—maybe in a week or so—
I finally got him out my door.
"And now," I said, "Back to my score."

Next did the ringing phone intrude into my studied solitude,
Clanging louder, ever shriller, till I could not stand it more.
'Twas someone of good intent, indeed, the booster president.

Thus twenty minutes more were spent with one I did not dare ignore.
Plans for the chili feed were set, pizza sales were lagging yet.
Money was not coming in, more was needed—much, much more.
I tried to focus on the score.

Presently Tahellenbach, my principal, came in to talk
Of sundry senseless subjects that we'd talked about before.
Though his meaning was not clear, it was wise to lend an ear
So I tried to pay attention as he mumbled more and more.
What he had hoped to gain, I could never ascertain
But I think he felt much better as he headed for the door.
"Oh, no!" I sighed, "It's half past four."

With firm-set jaw and pen in hand, I got back to work I'd planned,
Scanned a page and marked and scanned, paused and scanned and marked some more.
Again I heard the sound of tapping, then a louder, harder rapping,
Changing now into a thumping, thumping sound that shook the floor.
Glancing up I faced the Farkles, peering through the office door.
Only Farkles—nothing more.

"I'm busy now," I loudly said. "Please pick another time instead.
I've got a lot of work to do—I need some time to mark this score."
"You really need to fix my flute," Fannie said.
" 'Cause it won't toot.
I huff and puff until I'm blue, and I had Freda try it too.
It seems no matter what I do, it just don't sound good anymore."
Fixing the flute was a major chore.

Intently now I scanned the score, till interrupted by the roar

Of Rembrandt's high-pitched polisher grinding at
the bandroom floor.
In vain I tried to concentrate, then noticed that
the hour was late—
Much later than the night before.

I donned my coat and locked the door.
Rembrandt sang as he waxed the floor.
"Good night!" he yelled above the roar. I waved
back as I walked away.

The wind was cold against my face and quickly I
increased my pace.
I glanced up at the clouds of gray.
Tomorrow was another day.

*Phil Fahrlander is a retired band director from the
Minden Public Schools in Minden, Nebraska. This arti-
cle originally appeared in the October 1998 issue of the*
Nebraska Music Educator. *Reprinted by permission.*

Learning To Play in Tune
by Wayne E. Goins

What a joy it is to play in an ensemble!
There are literally hundreds of thousands of great selections to be heard
and performed in every genre, be it marching,
symphonic, orchestral, or jazz. There are also great
ensembles with fresh, energetic students waiting to
play music. And then there are motivated band
directors waiting to conduct the great music performed by the energetic students. All is right with
the universe. And then it happens: the one single
element that can bring the entire world crashing
down like a house of cards—bad intonation. It's a
menace that no living ensemble conductor can
escape. It creeps up on you at any time, and has an
impact of such magnitude that it can pull any
advanced ensemble, sophisticated composition, or
accomplished conductor down to what sounds
like a beginner-level exhibition. How does this
happen?

There are several major areas that all directors
should examine if they are indeed serious about
gaining control over this ever-present monster.
Therefore, to significantly improve the quality of
intonation in your ensembles, the following topics
are hereby suggested for experimentation. Any
one or combination of these items should bring
noticeable results to everyone involved—you, your
ensemble, and equally, if not more importantly,
your audience.

'Beatless' Tuning
A typical ensemble rehearsal begins with the
director who finds a starting pitch (for instance,
B-flat) and instructs the ensemble to tune to that
note. Contrary to popular belief, that may not be
the most effective way to get your ensemble on
the same wavelength. Many ensemble directors
have begun to realize this. Ed List, one of the

foremost authorities on developing intonation
skills for large ensembles, is a strong advocate of
the concept of 'beatless' tuning. He believes that
hearing a pitch as 'sharp' or 'flat' is not the primary goal; the real objective, according to Lisk, is
to recognize the beats that occur as a result of two
pitches that do not vibrate at the same speed, and
adjust accordingly. The alteration made on the
instrument to perfectly align the pitches up or
down is not relevant; the task is to listen for the
speed of vibrations and adjust until they gradually
slow down, ultimately ceasing altogether. There
are definite advantages to this approach, and upon
closer examination, one of them soon becomes
obvious; it reinforces the idea that students should
learn to hear for themselves, thus developing good
listening skills from the very beginning, instead of
solely depending on the director for a responsibility that they themselves should accept.

The second benefit, which may be even more
important, is that it reinforces the idea of constantly monitoring the pitch, from the beginning
to the end of the performance. This is in stark
contrast to the habits that many musicians develop, which is to tune at the beginning of the
rehearsal, and then forget it. Yet there are any
number of aspects that may affect the pitch during
performance. Using this approach ensures that all
members of the ensemble are not only acutely
aware of their sound, but are making a conscious
effort to hear their pitch as it relates to those sitting on either side of them, their section, and the
band as a whole.

Pitch Tendencies on the Instrument
One aspect of the tuning process that has an enormous effect on the sound of the ensemble is the
natural tendencies of the instrument itself. This is
an issue that should never be overlooked or under-
estimated by ensemble directors. To the contrary,
learning and memorizing the particular tendencies

of each instrument can save much time, energy, and frustration for both student and teacher.

For example, the notes B-flat, B-natural, and C below the staff on the trumpet have a tendency to be flat, while the low C-sharp and D will be sharp. In similar fashion, the G and A above the staff will be sharp, while the B-flat—only a half step higher—will be flat. With trombones, the middle C tends to be flat, the F above the staff is sharp, while the G—only a step higher—will be flat. For saxes, the low F to B-flat is flat, while the pitches generated by the palm keys are generally sharp, as well as those notes generated by the octave key.

Although these are but a few examples of pitch tendencies, there are many more instances that occur as a result of the partial series found in music. Those directors who are well-aware of these variances have a better chance at maintaining an ensemble that plays in tune most of the time.

Breath Support

It comes as no surprise that one of the leading causes of bad intonation occurs as a result of a lack of breath support. Consequently, young players who do not blow a sufficient amount of air through the horn will not play in tune. What typically happens is this: the student does not fill the lungs with enough air initially, and they try to compensate for the pitch deficiency by altering their embouchure, which usually amounts to a thin, pinched sound. The cumulative effect is that the entire ensemble will tend to play sharp because the players are overblowing in an attempt to make up for the lack of volume and tone that can only be created by a good, steady air stream. If ensemble directors are constantly aware of this, they can, in turn, remind students to continually monitor themselves by sitting up straight when they play, maintaining the proper angle of the instrument to their lips, and striving to produce the largest, roundest tone possible.

This last point cannot be stressed enough; without good tone, the time spent on developing an individual's pitch accuracy is practically useless. It is imperative, therefore, to instill in students at an early age the importance of proper technique to create breath support, which undoubtedly leads to better intonation. Technique, tone, and intonation—the three are inextricably linked.

Embouchure

Using the proper embouchure in performance is crucial to the ensemble's sound. Although which technique works best has and will always be subject to debate among directors, there really is only one criteria: the method that produces the fullest, most consistent sound is the one to use. Still, there are as many different teaching styles as there are directors. This becomes readily apparent when examining the wide variety of approaches to embouchure among students in ensembles. The situation is complicated by the fact that the director of the ensemble may not be as versed on one instrument family as another, and as one might expect, the instrument he or she plays is the one they know best. While it might be unrealistic to expect the director to become an instant expert on every instrument in the ensemble, it is not unreasonable to suggest here that every director should take the time to invite a specialist for each family of instruments to sit in on a rehearsal or two and give a 'checkup' to each member of the band. The results may be surprising.

Equipment

Every director wishes each member of the ensemble could afford to purchase the best instrument available. This is because the quality of an instrument has everything to do with intonation. It is sometimes difficult to convince students, parents, and even administrators that, in many instances, the level of craftsmanship used to make instruments has a major influence on how well students perform, not to mention their self-perception of musicianship. Yet it is a worthwhile endeavor to encourage every participant to get the most affordable instrument as early as possible. This is important because our ears adapt very quickly, and one can easily become comfortable with an excellent sound just as quickly as becoming complacent with a poor sound.

When deciding on which model will be bought, both students and teacher should be mindful of the effect that each particular brand will have on the student's individual tone, as well as the ensemble's overall sound. Then there are differences in tone within the same brand or model, which should also be taken into consideration. In addition, accessories such as reeds, mouthpieces, and headjoints play a large role in defining the sound. There are rare instances, however, where the instrument itself is out of tune, and no amount of adjusting can overcome or compensate for the inherent intonation problems. Still, it stands to reason that the more an instrument costs, the fewer intonation problems one may expect to encounter.

Tuning in Context

This may sound a little strange, but how much good does it actually do to tune to a B-flat if the first chord of the composition is an A major chord? The point here is that in addition to the standard, comfortable tuning notes of concert B-flat or F, there is an awful lot of information that can be gained as a result of making tuning adjustments that are related to the actual tune being performed. There are many advantages to this approach, the most obvious being that it sends a message to students that process of tuning is not an isolated event, but one that is directly and continually connected to the composition.

Secondly, it gives the ensemble an opportunity to extricate specific areas of the piece and focus on the quality of resonation of the chord structure, which, in part, depends on the voicing of the chord. Because each voicing naturally produces a different kind of resonance, both director and student can make the proper intonation adjustments based on three things: what degree of the chord each instrument is playing, what register of the instrument they are in, and what the proper balance of tone and volume should be at that particular spot in the piece. This method is significantly more effective for the purpose of hearing where intonation problems are 'hiding' in the music.

Resonance

We have already discussed that a great deal of the problem related to tuning is hidden in the fabric of bad posture, lack of breath support, bad equipment, instrument-related pitch tendencies, and other things. One of the most enlightening discoveries about intonation occurs when one realizes that an ensemble that plays well in tune is substantially more powerful as a unit than one that does not. In many cases, a smaller-sized ensemble can out-perform a larger group if they play with 'beatless' tuning because the notes no longer cancel each other out. The ensemble is truly in harmony with itself; thus, the entire ensemble resonates together. Many ensembles mistakenly try to recreate this power (which emanates from playing in tune) with the inadequate substitution of sheer volume, generally causing members of the ensemble to over-blow—the very thing that leads to intonation problems to begin with, just as we mentioned earlier. On the other hand, it is such a pleasurable experience to hear a small ensemble that produces a sound twice its size—the natural result of good intonation.

Closing Thoughts

The time spent working on developing intonation is well worth the effort. Here, as a final word, is a short list of do's and don't's that will make your ensemble sound better every time.

Don't:

- Don't tune to only one note; find chord voicings within the composition that resonate; teach students to listen and adjust.
- Don't back away from dissonance; learn to remove it by altering the embouchure until beats are removed.
- Don't just tune up first and forget it; tune again after the instruments are warmed up.
- Don't tune to section leaders who have bad tone; tune to those who produce the largest, roundest tone.
- Don't think the problem is solved quickly, easily, or permanently.

Do:

- Develop listening skills by using the 'beatless'-tuning process.
- Learn to adjust embouchure before adjusting the instrument.
- Tune to the key/chord you're going to be playing in the composition.
- Commit instrumental tendencies to memory (pairing students to use 'pitch tendency' sheets works well).
- Develop students' tone, and good intonation will follow.
- Remember that good intonation leads to more power and volume.

In Part Two of this article, we will discuss specific solutions for better intonation, including an in-depth explanation of how to use pitch tendency sheets for a better sounding ensemble. Until then, good luck, and keep striving to make good music.

Wayne E. Goins is assistant professor of music and director of the jazz program at Kansas University in Manhattan, Kansas. This article originally appeared in the Winter 1999 issue of the Michigan Music Educator. *Reprinted by permission.*

Learning to Play in Tune, Part II

by Wayne E. Goins

In Part I of this article, we discussed the conductors' dilemma of constantly battling the problems associated with intonation. The primary areas mentioned for consideration when attempting to resolve bad intonation included: using the 'beatless'-tuning method; becoming aware of natural pitch tendencies on the instrument; using breath support; using proper embouchure; buying good equipment; tuning in musical context; and finally, reaping the positive effects of resonance as a result of good intonation throughout the ensemble.

In this article, we will discuss specific solutions that can help lead to better intonation for your ensembles. More specifically, there are two methods presented here that are intended to serve as a means of addressing intonation on both an individual and collective basis: pitch tendency sheets and function chorales.

First, we will address the effective use of tendency sheets as a method of isolating specific pitches in each band member's everyday performance. To begin with, there are two specific areas to be investigated if we wish to isolate the problem: (a) the natural tendencies of the particular instrument to go flat or sharp in certain areas within the range of notes, and (b) the natural tendencies of the players themselves to go sharp or flat, which may occur as a result of either their embouchure, their reeds/mouthpieces, or possibly a combination of both.

Pitch Tendency Sheets

One of the most effective ways for each student to locate his or her own problem areas on the instrument is to observe the pitch location over a designated period of time. This is a very logical way to notice if there are any consistent patterns of behavior in the mechanics of the instrument or flaws in performing technique of the student. The 'Pitch Tendency Sheets' (See figure 1) are designed to identify each pitch individually and throughout the entire range of the instrument. Here's the procedure:

1. Have each student team up with a partner. Student 'A' will be the performer, while student 'B' serves as a 'pitch monitor.' Both students are to find a quiet location, preferably a practice room.
2. Student 'A' takes a few minutes to get the instrument warmed up by running a few scales, arpeggios, or musical passages, until he or she feels comfortable and ready to play.
3. Student 'A' then plays each chromatic note individually, starting from the middle range of the instruments and proceeding upwards or downwards in chromatic succession, covering three octaves.
4. Student 'B,' using a standard tuning device, compares the pitch of the student to the indication of the tuner, and records (a) whether student 'A' is sharp or flat, and (b) by how many cents in either direction.
5. Student 'A' proceeds to the next chromatic pitch, and the process is repeated until all the pitches are played and documented.

It is important to note, however, that the student performing should not look at the tuner, as this may have an effect on natural performing tendencies. The complete procedure should be done three times, either in successive days, or over an entire week by putting a day of no activity (i.e., Tuesday, Thursday) in between testing days (Monday, Wednesday, Friday).

Examining the Chart

Once the data has been collected and entered for all twelve pitches on all three days, then all one has to do is to look for patterns of consistency in regard to flatness or sharpness. If, for example, a bass clarinetist observes that for all three days, the note 'G' in the first octave has a strong tendency to be sharp by 10–15 cents, there is a strong possibility that the phenomenon may be occurring every time the note is played. The pitch, therefore, can be compensated for by dropping the jaw in order to alter the embouchure so that every time that particular note is encountered, an adjustment is made automatically so that the student is better in tune with the ensemble. In other cases and with other instruments, maybe an alternate fingering (trumpets, for example) is the key to better intonation for certain pitches.

The clear advantage to the continual use of pitch tendency sheets is that, if students commit their tendencies to memory and make their adjustments in real time when performing a piece within the ensemble, the difference can be astounding. Obviously, to achieve visible (or in this case, aural) results, the entire ensemble has to be committed to the cause of striving to improve their overall ensemble sound. Indeed, it is every band director's dream to have each individual member in the band show such concern about

Figure 1. Wind Instrument Pitch Tendency Chart

| Name | Instrument | Make and Model |

Instructions

1. Work in pairs using a metered tuning device (strobo Conn, Korg, etc.).
2. While playing each pitch, have your partner indicate on the chart whether the pitch is sharp or flat (circle symbol) as well as number of cents sharp or flat. *Note:* the player should not look at the tuner.
3. This is to be done three separate times (once each week), correcting the deficiencies each time.
4. This assignment must be completed by _____.

	1st Reading Date: Recorder:	**2nd Reading** Date: Recorder:	**3rd Reading** Date: Recorder:
A	Octave 1: ♭ ♯ cents_____ 2: ♭ ♯ cents_____ 3: ♭ ♯ cents_____	Octave 1: ♭ ♯ cents_____ 2: ♭ ♯ cents_____ 3: ♭ ♯ cents_____	Octave 1: ♭ ♯ cents_____ 2: ♭ ♯ cents_____ 3: ♭ ♯ cents_____
A♯ B♭	Octave 1: ♭ ♯ cents_____ 2: ♭ ♯ cents_____ 3: ♭ ♯ cents_____	Octave 1: ♭ ♯ cents_____ 2: ♭ ♯ cents_____ 3: ♭ ♯ cents_____	Octave 1: ♭ ♯ cents_____ 2: ♭ ♯ cents_____ 3: ♭ ♯ cents_____
B	Octave 1: ♭ ♯ cents_____ 2: ♭ ♯ cents_____ 3: ♭ ♯ cents_____	Octave 1: ♭ ♯ cents_____ 2: ♭ ♯ cents_____ 3: ♭ ♯ cents_____	Octave 1: ♭ ♯ cents_____ 2: ♭ ♯ cents_____ 3: ♭ ♯ cents_____
C	Octave 1: ♭ ♯ cents_____ 2: ♭ ♯ cents_____ 3: ♭ ♯ cents_____	Octave 1: ♭ ♯ cents_____ 2: ♭ ♯ cents_____ 3: ♭ ♯ cents_____	Octave 1: ♭ ♯ cents_____ 2: ♭ ♯ cents_____ 3: ♭ ♯ cents_____
C♯ D♭	Octave 1: ♭ ♯ cents_____ 2: ♭ ♯ cents_____ 3: ♭ ♯ cents_____	Octave 1: ♭ ♯ cents_____ 2: ♭ ♯ cents_____ 3: ♭ ♯ cents_____	Octave 1: ♭ ♯ cents_____ 2: ♭ ♯ cents_____ 3: ♭ ♯ cents_____
D	Octave 1: ♭ ♯ cents_____ 2: ♭ ♯ cents_____ 3: ♭ ♯ cents_____	Octave 1: ♭ ♯ cents_____ 2: ♭ ♯ cents_____ 3: ♭ ♯ cents_____	Octave 1: ♭ ♯ cents_____ 2: ♭ ♯ cents_____ 3: ♭ ♯ cents_____
D♯ E♭	Octave 1: ♭ ♯ cents_____ 2: ♭ ♯ cents_____ 3: ♭ ♯ cents_____	Octave 1: ♭ ♯ cents_____ 2: ♭ ♯ cents_____ 3: ♭ ♯ cents_____	Octave 1: ♭ ♯ cents_____ 2: ♭ ♯ cents_____ 3: ♭ ♯ cents_____
E	Octave 1: ♭ ♯ cents_____ 2: ♭ ♯ cents_____ 3: ♭ ♯ cents_____	Octave 1: ♭ ♯ cents_____ 2: ♭ ♯ cents_____ 3: ♭ ♯ cents_____	Octave 1: ♭ ♯ cents_____ 2: ♭ ♯ cents_____ 3: ♭ ♯ cents_____
F	Octave 1: ♭ ♯ cents_____ 2: ♭ ♯ cents_____ 3: ♭ ♯ cents_____	Octave 1: ♭ ♯ cents_____ 2: ♭ ♯ cents_____ 3: ♭ ♯ cents_____	Octave 1: ♭ ♯ cents_____ 2: ♭ ♯ cents_____ 3: ♭ ♯ cents_____
F♯ G♭	Octave 1: ♭ ♯ cents_____ 2: ♭ ♯ cents_____ 3: ♭ ♯ cents_____	Octave 1: ♭ ♯ cents_____ 2: ♭ ♯ cents_____ 3: ♭ ♯ cents_____	Octave 1: ♭ ♯ cents_____ 2: ♭ ♯ cents_____ 3: ♭ ♯ cents_____
G	Octave 1: ♭ ♯ cents_____ 2: ♭ ♯ cents_____ 3: ♭ ♯ cents_____	Octave 1: ♭ ♯ cents_____ 2: ♭ ♯ cents_____ 3: ♭ ♯ cents_____	Octave 1: ♭ ♯ cents_____ 2: ♭ ♯ cents_____ 3: ♭ ♯ cents_____
G♯ A♭	Octave 1: ♭ ♯ cents_____ 2: ♭ ♯ cents_____ 3: ♭ ♯ cents_____	Octave 1: ♭ ♯ cents_____ 2: ♭ ♯ cents_____ 3: ♭ ♯ cents_____	Octave 1: ♭ ♯ cents_____ 2: ♭ ♯ cents_____ 3: ♭ ♯ cents_____

intonation, and take an active part in remedying the situation.

There is, however, still one caveat that one cannot forget; there is always the reality that the results of the three-day trial may be affected by the make and model of the instrument, the choice of mouthpieces or reeds used, and any number of other external factors. For this reason, it is strongly urged that each student choose to do his or her own 'research project,' so to speak, and experiment with various aspects of instrument setup in order to find out which combination of embouchure, instrument, fingerings, mouthpieces, etc. will give them the best overall results for accurate intonation. And with every three-day trial, each student will have a much more knowledgeable relationship with his or her instrument and will know the pitch tendencies for every note.

Function Chorales

While pitch tendency sheets are used primarily for individual development, the purpose of 'function chorales' is to enhance students' ability to develop a higher level of discriminatory-listening skills in a group setting. Composer Stephen Melillo designed twenty-two function chorales which accomplish multiple tasks simultaneously; they are designed to teach ear training through the development of skills in the areas of intonation, tuning, and music theory.

The strength of using this system lies in its diversity. The function chorales are designed to be used by all ensembles of any size, and can be performed by students of all ages and in any key. Naturally, each chorale is written in four parts. Therefore, no matter what the size, the entire ensemble is divided into the four traditional sections of soprano, alto, tenor, and bass. Each function chorale uses numeric notation, which allows the musician to 'see' where a pitch will sound before it is played. The advantage of the numeric system is that each section is able to switch parts so that every member of the ensemble has the opportunity to play the roles of soprano, alto, tenor, and bass. Each member is encouraged to adjust their chosen parts to fit the octave range that is most comfortable to them.

For the band director who uses this system, it is important to realize what can be accomplished if properly applied to the rehearsal. For example, some short range goals might be to increase each students' awareness of intervals, vertical chord voicings, horizontal movement. Yet another goal might be to instill greater intonation

throughout the entire ensemble by encouraging each member to listen for balance in volume among sections.

Similarly, some long-range goals might include developing listening skills to the level where there is 'beatless' intonation not only within, but across each section. These chorales can be used for concert, symphonic, or jazz ensembles. Because many jazz musicians are accustomed to using both Roman numerals for chord progressions, as well as extended chord voicings, many members of the jazz ensemble will find this particular system to be quite familiar, and, therefore, an even more enjoyable experience. Once the band director and students are both familiar with the system, added musical elements such as dynamics, tempo changes, fermatas, etc., can be added to create the most musical experience for the ensemble.

Getting Started

There are two preparatory exercises which are designed before beginning the twenty-two exercises. The first is a drill which serves to develop students' ability to hear each note in a major scale as a number in a series of seven numbers. Because the maximum benefits can be derived from this system by playing each exercise in every key, it is suggested that every student be able to play all of their major scales in the cycle of fourths (F, B-flat, E-flat, A-flat, D-flat, G-flat, C-flat, F-flat) and the cycle of fifths (F, C, G, D, A, E, B)

Once this is accomplished, slight alterations to any degree of the scale creates any desired mode. The result is that students can learn all of their modes in a simple manner. For example instead of discussing modes in an unfamiliar way, one might explain the mixolydian mode not as the fifth mode in the diatonic series, but as a major scale with a lowered 7th degree, which is an explanation which is generally much more palatable to the uninitiated.

The second listening exercise involves a portion of the overtone series. Students begin by starting on a concert pitch in unison (C), and moving down to the fifth of the key (G), then down to the octave of the original concert pitch. Do this exercise starting on concert B-flat, and repeat in descending half steps down to E, for a total of 7 repetitions. The rhythmic pattern will be half note, half note, whole note. Melillo's unique notation system is a practical, yet efficient use of space (see the Function Chorale in figure 2). Hidden in the diagrams are all the components needed to reproduce the desired musical state-

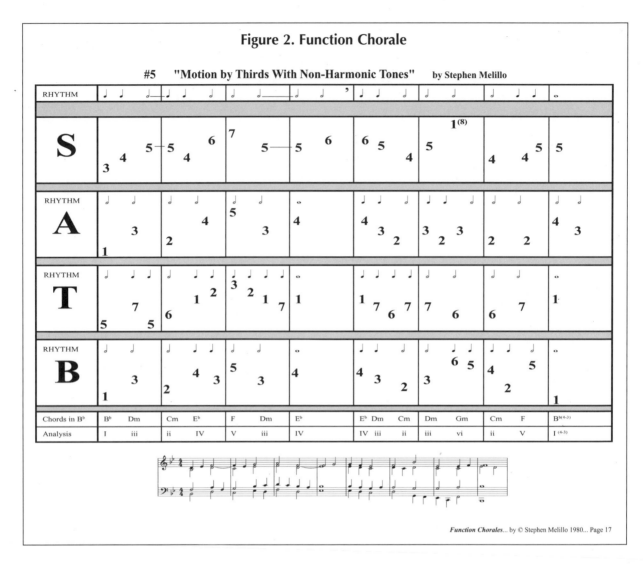

Figure 2. Function Chorale

#5 "Motion by Thirds With Non-Harmonic Tones" by Stephen Melillo

Function Chorales... by © Stephen Melillo 1980... Page 17

ments intended by the author. Observe the following aspects that are included in each of his original arrangements:

1. Each *rhythm* of each exercise is written in whole notes, half notes, and quarter notes. The note values are kept as simple as possible for easy reading, while maintaining the integrity of the four-part chorale tradition.
2. The *note values* can be determined by how many numbers (which represent scale degrees) are in each 'measure,' which is represented by a box or frame.
3. The vertical *harmony* is distributed among the four sections of SATB.
4. The horizontal *melody,* or contour, is determined by the relative placement of the number inside the frame. In other words, a '5,' or fifth degree of the scale, would be physically located in a higher position in the frame space than a '3,' or third.

5. The *form,* or chord progression, is determined by the specific notes designated to each section (SATB) as one moves across each frame.

At the bottom of each of the twenty-two exercises, the four-part chorale is written out in standard notation, along with an accompanying traditional Roman numeral analysis. This can be covered or whited out on the photocopied pages as an exercise for students to develop their ability to 'see' what they hear. Each chorale uses common chord progressions from the diatonic system, and by altering the basic structure of each individual chord, creating the type of vertical and horizontal movement that is regularly encountered in classical, jazz, and blues chord progressions.

Maximum Benefits

Because this system is based primarily on theoretical principles, there is no standard written notation, and each exercise is written by numbers, which serves two purposes. First, it increases the listening skills of students who no longer have written notation as a distraction, thus allowing them to hear with more accuracy. Secondly, it strengthens the students' mental images of where a note lies in the vertical scheme.

Closing Thoughts

It is hoped that these two methods will help both band director and students experience a more positive experience as a result of better intonation. Although there are undoubtedly other methods

and approaches by those who have devised ways to combat the ever-present intonation problem, with a conscious effort, these two approaches are good places to start and can serve as first steps on a long journey toward experiencing the joy that accompanies musical consonance.

Wayne E. Goins is assistant professor of music and director of the jazz program at Kansas University in Manhattan, Kansas. This article originally appeared in the Spring 2000 issue of the Michigan Music Educator. *Reprinted by permission.*

The Gender-Stereotyping of Band Instruments
by Christopher S. Harvey

The Problem

Many factors are involved in the instrument-selection process. Common influences on students when choosing an instrument include: the sound of the instrument; the influence of music teachers, parents, and friends; the availability of the instrument; and the size of the instrument (Fortney, Boyle, & DeCarbo, 1993). Previous research has shown that the gender association of certain instruments also plays a role in the instrument selection process (Abeles & Porter, 1974; Delzell & Leppla, 1992; Griswold & Chroback, 1981). The attitudes and preferences of young children, middle school students, college students, and adults toward various instruments have been investigated by other researchers such as Abeles and Porter (1974), Byo (1991), Fortney, Boyle, and DeCarbo (1993), and Griswold and Chroback (1981).

Some implications of instrument preference for music teachers have been presented in a survey of related literature by Coffman and Sehmann (1989). Coffman and Sehmann have summarized the findings of various researchers by making the following observations: (a) young children do not show preference for particular instruments (Geringer, 1977), (b) the sex-stereotyping of instruments first appears in children around the third grade (Abeles and Porter, 1974) and lasts through adulthood (Griswold and Chroback, 1981), (c) parents choose instruments that are sex-stereotyped for their children (Abeles and Porter, 1974), and (d) the gender of the per-

former affects the sex-stereotyping of instruments (Abeles and Porter, 1974). Thus, it seems that some students may be limiting their music opportunities by choosing to play instruments that are stereotyped as being appropriate only for a certain sex of player.

The main purpose of this study, therefore, was twofold: (a) to discover which instruments of the band are stereotyped by gender and (b) to investigate the characteristics of the instruments which cause them to be viewed as either masculine or feminine. A secondary purpose of the study was to examine if the instrumental ratings vary by sex.

The researcher decided to include only the following band instruments in the study: flute, clarinet, saxophone, trumpet, French horn, trombone, tuba, and snare drum. Likewise, only the association of size, pitch, and volume of the instruments to gender-stereotyping was investigated. The fact that all participants in this study were volunteers was the primary limitation of the study.

The term gender-stereotyping rather than sex-stereotyping has been used for the purposes of this study. *Sex* refers to the biological characteristics of men and women whereas *gender* is used to describe behavioral characteristics (Archer & Lloyd, 1982). For the purpose of this study, an instrument that is considered "masculine" is one that a boy is more likely to play while an instrument that is considered "feminine" is one that a girl is more likely to play. Furthermore, in this study, the *pitch* of an instrument refers to the relative highness or lowness of an instrument's sound. The *volume* refers to the relative loudness or softness of an instrument's sound.

Related Literature: Instrument Gender Association

Attitudes of Elementary School Children

Several studies have examined the issue of gender associations with musical instruments. Geringer (1977) studied children's preferences by observing their behavior. Geringer and his assistants observed 40 children, ages three to five, who had had no previous musical training. Students were found to show no preference toward any instruments. Abeles and Porter (1978) also found that sex-stereotyping of instruments did not occur in children who were in the third grade and below. However, by fourth grade, male students were more likely to prefer those instruments thought to be masculine, and female students were more likely to prefer those instruments thought to be feminine.

In a recent study dealing with fourth-grade students' instrument preferences, Delzell and Leppla (1992) compared data concerning gender association of instruments with the findings of earlier research studies by Abeles and Porter (1974) and Griswold and Chroback (1981). It appears that certain instrument preferences have changed noticeably. The saxophone has gained in popularity while the trumpet has dropped. Gender association was not given as a reason to play a first-choice instrument in the study, but it was given as a reason not to play a last-choice instrument. Delzell and Leppla concluded in their study that gender associations with instruments have decreased since 1978. Associations by gender may have lessened because of the Title IX laws and the fact that society in general has increased its sensitivity to the issue of gender stereotyping (Delzell & Leppla, 1992).

Attitudes of Middle School Students

In a study investigating middle school band instrument choices, Fortney, Boyle, and DeCarbo (1993) presented a survey to 990 middle school students from 13 middle schools in Florida. The results of this study showed strong gender-associations with certain instruments. Specifically, the flute and clarinet were chosen most often by female students while the members of the brass family and percussion were most often selected by male students. These results support previous research on gender-stereotyping of instruments (Abeles & Porter, 1974; Delzell & Leppla, 1992). Middle school music teachers, parents, and friends were listed as other influences in the instrument selection process.

Attitudes of University Students

Abeles and Porter (1978) presented college music majors and nonmajors with paired comparisons of eight instruments. Subjects were asked to circle the instrument they considered to be more masculine. The instruments were then ranked from most feminine to most masculine in the following order: flute, violin, clarinet, cello, saxophone, trumpet, trombone, and drum. No significant difference was found between the rankings of music majors and those of the nonmajors.

In a similar study, Griswold and Chroback (1981) surveyed music majors and nonmusic majors concerning the sex-stereotyping of instruments. In contrast to Abeles and Porter (1974), music majors and nonmajors rated the instruments differently. Music majors were more prone than nonmusic majors to rank the instruments in a masculine direction (particularly the clarinet and string bass). The Griswold and Chroback study included an examination of 15 instruments as well as the instrumental and choral conductor. Instruments rated as feminine included harp, flute, piccolo, and glockenspiel, while saxophone, drum, trumpet, string bass, and tuba were rated as masculine.

Masculine and Feminine Stereotypes

In a study investigating masculine and feminine stereotypes, Williams and Bennett (1975) asked university students to choose from a list of 300 adjectives that were associated with either men or women. Among the adjectives that were associated with women were gentle, meek, and mild. Adjectives associated with men included assertive, dominant, forceful, and loud. Perhaps some connection can be made between these adjectives associated with gender and the roles of the instruments that are associated with a certain gender. For instance, in both the Abeles and Porter (1978) and Delzell and Leppla (1992) studies, the drum (typically a loud instrument) had the strongest masculine association and the flute (a gentle instrument) the strongest feminine association.

In a similar study, four groups of university students were asked to classify 400 adjectives in order to find those that described characteristics of men and women (Bem, 1974). Gentle, soft-spoken, and tender were among the adjectives found to have feminine connotations in the *Bem Sex Role Inventory*. Among the masculine adjectives were aggressive, forceful, and dominant.

Spence, Helmenrich, and Stapp (1975) developed the *Personal Attributes Questionnaire* in order to find those characteristics that were female-valued items, male-valued items, and sex-specific items. In this study, the enjoyment of music and the arts was found to be a female-valued item. Aggressive, dominant, and loud were all adjectives that were found to be sex-specific to males. Again, a connection can be made with these adjectives and the roles of those instruments that are stereotyped by gender in the band.

Parental Influences on Sex-Stereotyped Activities

Abeles and Porter (1978) also examined adult attitudes toward musical instruments. Each subject was asked to indicate the top three choices of an instrument they would like their fifth-grade son or daughter to play. Their options were: cello, clarinet, drums, flute, saxophone, trombone, trumpet, and violin. The instruments most often chosen for boys to play were the drum, trumpet, and trombone. The flute, clarinet, and violin were chosen most frequently for girls to play. These results are consistent with other studies regarding the sex-stereotyping of musical instruments (Delzell & Leppla, 1992; Griswold & Chobrack, 1981).

Furthermore, research has verified that parents encourage sex-typed activities. It has found that boys are more likely to receive disapproval from their parents for engaging in activities that are sex-typed as female activities than girls are for engaging in activities that are sex-typed as male activities (Macoby and Jacklin, 1974). Simply put, the literature indicates that it is more acceptable for a girl to be a "tomboy" than for a boy to be a "sissy." In a study concerning sex-typed activities, Lansky (1967, cited in Macoby & Jacklin, 1974) reported that parents did not object to girls engaging in typical male activities. However, parents reacted negatively when a boy chose a typical female activity.

These findings explain why it is more common to find males playing instruments that are categorized as masculine (e.g., trumpet, trombone, snare drum) than it is to find males playing instruments that are categorized as feminine (e.g., flute and clarinet).

Methodology

The subjects were 20 undergraduate and graduate students, both males and females, who were enrolled in summer courses at the University of North Dakota. The subjects were volunteers over the age of 18 who resided in a residence hall. Some subjects had had previous band experience and some had not.

A three-part researcher-constructed survey was used to gather data about gender stereotyping. Subjects completed the five-minute survey in the study lounges in their residence hall. A test-retest reliability coefficient of .95 was obtained with a sample of five subjects who took the test twice. The researcher administered the survey both individually and in small groups. On the first section of the survey, subjects were asked to provide descriptive information concerning their sex and years of experience in a school band program. In the second part of the survey, students were asked to rate eight band instruments on a Likert-type scale constructed by the researcher.

The third section of the survey investigated why the instruments are characterized as "masculine" or "feminine." Subjects rated the size, volume, and pitch of the eight instruments on the same Likert-type scale as in the second part of the survey. These 24 questions were ordered in a random manner on the survey by selecting each question out of a box individually. The researcher's choice of the particular characteristics (size, volume, and pitch) of the instruments was based on a study by Fortney, Boyle, and DeCarbo (1993). In this study, sound was given most often as an influence on instrument choice in middle school students and since pitch and volume are two important factors that make up an instrument's sound, they were selected for inclusion in the present study. The size of an instrument was also given as an influence on instrument choice in the same study.

Analysis

The mean ratings and standard deviations for the eight instruments examined in the study are displayed Table 1. The instruments are placed on a continuum from feminine to masculine. The flute was rated as the most feminine while the tuba was rated the most masculine.

Table 2 examines the gender rating for instrument pitch. The results were similar to the results in Table 1 with the exception that the snare drum (a nonpitched instrument) was ranked higher than the trumpet and saxophone.

Means for instrument size are reported in Table 3 and again the results are similar to those in Table 1. Although the ratings of the trumpet and saxophone differ from the overall ratings reported in Table 1, the remaining instruments occupy their same positions on the feminine-masculine continuum.

Means for the gender rating of instrument volume are reported in Table 4. While the means differ slightly, the instruments occupy the same positions in the feminine-masculine continuum as in Table 1.

The mean gender ratings of the instrument total (pitch + size + volume) in Table 5 were consistent with the overall mean gender ratings of the instruments as reported in Table 1.

An ANOVA (analysis of variance) procedure indicated that there was no significant difference in the overall mean gender instrumental ratings of the male and female subjects.

Table 6 displays the Pearson-Product-Moment correlation coefficients between the mean gender ratings of the instrument characteristics (size, volume, and pitch) and the total mean gender ratings of the instruments. All coefficients were significant at a $p<.05$ level.

The size, volume, and pitch were all shown to have a significant relationship with the total mean gender ratings of the instruments. However, the relationship between each characteristic and the total mean gender rating varied by instrument. For

instance, the size of the clarinet, saxophone, and tuba had the highest relationship with their total mean gender ratings. Likewise, the volume of the flute and trombone and the pitch of the French horn, trumpet, and snare drum had the highest relationship with their total mean gender ratings.

While the pitch of the French horn, trumpet,

Table 1. Mean Gender Rating of Instrument

Instrument	Mean	Standard Deviation
Flute	4.10	.97
Clarinet	3.85	.58
French Horn	3.30	.73
Saxophone	2.65	.67
Trumpet	2.30	.57
Snare Drum	2.15	.67
Trombone	1.85	.67
Tuba	1.70	.87

1 = very masculine   5 = very feminine $N = 20$

Table 2. Mean Gender Rating of Instrument Pitch

Instrument	Mean	Standard Deviation
Flute	4.10	.85
Clarinet	3.70	.66
French Horn	3.20	.70
Saxophone	2.55	.61
Trumpet	2.50	.69
Snare Drum	2.60	.68
Trombone	2.10	.48
Tuba	1.65	.67

1 = very masculine   5 = very feminine $N = 20$

Table 3. Mean Gender Rating of Instrument Size

Instrument	Mean	Standard Deviation
Flute	3.85	.93
Clarinet	3.40	.75
French Horn	3.05	.61
Trumpet	2.80	.41
Saxophone	2.50	.83
Snare Drum	2.45	.51
Trombone	2.05	.51
Tuba	1.55	.46

1 = very masculine   5 = very feminine $N = 20$

Table 4. Mean Gender Rating of Instrument Volume

Instrument	Mean	Standard Deviation
Flute	4.10	.72
Clarinet	3.20	.79
French Horn	3.10	.79
Saxophone	2.75	.51
Trumpet	2.25	.64
Snare Drum	2.20	.77
Trombone	2.00	.46
Tuba	1.40	.60

1 = very masculine   5 = very feminine $N = 20$

Table 5. Mean Gender Rating of Instrument Total (Pitch + Size + Volume)

Instrument	Mean	Standard Deviation
Flute	12.05	1.93
Clarinet	10.30	1.34
French Horn	9.35	1.79
Saxophone	7.80	1.44
Trumpet	7.55	1.28
Snare Drum	7.25	1.48
Trombone	6.15	.99
Tuba	4.60	1.60

3 = very masculine   15 = very feminine $N = 20$

and snare drum yielded the highest correlation coefficients, the pitch of the remaining five instruments indicated the lowest relationship with their total mean gender ratings. The volume of the trumpet, the size of the French horn, and the size of the snare drum were the variables with the lowest relationship to the instrument's total mean gender ratings.

Conclusions

The data gathered in this study confirm that certain instruments of the band are strongly stereotyped by gender. The flute and clarinet were rated as very feminine while the trombone and tuba were rated as very masculine. These results are consistent with a study conducted by Griswold and Chroback (1981). While the method used to gather the data differed, the instruments were located in the same positions on a feminine-masculine continuum in the two studies.

A moderate to high correlation (.41–.96) was found between the pitch, volume, and size of all the instruments with the total masculine and feminine ratings of the instruments. This would suggest that these characteristics (pitch, volume, and size) are all factors that contribute to the instrument's perceived masculinity or femininity. However, it seems that different characteristics were more strongly associated with the total mean gender rating depending upon the instrument.

The results of this study may be used by band directors in the formulation of strategies for counteracting bias in the instrument selection process. For example, perhaps more girls would be interested in playing those instruments that are considered masculine (trombone and tuba) if they did not have to carry such a big instrument to and from school. In order to accomplish this, a school could provide these instruments for students to use at home. A strategy for encouraging boys to select instruments that are considered feminine (flute and clarinet) might include the demonstration of these instruments by male performers.

Some directors may not wish to actively recruit band members to play certain instruments solely for the purpose of lessening gender-stereotypes. However, all directors must provide a positive learning atmosphere for those students who choose to play instruments that are perceived as inappropriate due to their gender associations. Students must also be aware of the implications of playing a gender-stereotyped instrument that others deem inappropriate. This holds true especially for boys who choose to play the flute or clarinet,

Table 6. Pearson-Product-Moment Coefficient between the Mean Gender Ratings of the Instrument Characteristics and the Total Mean Gender Rating of the Instrument	
Variables	r
Flute	
Size	.7923
Volume	.8305
Pitch	.6999
Clarinet	
Size	.7076
Volume	.7051
Pitch	.4061
Saxophone	
Size	.7974
Volume	.5591
Pitch	.5574
French Horn	
Size	.7141
Volume	.8717
Pitch	.9575
Trumpet	
Size	.7235
Volume	.6618
Pitch	.8089
Trombone	
Size	.7149
Volume	.8126
Pitch	.5598
Tuba	
Size	.8392
Volume	.8324
Pitch	.6592
Snare Drum	
Size	.6782
Volume	.7399
Pitch	.8347

All coefficients displayed were significant at the $p<.05$ level; $N = 20$.

the two most "feminine" instruments. Boys may choose not to play these instruments because of the ridicule they may be subjected to by their peers. In order to alleviate such negative pressure, directors must work to educate students that there is no such thing as a "boy's instrument" or a "girl's instrument." This concept should be stressed during the instrument selection process as well as throughout a student's instrumental career.

Furthermore, because parents are an important influence in the instrument selection process (Abeles & Porter, 1974), they too must be aware of the issue of gender stereotyping. The lessening of gender stereotyping of band instruments may occur through a combination of a gender-neutral approach to the instrument selection process by both the director and the parents of band students.

The researcher suggests that a specific member of the saxophone family (i.e., soprano, alto, tenor, baritone) be used in further research. Since the size of the saxophone was shown to be related to the total mean rating of the saxophone, different members of the saxophone family would most likely show different mean gender ratings. The researcher also suggests that the attitudes and preferences of current band students be investigated in further research. The reasons these students give for selecting their particular instruments may be helpful for directors in assessing the gender associations of instruments in the band.

In conclusion, this study shows that gender stereotyping of band instruments does exist. The results of this study may encourage directors to take a gender-neutral approach to the instrument selection process that will allow both male and female students equal musical opportunities and experiences.

References

Ables, H. F., & Porter, S. Y. (1978). The sex-stereotyping of musical instruments. *Journal of Research in Music Education, 26,* 65–75.

Archer, J., & Lloyd, B. (1982). *Sex and Gender* (2nd ed.). New York: Cambridge.

Bem, S. L. (1974). The measurement of psychological and androgyny. *Journal of Consulting and Clinical Psychology, 42,* 155–162.

Byo, J. (1991). An assessment of musical instrument preferences of third-grade children. *Bulletin of the Council for Research in Music Education, 110,* 21–32.

Coffman, D. D., & Sehmann, K. H. (1989). Musical Instrument Preference: Implications for music educators. *Update: Applications of Research in Music Education, 7,* 32–34.

Delzell, J. K., & Leppla, D. A. (1992). Gender association of musical instruments and preferences of fourth-grade students for selected instruments. *Journal of Research in Music Education, 40,* 93–103.

Fortney, P. M., Boyle, J. D., & DeCarbo, N. J. (1993). A study of middle school band students' instrument choices. *Journal of Research in Music Education, 41,* 28–39.

Griswold, P. A., & Chobrack, D. A. (1981). Sex-role associations of music instruments and occupations by gender and major. *Journal of Research in Music Education, 29,* 57–62.

Lansky, L. M. (1967). The family structure also affects the model: Sex-role attitudes in parents of pre-school children. *Merill-Palmer Quarterly, 13,* 139–150.

Macoby, E. M., & Jacklin, C. N. (1974). *The psychology of sex differences.* Stanford, CA: Stanford University Press.

Spence, J. T., Helmenreich, R., & Stapp, J. (1975). Ratings of self and peers on sex role attributes and their relation to self-esteem and conceptions of masculinity and femininity. *Journal of Personality and Social Psychology, 32,* 29–39.

Williams, J. E., & Bennett, S. M. (1975). The definition of sex stereotypes via the adjective check list. *Sex Roles, 1,* 327–337.

Christopher S. Harvey is director of bands in Hazen, North Dakota. This article originally appeared in the May 1995 issue of the North Dakota Music Educator. *Reprinted by permission.*

The First Five Minutes, or Don't Trip over the Mechanics

by Dave Killam

Who controls the first five minutes in your classroom? Probably precisely whoever will exercise control for the remainder of the period. Think on that.

A new band director was recently observed as students entered her room. One of the first to arrive immediately engaged this director in conversation, a really friendly chat clearly revealing good student-director rapport. Yet in the meantime, what were the remaining band members doing?

Some were following the example being set. They were engaging in their own private conversations. One couple tried out each other's instruments, always a delight from the perspective of the musical instrument repairman. Another twosome were engaged in jovial banter eventually turning into a poking contest. The noise level was rising.

Still other students started blowing "warm-up" sounds. More than a few of these bore little similarity to what most of us think of as legitimate warm-ups. Eventually one such sound went clearly beyond reasonable limits, at which point our beginning band director suddenly awoke to what was transpiring and raised the decibel level another several notches by screaming, "Who did that?"

There's no need to describe the scenario further. It may already be way too familiar to some. Breaking out of such patterns, however, demands a combination of self-discipline and adherence to preestablished rules alien to certain contemporary settings. And by "self-discipline" I refer to that of the director, not the students.

How easy it is to engage in pleasant conversation with a student or colleague at the precise time when our attention needs to be most keenly focused on the class as a whole. Some administrators even are frustratingly slow to realize that disruptions in the middle of a class, when things are orderly, often infringe far less than disruptions at passing time when decorum may be in a state of flux. (How's that for a euphemism?) Of course, we all know that no competent administrator would ever interrupt merely to assert authority or satisfy his own ego.

Learning starts the moment the student enters your room, particularly learning as regards expectations. Either said student decides what mode of entry is appropriate, or you the teacher decide. Which do you prefer? If you, the teacher, have placed yourself in the position of not even being aware of the varying attitudes and behaviors evidenced as your class arrives, you have relinquished a certain degree of control before you've even established it, and when working with students of varying ages, it can be mighty difficult to regain such prerogatives once youngsters have taken them over.

Let me propose an entirely different scenario. The teacher stands at the door as the class enters. Written on the blackboard are instructions to be carried out the moment the student is seated. These could be putting music in rehearsal order, checking certain trouble measures in a designated piece, checking fingering charts or reviewing less familiar scales. The possibilities are endless. How might your students respond to the blackboard directive, "We will warm up with a D minor melodic scale; the last two students seated and ready to play will be called upon to play their scales individually," or perhaps, "I have some free music materials I am discarding. First choice will be given to today's most helpful student (most hard working, best prepared, most considerate, etc.)"—again possibilities limited only by a teacher's imagination and preparation, but perhaps most importantly directed by concerns and needs arising from prior rehearsals.

As the class enters, one individual is overly loud. The teacher, immediately aware of such, calls said student aside for a one- or two-word reminder, not a conversation nor even an exchange. This reminder is rendered in a voice sufficiently subdued to both set the tone for the classroom and avoid embarrassing the student. Please note the term was reminder, not reprimand. Reprimands may also occasionally be in order, but if used when not justified, quickly become meaningless, ineffective, or worse, actually counter-productive.

Another student approaches with a broken instrument but is immediately sent to his seat with instructions to review band rules. These rules include the admonition, "Class time will be spent on class matters; individual needs will be addressed on personal time. Instrument repair problems are to be brought to the director's attention before school, after school, at home, or whatnot, but *never, ever* immediately prior to or during a rehearsal."

A band director standing in front of umpteen idle instrumentalists and taking that time to ascertain what is wrong with one individual's instrument more than likely has his head involved in the wrong examination.

Finally, no sound is produced on any instrument until the director plainly calls for it. How many problems in your band room could be remedied by adherence to this one simple principle?

Another activity that should never take place in rehearsal time is a director's searching for music. The search should always be done by the student (or band librarian) and in a manner so as not to disrupt the rehearsal.

But enough about band. Inattention to mechanics can trip a teacher up just as quickly in any class. How would you introduce rhythm band instruments to a second grade?

A parent with small daughter in tow once visited my home. The three-year-old quickly spied a song flute on my kitchen table, whereupon her mother told her, "You may pick it up, dear, and look at it but you're not to blow into it." How lovely it would have been to see the little dear tenderly pick up the flute, look it over really carefully and then gently return it to the table without blowing it. Except, of course, that's not what happened, and naturally the mother had to follow up by disciplining her very naughty child. Foolishness. Our very first responsibility is to be sure expectations are not only understood but are also reasonable and age appropriate.

The teacher who walks into a room, and hurriedly places a rhythm band instrument on the desk of every second grader is asking for bedlam.

Imagine this approach: You walk into the room with a closed box and announce, "I've got some really fun things in this box, and Jill will be the first to get one because I like the nice, quiet way she's sitting up and paying attention." (Slight pause while all emulate Jill's exemplary attentive attitude.)

"But I have to warn you about the instruments in this box. Some of them are naughty at times. Some of them might try to play with your hands and make noises before they should. So I'll tell you right off if anyone is unlucky and gets a naughty instrument that tries to play with their hands, we'll put it right back in the box really quickly. Now, who thinks if I put an instrument on the corner of their desk, they can make sure it doesn't try to touch their hands until I say it's time to pick it up and play it?"

And to the teacher who says, "Do I have to go all through something like this?" I respond, "If you don't, you're apt to go through something much worse." And of course this is not the only possible approach. It's but one suggestion, but one that's been tried, tested, and found effective. The point is merely that if you don't properly deal with the simple mechanics of passing out rhythm instruments, the rest of your lesson plan content may get lost in the shuffle.

When your chorus enters, are assigned chairs already in place with a folder of music on each, and again a note on the board immediately directing attention? (e.g., In which piece did altos encounter a tricky enharmonic change last rehearsal, and what was the lesson learned?)

Does your recorder group sound notes before you're ready? Have you taken steps to prevent such, especially steps like not taking too long getting ready?

Do you allow a fourth grader to be thumbing through a book when he should be pointing to notes on a designated page as he listens to you sing these notes?

Stop suddenly and unexpectedly: "How many were pointing to the third note in the seventh measure?"

As hands tentatively start to rise, "Oh, really, that's too bad, you must have lost your place, how many were in the tenth measure?—Gee wiz, you got lost too. Guess we'll have to try it again, and I'm going to walk around as I sing and see how many pointing fingers are staying right with me in the book." Remember if you let a trend develop wherein students know just what you're going to say next, they no longer have any reason to heed.

Don't expect more than passive listening unless you find a way to physically involve the student, and don't expect learning to take place automatically. Check to see if it's happening. Find your own methods of checking, but don't assume just because "you taught it, they caught it." Don't assume either that because they're in the same room they're necessarily with you. Sometimes you have to make a point of being with them—nicely, of course.

Do you say to your first graders "stand up," or do you say, "When I close my eyes everyone is going to stand so quietly that I don't hear anyone move and when I open my eyes I'll get a big surprise."

Why bother?? For one reason, because in our profession particularly, any excess sound is an assured enemy of quality instruction where we want to focus on those sounds that are musically correct.

Lesson plans—yes, sequential learning—crucial, varied content matter, to be sure, but, if you don't first master the mechanics of getting from here to there in an orderly expeditious manner, you're unlikely to achieve much of any of the rest of it.

Retired after thirty-five years as a music educator, Dave Killam of Colebrook was New Hampshire Teacher of the Year in 1974 and was inducted into the New Hampshire Music Educators' Hall of Fame in 1999. This article originally appeared in the September 1999 issue of New Hampshire's Quarter Notes. *Reprinted by permission.*

Preparing the Band for Contest
by Alan LaFave

The title of this article is a bit misleading. I've seen this title used many times for clinics and presentations at various conferences, but the reality is there is not one single key item that will magically prepare your band for any performance. We must constantly work at many concepts on a daily basis. Every performance we give can create anxiety and feelings of nervousness and uncertainty. I don't believe it is possible to have a good performance unless the rehearsals preceding the performance are good. There is an old saying:

Bad rehearsals	=	Bad performances
Fair rehearsals	=	Fair performances
Good rehearsals	=	Good performances
Great rehearsals	=	Great performances

Have you ever noticed how focused students get when the performance is just around the corner? It's amazing how the level of concentration and dedication seem to improve as the performance looms closer on the horizon. I'd like to share with you some ideas on how to improve the rehearsal techniques to enhance concentration and dedication from day one.

First, try to emphasize that the important issue here is the rehearsal. The *process* needs to become more important than the *product*. If the learning process is excellent, the final product has a greater likelihood to be also. I believe one of the best things we can teach our students is how to practice and approach their instruments. A systematic routine in which important concepts such as tone, technique, articulation, rhythmic awareness, and musical sensitivity is more preferred than placing all of the emphasis on one big performance such as large group music contest or All-State auditions. The final result in preparing for one big performance will be just that—one big performance. Isn't it better to focus on a way of rehearsing and practicing that will have a long-term payoff? In my opinion, the answer is *yes*.

Second, make sure you are a consistent conductor. I realize this is somewhat of a generalization, but if you cannot maintain a consistent tempo on the same piece from rehearsal to rehearsal, you are doing your ensemble a terrible injustice. They never know what to expect. Being consistent includes not just tempo, but stylistic indications as well. If you are working on balance and ask for a specific part to be more or less prominent, don't continually change your mind. This will lead to confusion and frustration on the part of your players.

Third, good intonation is a continuous developmental process. Most bands with intonation problems play sharp. Our ears tend to hear and accept sharpness as a good thing. Why? Bands which play on the sharp side of pitch tend to sound bright and brilliant. Many directors think this is a good thing. Conversely, bands which play flat tend to sound dull and unfocused. Bands which play in tune have more resonance and depth to the tone color. There is certainly more beauty in the sound, and good balance is easier to achieve. We must train our students to listen more critically during the entire rehearsal, not just during the five minutes spent tuning at the beginning of rehearsal. The biggest problem with hearing sharpness as good is that it can become self-defeating after a while. If the pitch continues to rise, as it often does due to physical factors such as heat and humidity, sooner or later everyone will be fighting with each other. A clarinet player can only push in so much. Sooner or later they will be playing with such tight embouchures that they will practically have to bite a hole in their lip to get in tune. If you are in a performance and you sense the pitch is going wayward, please take a moment to retune. This is something we all do in rehearsals. Concert situations should be no different. Dr. Richard E. Strange, Director of Bands at Arizona State University, has devised a step-by-step procedure for band tuning. I highly recommend this approach:

1. Start with instruments assembled exactly the same as when last in tune to the level of A = 440 Hz. (i.e., barrel joints, mouthpieces, and slides the same distance in or out).
2. "Warm up" all wind instruments thoroughly to equilibrium temperature before beginning this (or any) tuning procedure.
3. Sound tuning pitch (concert F) by electronic or mechanical means (always being certain to use A = 440 Hz. pitch level). Make sure the tuner is calibrated correctly. *on piano ?*
4. Have entire band match pitch by humming (it focuses their attention even more and puts the pitch into their heads).
5. Have each section tune in rotation, starting with low-pitched sections and proceeding to high-pitched sections (suggested order: tubas, euphoniums, trombones, horns [on transposed middle C, and then an octave above to tune the B-flat side], trumpets, bass clarinets, bassoons, B-flat clarinets, flutes, and piccolo).
6. Then have the entire band tune instruments at the same time at a mezzo-piano level. (No E-flat instruments while tuning to concert F. Their turn will come later.)
7. Tune section members individually if needed. Have each individual match pitch with tuner and then adjust pitch.
8. Sound concert A. (Do not hum or sing, just listen; A is too high to sing comfortably).
9. Have string bass(es) tune open strings (band absolutely quiet). *electric bass?*

10. Have oboes, saxophones, and French horns (again) tune as a section, then one at a time if needed on concert A.
11. Have all other instruments make one more check using concert A if you wish.
12. Check individuals and sections constantly during rehearsal.
13. All players must check themselves constantly during rehearsals and concerts. Listen carefully at all times and avoid the tendency to "drift sharp."
14. Think and hear A = 440 Hz. for beautiful, resonant tone quality and more perfect intonation.

While this may seem complicated, this entire process should take less than five minutes. Making it a part of your daily rehearsal routine will certainly improve your students' awareness of pitch if nothing else. By improving their ability to hear the difference, your band will undoubtedly begin to approach good intonation as a prerequisite to good performing. One last personal note on tuning. Please avoid "going around the band" with your tuner facing the student. Anyone can manipulate their instrument to get the needle straight up and down. Train your students to hear the difference instead of seeing the difference.

Alan LaFave is director of bands and dean of the School of Fine Arts at Northern State University in Aberdeen, South Dakota. This article originally appeared in the Spring 1996 issue of The South Dakota Musician. *Reprinted by permission.*

Make Music! Don't Just Play Notes!

by Rusty Logan

How many times have we made the above statement during a rehearsal of our ensemble? Do the students understand what we want? Do we, as directors, know what is needed to make this happen? When I start thinking about what I want when this statement is made, I realize there are at least 10 important elements that go into producing a musically satisfying band performance.

Duration

Give every note a full life of its own. Never shorten long notes or allow them to diminish unless such directions are given. Changing the duration of notes can cause major phrasing and balance problems throughout the entire ensemble.

Shaping

Give shape to long notes as well as to those that repeat on the same pitch. Never allow them to sit and do nothing. Creatively shape the sustained notes by listening to the musical ideas that are taking place around them. Shape the ideas of the composer, while remaining true to his style.

Contour

Give each part—melody, harmony, rhythm, counter melody, bass—a directional contour of its own. Form individual parts in relation to the others surrounding it. Teach the percussion section, as well, to give every line direction. Each section will feel the importance of its part by giving attention to the contour of the musical line.

Blend

Form a musical concept of the blend you want from the ensemble before stepping on the podium. Whether this concept is bright, dark, or mellow, start by blending parts, sections, families, and then the entire ensemble. Concentrated listening, enhanced by the knowledge of what to listen for, works wonders if done regularly.

Balance

Teach the idea of balance to your group by showing how vertical and horizontal relationships are affected by dynamics, tessitura, special effects, etc. To obtain good balance, have the band sound a chord starting with the bass instruments alone, followed by the treble ones, adding more instruments until the top of the band's range is included. Ideally, all the parts should be sounding equally. When a weak voice occurs in an ensemble, balance the group in relation to this voice. Though most directors do not think of balancing an ensemble from the top down or middle out, when necessary, it is possible.

Phrasing

Marking the phrase design and making students aware of it is important. While a phrase can be as short as two measures or as long as five or more, it needs to be outlined in relation to the other phrases around it. As a general rule, if there is some doubt about where a phrase ends, players should make a long phrase to enhance the overall feeling of shape and melodic direction.

Stress

Explain to your students that all pitches do not have equal stress. Point out and have students mark the pitches that require stress within each phrase. Also mark the high point in the phrase or the note which the line tends to stress. Stress definition is important to the flow of the phrase.

Articulation

Base articulations and special effects on the concept of a long, full sound. Work backward toward the shorter, detached articulations. Articulation affects how certain notes will be performed. I think of every note as having three parts: a front, middle, and back. Depending on the type of articulation in use, I have the ensemble play just the front of the note (staccato), into the middle (marcato), or all the way through the note to its back (legato) to get the proper effect.

Attacks

Make sure attacks reflect the proper mood of the phrase or section. All attacks should be on time, well defined, and controlled. Some players do not understand that the attack takes place only on the tongue's backstroke, and not when the tongue contacts the reed, teeth, or gums.

Releases

Make releases come alive. The performer needs to know what takes place before and after the release (changes in dynamics or the articulation, time for breathing, etc.). He also should know how to release the tone (a slight lift, a ring, a snap), and what section or player to release with.

These 10 points should help band directors, as well as students, understand the phrase, "Make Music: Don't Just Play Notes," a little more. Although this information alone will not answer all the questions, it should help you get started.

Rusty Logan is director of bands at Auburn High School in Auburn, Alabama. This article originally appeared in the March 1996 issue of Alabama's Ala Breve. *Reprinted by permission.*

On the Road Again
by Stephen McGrew

You have decided to take your band on the road. See how it "plays in Orlando," so to speak. Assuming you have already resolved the philosophical educational issues, it is now time to begin the "nuts and bolts" planning for the trip. This article is for the novice—a director who has not previously taken his or her ensemble, say, out of state or out of the country. Since traveling with school performing groups is by no means in its pioneering stage, this brief article will deal mostly with general planning and sequence. Helpful tips to use or not will also be on the menu.

"Appetizer"
Scheduling the Trip
The exact dates of the tour should be placed on the school calendar at least *one* year in advance. You have already done activity and venue research, so administrative and board approval will also be sought at this time. Band boosters should be brought into the loop, also. A brief article in the local media will help plant the seed early. In this article, include your educational justification of the tour, number of performances, and anticipated audience.

"Salad & Rolls"
Select a Tour Consultant/Agent
Once you have approval of the tour and the dates, it is time to contact a travel consultant. There are many reputable companies ready and eager to take your ensemble just about anywhere. Many tour consultants display at the IMEA Convention each January. They also run ads in professional journals such as the *Musicator* and *Music Educators Journal.* You should also talk with as many colleagues as possible who have travel or tour experience. The decision you make here could make the difference between a merely *tolerable* trip and a truly *memorable* trip.

Most directors interviewed strongly agree that it is advisable to insist on a tour guide who accompanies the group from departure to return.

This arrangement will ensure that the director has time to concentrate on the performances. From the time the buses leave the parking lot, the tour guide should take care of *all* details—schedule, personnel, hotel room assignments, meals, itinerary—*everything* aside from the group's performance responsibilities.

Once you have decided tentatively on a travel company, insist on a list of references, then call several of the directors and ask them to describe their level of satisfaction with the tour company.

Transportation
Satisfied with your choice of tour/travel company? Leave a deposit with them to guarantee hotel and travel arrangements. Note: Some travel companies will bid transportation costs and give the director and/or band booster committee the option of selection. If this is so, be sure the bids include type, year, and size of coaches (buses). Also seek out references for coach lines. Most travel company recommendations will be valid. After all, they want your group to have the best experience possible, and nothing is worse than traveling in gimpy coaches.

Accommodations
A good rule of thumb to follow is to select, through your travel company, the best hotel your group can afford. Also, go with housing that has only interior hallway room access. This makes supervision and security much simpler. The safety issue is obvious. Hotels that are experienced with group assignments and conventions are preferable to the less experienced and less expensive.

Budget and Fund-Raising
No doubt your band booster association has a growing balance for such undertakings. Hopefully this is the case. At any rate, fund-raising specific to this cause should kick in immediately—subject for another article? There are many unique fund-raising activities that call for absolutely no up-front money. Band booster associations may be familiar with some of them. Most directors and booster officers interviewed stated that they make it mat-

ter of practice to design all of their fund-raising as pre-sales, sponsorships, or pledge-a-thon efforts, avoiding campaigns requiring a purchase in advance that can result in leftover inventory to be shipped back or "eaten"—sometimes literally.

Performance Venues

The possibilities are endless. Not a day goes by without "invitations" arriving in the mail or the phone ringing off the hook offering unique performance possibilities. This decision is usually made very early. One to two years in advance of the tour is a good time to do some leisurely research via conventions, friends, and colleagues. Again, search out references and seek their level of satisfaction with the festival or competition.

"Main Course"
The Year is Here

As you have probably gathered by now, most of the hard work is done a year or more ahead of time. The year of the tour will be one of making application tapes, arriving at a precise number of students making the tour, and working with the booster organization's finance committees.

Make yourself available for service club programs. They are most appreciative and will want to contribute to your cause once they hear of the exciting plans. Now is the time for a media blitz. Concentrate on local and school newspapers, but don't neglect the regional newspapers and radio/television outlets.

As time draws near for your first extended tour (five or more days), you may be experiencing some anxiety. Not to worry. All the time you spent researching one and two years ago will pay off. Have confidence in your tour consultants. They are very experienced and professional. Once the trip starts, just enjoy. On my first out-of-state trip, when leaving the parking lot with 160-plus band students, and chaperones, my tour consultant must have seen my very pale face. He looked straight at me and said, "Now, from this point on, you just take care of the band's performances. Leave the rest to me." Ah! Music to my ears!

Figure 1. Tour Checklist

1–2 Years in Advance of Tour
____ Do Research on possible performance venues
____ Begin gathering information and references on tour companies
____ Investigate possible tour timing—school calendar, etc.
____ Inform booster organization of possibilities

1 Year in Advance of Tour
____ Set dates of tour
____ Get administrative and school board approval
____ Check with boosters on financial standing; establish goals
____ Media release
____ Select tour company & set initial planning session
    a. Length of tour
    b. Possible itinerary
    c. Approximate cost per student
    d. Transportation
    e. Accommodations
____ Financial arrangements
    a. Student's share
    b. Boosters' share
____ Publicity

The Year!
____ Publicity, publicity, publicity
____ Exact count of participants
____ Letter of intent—deposit due
____ Health forms & insurance numbers
____ Final tour meeting with parents and students
____ Final meeting with chaperones and tour guide
    a. Handbook
    b. Assignments
    c. ID T-shirts
____ Departure—have media present at departure and return for pictures.

Stephen McGrew is director of bands at Seymour High School in Seymour, Indiana, and is currently editor of the Band Stand column of the Indiana Musicator. *This article originally appeared in the May 1999 issue of the* Indiana Musicator. *Reprinted by permission.*

Listening
by Nedo Pandolfi

Discriminate Listening

A keen sense for listening as required in a musically sensitive ensemble can be indispensable for a student's individual progress, not to mention the success of an ensemble in communicating with an audience. At first glance, this statement sounds like a no-brainer. Of course, you say; how can anyone profess to do anything worthwhile if they don't listen in a musical setting? Well, this lack of discriminate listening may be prevalent not only in young student groups but also in aspiring young professionals.

A Young Professional's Experience

I must confess that as a recent graduate playing principal trumpet in the Florida Symphony Orchestra and the National Orchestra in Montevideo, I was mainly concerned with playing my part and seeing to it that the outcome of my performance was musically acceptable. I had been playing principal trumpet in the orchestra in Montevideo for two years. After a performance of *Pictures at an Exhibition,* the retired concertmaster of the orchestra who had attended all the concerts approached me. He shook my hand as he made an observation and said, "I have been listening to you for the past two years, and I believe that you have finally made the transition from soloist to an orchestral musician." I thoroughly understood what he meant. Performing in the orchestra had become a more enjoyable experience. I was now more concerned about fitting in to enhance the total effect of the composition. My own playing, although important, became secondary to the ensemble. The transition had been made with benefits to the orchestra and myself.

A Natural Reaction

It is natural for young musicians with a limited amount of experience in ensemble playing to focus their attention on their own playing with only a peripheral concern for what is happening around them. I can't count the number of times that a student would evaluate a performance according to how he played his part. The overall effect of the performance could very well have been excellent but if that individual did not perform up to his expectations he would inevitably feel upset.

Undue Pressure

Students put too much pressure on themselves when they isolate their part from the ensemble. The result is usually a performance that is less than desirable, shattered nerves and a negative experience to boot. Who needs it?

The sooner the person responsible for the performance of an ensemble solves the problem of listening, the quicker the experience turns from frayed nerves and disappointed results to a very positive and enjoyable experience for everyone.

Promote Good Listening Habits

A rehearsal should be predominantly a session for listening. The conductor sets the tone of the rehearsal. It becomes his responsibility to see to it that the students are focusing on those aspects of the composition that give them a clear understanding of the desired outcomes.

Giving the students something to listen for or to, can and will usually get their attention. This can mean focusing on just about any aspect of the composition such as an articulation, a phrase, intonation, a particular chord structure, a specific rhythmic figure, etc.

Listening carefully to a specific component of a composition is gradually developed to include the total full-bodied sound of the composition. Then, and only then, will the student enjoy the experience of making music. Developing a delicate sensitivity to listening guarantees musical integrity.

Fitting In

The total musical experience requires that the student hear the entire composition and how his individual part fits in. Coming to this realization, the individual performer begins to appreciate how his part, however important, is secondary.

As a result, attention is given to the entire ensemble. The performer listens to how his part contributes, makes an effort to blend with his musical surroundings, and becomes more relaxed realizing that a single error does not destroy the overall outcome of a performance. He is now a part of an entire musical statement not an isolated component of it.

Conductors' Responsibility

While the conductor may be listening to the entire composition, it is very likely that most student musicians only listen to their own part and then not in a very discriminating way. It is the conductor's responsibility to promote this most demanding of all aspects of music making.

I have found that the one most important word in a conductor's vocabulary is "listen." Everything that happens on the podium must involve the act of listening. It is not the baton that dictates how an ensemble will perform but how successful the conductor was in getting the musicians to listen and react to what they were hearing.

Granted that a good baton technique may be helpful and necessary. Yet, it must be placed down on the list of priorities. Interaction between musicians should be predicated on listening to each other and executing in harmony with one another. This can only be accomplished through a very high degree of discriminate listening. A teacher needs to emphasize listening in all aspects of music, be it in a private lesson or in an ensemble.

Reality Rears Its Ugly Head

When a student listens to his playing on a tape recorder, his reaction never ceases to amaze me. The look of astonishment and disappointment usually follows disbelief and protest, blaming the quality of the tape recorder. Our subjective hearing usually fools us. We have in mind what we want to hear but it is not often that what we intend and what is produced coincides. Developing a sense for accurate listening demands a great deal of attention. It is no easy task to differentiate between what is produced and what one thinks is produced. Subjective listening is very prevalent among students and high school music directors alike.

Without meaning to make any disparaging remarks about music directors, we are sometimes victims of conditioning over a period of time. Our everyday environment is not the highest level of musical achievement. It can very easily be a conditioning factor that comes into play in evaluating a performance. We unconsciously turn off sounds that on other occasions would be offensive.

I have yet to meet a music director who is not musically very sensitive when listening to an ensemble. He is keenly sensitive to balance, intonation, rhythmic accuracy, transparency, phrasing, and any other component of a performance. And yet, when in front of his own ensemble, many of these seemingly obvious talents leave him. We must always guard against subjective listening of our own groups.

Some Suggestions

Taping a rehearsal session will correct many problems. It will alert you to errors that may have gone unnoticed during the rehearsals. It may also give you an objective view in evaluating the success or failure of your approach. I have learned more about my failings from recordings of my rehearsals than from any articles I may have read. *Awareness gives us the information needed for change.*

Focus your attention on listening to a specific section and solving the problems inherent in that specified portion. The clearer and more transparent it becomes, the more we are apt to raise our standards for the remainder of the composition.

Get the students involved in making observations and corrections. Ask students to make suggestions. It can be very revealing and rewarding.

Always Take One More Step

When you feel that a section has improved, then go one step further with it. If you listen carefully you will not be satisfied. If you listen very carefully you will never be satisfied. At this stage you will be teaching something of worth. The more you listen, the more you will be asking of your students. The more you ask of your students, the more they will be learning. The more they learn through listening, the more enjoyment they will have in the performance of music.

We, as teachers, are in control of how much we are willing to give to our students. The satisfaction we receive from complete commitment to the highest standards possible cannot be compared to anything known to man.

The effort required achieving this makes it worthwhile. Listen, listen, listen, and then listen more carefully. It can change your life and the lives of the hundreds of students with whom you come in contact.

Nedo Pandolfi is a consultant, working with band directors throughout New England. This article originally appeared in the Fall 1998–1999 issue of the Rhode Island Music Educators Review. *Reprinted by permission.*

Rehearsal Techniques Revisited: Setting up a Learning Environment Conducive to Making Music
by Nedo Pandolfi

Before I begin, let me make it very clear that some of my techniques are very personal and particular to my own methods of teaching. I have been successful with them; used them consistently; made many changes over the years; and had I continued teaching, many more changes would have occurred. If sharing these thoughts with you helps in this very difficult profession, I will have accomplished my goal.

A conscious effort to improve techniques has been prominent since my first days of teaching. That is the only constant that I can recall. I am sure that most of us can relate to the aforementioned statement, realizing that everything changes from one moment to the next. What works in one situation may produce chaos in another.

Experience
A key to good rehearsals is having options for any situation that may arise. This comes from experience and dedication in a labor of love. Experience usually means that you are not surprised by anything that may come to pass in a rehearsal. You are prepared to cope.

Dedication
Dedication signifies that you are always looking for ways to improve.

Labor of Love
Labor of love indicates that you will go to great lengths to see that the highest standards possible are observed in the practice of music performance.

(The above definitions are mine and certainly not Webster's.)

Unless that kind of commitment is present I would suggest that you read no further, for you should find other means of earning a living. You will do yourself and students a great service. Be assured that the salary you may receive is not commensurate with the effort needed to have a successful music program. Having said that, let us go on to some basics in rehearsal techniques.

Complete Silence Required
Working with music requires that participants in a rehearsal maintain complete silence. Would you expect an artist to paint in bad lighting or work on a canvas in darkness?

Consequences of anything other than silence:

1. Listening as required in a musical ensemble is impossible.
2. A relaxed situation is impossible for you and your students.
3. Learning from each other is impossible.
4. Infringement on the rights of students to learn through listening.
5. Respect for the music is nonexistent.
6. Comments made from the podium become ineffective.

These are but a few of the more obvious reasons why complete silence is mandatory. Neglecting to make this a top priority from the get-go will certainly invite failure.

Setting Standards
Standards are set with the belief that your level of expectations will raise the level of students' expectations. Demand little. Receive little. And unless you wear earplugs, the frustration level will be unbearable.

A first experience with a group is usually not a problem. The students' curiosity about you and your abilities is uppermost in their minds. You can keep it that way if you have complete musical control. Maintaining the status quo requires knowledge of the score and a clear understanding of your musical expectations.

If your musicianship is weak, your leadership will be fragile, inhibiting your ability to communicate musically, and losing the respect of your students. *Weak musicianship breeds noise.*

Involve Everyone
Attention to the musical needs of all your students is essential. The last chair clarinetist is expected to have an identical set of expectations as the solo player. A good ensemble depends on everyone sharing in the responsibility of executing their part in a musically appropriate manner.

Individual Attention
When a problem in execution needs to be addressed, students should be expected to play their parts alone. This is a sensitive situation, carefully orchestrated over a period of time. It is prudent to begin with your more experienced players who are technically advanced and confident of their abilities.

Use discretion and knowledge of the personality involved. As time progresses, the students come to expect this procedure, gradually losing their inhibitions. The student needs to be successful with the particular problem addressed.

This technique will prove useful and productive when working with individuals or sections. It gives them the tools for problem solving. Promoting this method gradually becomes the norm in the eyes of the students. The fear of performing alone diminishes as the student learns to handle himself in performance situations.

Intonation

Create a consciousness for intonation beginning with the warm-up session. The objective requires that the students perform comfortably in the tonality of the music. The student must have control of the mechanics of the scale to accomplish this.

If a tonality appears unfamiliar to the student, it is ludicrous to expect that they can play in tune. It just doesn't happen.

I have expressed my views on the importance of extensive practice of scales and broken chords in past articles and the benefits derived therefrom.

One of the most obvious outcomes is the improvement in intonation and tone quality.

Mechanical Problems

It is impossible to grasp a feel for good tone quality and intonation until the mechanical problems are resolved.

Once the fingering and range problems are history, attention can be focused on intonation and tone quality.

Without focusing on intonation and tone quality in the beginning stages in the development of flexibility with scales, students automatically play better in tune as the tonality becomes familiar and easy to manipulate.

Working with a scale in all the modes becomes part of the process when coping with problems of intonation.

Volunteers

There are always volunteers ready to play a scale alone. (Bragging rights?)

The group listens for bad notes on a particular instrument; for example, throat tones on a clarinet; C-sharp and D on a trumpet; second line G on the B-flat side of a horn; etc. Students are able to pick these out and they gradually become aware of the imperfections of their own instruments, making adjustments accordingly.

Mutual Help Society

There is a great deal of helping one another with fingering problems which affect intonation, notably in the woodwind section and to a lesser degree in the brass section. As I stated before, the fear of playing alone gradually diminishes in the less capable performers. It is expected that all students will work on scales; even the least capable students reach a very high degree of proficiency in the execution of scales.

High Standards Become the Norm

As they become proficient in the manipulation of scales, they become very demanding in terms of intonation, tone quality, evenness of sound from one pitch to another, precision in rhythm, smoothness, and ease in performance.

Long-range results show refinement in their listening. Corrections in the above-mentioned areas are resolved quickly with excellent results.

Seldom will you need to spend time tuning up individuals before or during a rehearsal. This exercise has become the responsibility of the individual student and he accepts this willingly.

The sophistication the student has acquired in the art of listening puts the accountability on his shoulders and away from you, refreshingly allowing you to pursue other aspects of the music.

Music making becomes a more pleasant experience for all concerned.

Nedo Pandolfi is a consultant, working with band directors throughout New England. This article originally appeared in the Fall 1998–1999 issue of the Rhode Island Music Educators Review. *Reprinted by permission.*

1. Fingering
2. Range
3. Scale → Intonation + tone quality
4. Intonation
5. Rhythm precision

Warm-Up for a "Hot" Performance
by Dana Rothlisberger

"The tone of the ensemble was rich, full, and warm." "Good clear tone." "Fine, mature, well developed sound." "This group understands what good tone is all about." "What a musical performance! Congratulations!" These adjudicator comments reflect a superior ('hot') performance at a band festival. Engaging in a careful, structured, and consistent warm-up routine will aid each ensemble in gathering comments such as these at future performances.

Of course there are many components of a successful performance. Depending on how imminent the concert is, each conductor will have a set of personal priorities to focus on in preparation for the performance. The adjudicator remarks above deal with the criterion of tone. Tone is 'first among equals' in regards to the elements of a quality musical performance. A well focused daily warm-up routine is essential in developing tone. Each rehearsal must have a structured ensemble warm-up focusing on tone development for individual timbre as well as ensemble blend. At all times, and with encouragement from the conductor, the members of the ensemble must maintain concentration on the task at hand. The energy expended in the daily warm-up routine will pay dividends if all members of the ensemble buy into the concept and recognize their improvement. The balance, blend, and timbre of the group will improve if the warm-up is a regular and integral part of the routine which begins the rehearsal.

Athletes, physical trainers, and doctors always suggest that a thorough warm-up period precede any physical activity. The training session, practice, or game goes better if the participants have engaged in a thorough and comprehensive warm-up. So it is for the musician. Warming up is a time to get the muscles used in the production of sound stretched, limbered, and ready to go. The embouchure and breath support muscles need to be warmed up. If not, fatigue may quickly set in and the range and flexibility of the performer will be limited. An added benefit of the warm-up is that it provides an opportunity for the performers to mentally prepare for the rehearsal at hand.

Accountability for Conducting Gestures
I have heard the following from almost every conductor I have observed: "Watch me!" If we as conductors use that phrase, we must be held accountable. Every motion and every gesture has the potential for meaning. Conductors must be conversant and fluent in using these to communicate nonverbally to the ensemble. Just as when a performer makes a false movement with a fingering resulting in a wrong note, a conductor making a "false movement of the arm or hand might produce rhythmic wavering in the orchestra, or an incorrect dynamic."[1] Nicolai Malko relates the story about Hans Richter, one of the greatest post-Wagnerian conductors (1843–1913). When Richter was the chief conductor of the Vienna Opera he once made a rude remark to one of the double bass players. The man answered, "You are right. I made a mistake. But why do you speak so rudely? If your baton had a little bell at the tip, we would sometimes hear wrong notes too."[2] We should all be cognizant of our motions and gestures, and be clear and precise in communicating our desires to the ensemble. In addition to developing tonal concepts, the warm-up provides an excellent opportunity for the ensemble to be sensitized to the conductor's gestures.

Silence as a Prerequisite
Richard Floyd, Music Director for the Texas University Scholastic League of the University of Texas at Austin, says that "silence is the canvas upon which we paint music." I believe that it is important for us to hear the silence in the room. Too often we are so interested in getting started that we jump right into the rehearsal by going directly from talking to playing. An effective way to begin the warm-up is to bring the group to complete silence, and really listen to what the silence (or ambient noise of the room) sounds like. Let the group listen for about five seconds. Ask them to quietly blow air through their instruments in a low register. One or two breaths is sufficient. Then have the members of the ensemble select any low note they wish and play it softly on the conductor's gesture. As they play, each individual should concentrate on holding his or her pitch steady using proper posture, embouchure, hand position, breath support, etc. to maintain a well centered tone. On the conductor's next gesture, the ensemble should perform a low concert B-flat. The intent is that the ensemble, through performing a dissonant chord (everyone playing their note of choice) and then moving to a unison (B-flat), will listen and understand the difference in sound between the two, and become more sensitive toward matching the unison pitch of the ensemble.

Unison and Harmonization

Next in the warm-up routine is to perform a unison B-flat concert scale. That scale is used because a majority of band instruments are pitched in B-flat. (If necessary, work in sectionals with the horns in F and the E-flat saxophones on the pitches appropriate to their key.) The scale should be played using long tones, and should not be metric or rhythmic. The focus throughout is to center the tone, listen, and adjust. Ground rules John Paynter used during his warm-up routine include:

1. Always play with full breath support and try to produce the best possible tone.
2. Take a breath whenever you want to, in fact more often than you think you need it; even drop out if you feel the least bit of fatigue.
3. Leave and re-enter as graciously as you can.
4. Listen to the sounds in your section.
5. Listen to the sounds all around you in other sections.
6. Watch the conductor all the time.[3]

H. Robert Reynolds, in an interview with Joseph Casey, says "You should tune to exactly the same pitch every day, which is taken from a machine, because you must have a consistent reference point every day."[4] Prior to the organized warm-up at the beginning of the rehearsal, the students should use the tuner and adjust their slides or mouthpieces to the position where their instrument matches the reference sound. As the warm-up proceeds, they should continue to be sensitive and make minor adjustments using the tuning slide as necessary, along with adjusting their embouchure, etc., to 'humor' the pitch. Each pitch that is performed needs to be tuned and must be played with good tone. Herein lies a major reason to use a warm-up routine. The routine provides an opportunity for the performers to concentrate on the elements of accurate intonation (along with tonal development) without the added pressure of reading rhythms and pitches in printed music.

Many years ago, I observed rehearsals conducted by Dr. William Revelli. I observed he would always begin the day, and after returning from each break, with the B-flat scale in unison on long tones. During the scale, he would gesture for varying dynamics, and work on balance and blend within the unison. Balance and blend are closely related, but not synonymous. "Blend has to do with timbral compatibility of two or more tones, balanced with the relative volume of two or more tones."[5] After going up the scale, and then down, without repeating the top note, Dr. Revelli would ask the ensemble to 'harmonize' the scale. The first group would begin, and when they reached scale degree 3, the second group would enter on scale degree 1. When the first group reached scale degree 5, the second group would be on scale degree 3, and the third group would enter on scale degree 1. Each group would then continue with the scale, up and down without repeating the top note, until they returned to a unison scale degree 1(see figure 1). The assignment of instruments to each group is arbitrary and can change from rehearsal to rehearsal, thereby giving each group a different sense of its place in the chord.

If a more traditional and consistent grouping is desired, it might be:

- Group I: Flute, piccolo, oboe, soprano clarinet
- Group II: Trumpet, horn, alto and tenor saxophone
- Group III: Tuba, trombone, bassoon, bass clainet, baritone saxophone

Percussion mallet instruments could be added to Groups I and II with the percussionists playing long rolls using soft yarn mallets.

A variation of this exercise is accomplished by using the second inversion of the triad as the basis for harmonizing the scale. To accomplish this, delay the entry of Group III until Group I has reached scale degree 6 and Group II has reached scale degree 4. This harmonic arrangement provides some delicious dissonance with resultant satisfying consonance on the resolution. It also eliminates parallel fifths. The ensemble will be able to perform the intervals of a second and learn to hold their assigned pitch straight, true, and steady while listening to the dissonance created with

---

Figure 1. Harmonizing the Scale in Root Position

Group I:	1	2	3	4	5	6	7	8	7	6	5	4	3	2	1			
Group II:			1	2	3	4	5	6	7	8	7	6	5	4	3	2	1	
Group III:					1	2	3	4	5	6	7	8	7	6	5	4	3	2	1

Figure 2. Harmonizing the Scale in 6/4 Inversion with Sustaining Tonic at End																				
Group I:	1	2	3	4	5	6	7	8	7	6	5	4	3	2	1	_____	1			
Group II:			1	2	3	4	5	6	7	8	7	6	5	4	3	2	1	_____	1	
Group III:					1	2	3	4	5	6	7	8	7	6	5	4	3	2	1	

other instruments (see figure 2). For both of these exercises, a valid option for each group is to hold scale degree 1 until Group III has arrived on the tonic. The dissonance created by scale degree 2 sounding with scale degree 1, and the resulting unison achieved on the resolution can help assist in bringing enhanced musicianship into the warm-up.

To develop and enhance pitch awareness and acuity, a proven technique is to have the students sing the warm-up. When students harmonize the scale by singing and also sing the six-four version, pitch awareness and intonation will rapidly improve.

Warm-Up Variation One

It is important to keep the warm-up routine from becoming perceived and performed as drudgery or 'just something to do before we get to the real music.' If the conductor allows the routine to become predictable, it "ceases to have meaning and the players stop paying attention to it."[6] I learned a very effective warm-up routine from Dale Kennedy when he conducted the Maryland All State Senior Band in 1986. It is a wonderful variation to use, for it breaks the scale up into segments and then 'magically' produces a harmonic progression. The players can focus on unison playing with good tone, balance, and blend. They can also learn to hear intervals in a linear fashion. A chord progression is achieved as the scale segments are superimposed upon each other. Throughout, intonation can be improved as the segments are performed in unison or in a harmonic progression. Although Dr. Kennedy used concert F for this warm-up, one could also use concert B-flat.

The first segment consists of performing scale degrees 1–2–3. Many times groups tend to play scale degree 3 sharp, and this segment provides a chance to work with the ensemble to bring the pitch down to where it needs to be. The next segment involves performing scale degrees 4-5-1. This segment represents an idiomatic harmonic chord progression found in much of the music

written in tertian harmony. It allows the ensemble to focus on the progression while providing the opportunity to listen to the interval of a fourth and fifth over the tonic in a linear fashion. The third segment involves the widest interval and requires the ensemble to both 'hear' and 'feel' the pitch prior to performing it. The third segment is made up of scale degrees 6-5-5. The rearticulation of scale degrees helps the ensemble to work on perfecting the articulation of a repeated note, with no one person or section making their individual presence known. The last two segments, four and five, allow for attention to notes in the upper part of the scale where the intonation usually starts to go sharp, and the balance tends to become top-heavy. These two segments encourage the ensemble to listen and correct these two problems. Segments four and five include degrees 6-7-8 and 8-7-8 of the scale, respectively. Figure 3 displays the various scale segments in order of presentation. As with the other portions of the warm-up routine, this exercise should be done in a nonmetrical fashion, using long tones, and expressing the conductor's wishes through nonverbal gestures. Once the individual segments have been performed, the 'magic' emerges as all the segments are performed at the same time. I like to assign the tubas to segment two (scale degrees 4-5-1), and then remaining members of the ensemble are asked to choose any one segment and to play their choice on my cue. The resulting chord progression allows the ensemble an additional musical experience upon which to enhance their musicianship in the areas of tone production, intonation, balance and blend. Figure 4 presents the superimposition of the scale segments showing the subdominant–dominant–tonic harmonic progression.

One of my colleagues, Dr. Joseph Briscuso, provides four additional scale segments that follow the same model as the Kennedy warm-up and can be used during the warm-up routine for work with unison performance as well as for material for chord progressions (see figure 5).

Figure 3. Kennedy Warm-up Routine Scale Segments				
Scale degrees:	1 – 2 – 3;	4 – 5 – 1;	6 – 5 – 5;	6 – 7 – 8; 8 – 7 – 8

Figure 4. Superimposition of the Kennedy Warm-up Routine Scale Segments

```
1 – 2 – 3
4 – 5 – 1
6 – 5 – 5
6 – 7 – 8
8 – 7 – 8
```

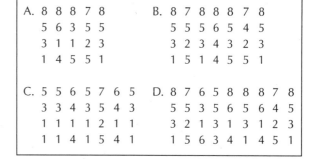

Figure 5. Four Briscuso Scale Patterns and Chord Progressions

```
A. 8 8 8 7 8          B. 8 7 8 8 8 7 8
   5 6 3 5 5             5 5 5 6 5 4 5
   3 1 1 2 3             3 2 3 4 3 2 3
   1 4 5 5 1             1 5 1 4 5 5 1

C. 5 5 6 5 7 6 5       D. 8 7 6 5 8 8 8 7 8
   3 3 4 3 5 4 3          5 5 3 5 6 5 6 4 5
   1 1 1 1 2 1 1          3 2 1 3 1 3 1 2 3
   1 1 4 1 5 4 1          1 5 6 3 4 1 4 5 1
```

Variation Two

As a college student, I studied trombone with Dr. Neill Humfeld. Dr. Humfeld in turn had studied with Emory Remington at the Eastman School of Music. I became knowledgeable about the famous Remington warm-up routine through my study with Dr. Humfeld. The opening section of this routine transfers very nicely to a full band warm-up exercise. Figure 6 illustrates the warm-up routine from concert B-flat to concert F.

The warm-up routine involves having the entire ensemble perform long tones on the pitches indicated. As can be seen in figure 6, it is an exercise that descends chromatically from B-flat, while returning to B-flat after each new pitch. Variations of this routine include having the ensemble sing it, having half the ensemble sing while the other half plays, having the brass players 'buzz' the exercise (or a portion of it), alternating from one instrument family to another for the next note, etc. It is obvious that conductor imagination and creativity are key ingredients in ensuring something interesting and musically appropriate is happening at all times during this as well as in any warm-up routine.

After the Warm-Up

The warm-up is not a place for technical development. That component of the rehearsal should be separated from the warm-up routine. The segment of the rehearsal immediately following the warm-up routine should focus on further musicianship development using music written in a chorale style. If the rhythmic and technical demands are minimal, and the harmonic content basically triadic, the ensemble can focus on the elements of musicality that will cause the ensemble to perform

in a musically literate fashion. I am personally fond of Lake's arrangement of *Sixteen Chorales by J. S. Bach*[7] because I find each of them musically satisfying. Each chorale provides a great opportunity for the ensemble to learn, understand, and experience what is required to perform 'easy' notes and rhythms in a musical manner. Each conductor has his or her own favorite chorale style music, be it the classic *Treasury of Scales,* an arrangement of chorales by Claude Smith, or a personal arrangement.

As we strive to consciously and meticulously engage our ensembles in a warm-up routine, the quality of tone will improve and the level of musicianship will be in the 'superior' category. Those who then hear our ensembles (be they parents, family, friends, adjudicators, or music lovers) will be favored with a rich, dark, warm, pure, full, characteristic tone performed at a tonally and musically sophisticated level. It is incumbent upon each of us to ensure that every member of the ensemble departs each rehearsal having had a positive, musical experience. The warm-up routine is a way to bring musical moments into the rehearsal.

Final Thought

John Paynter was a fine musician and one of the great intelligent men of the music profession. He touched the lives of many, many high school and college musicians and was an inspiration to all

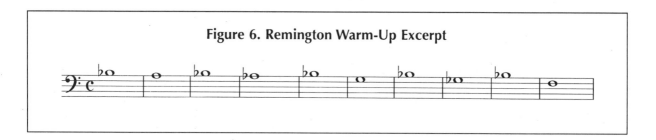

Figure 6. Remington Warm-Up Excerpt

who knew him. I had the opportunity to be his rehearsal assistant with a collegiate honor band in Oklahoma for a week during the summer of 1989. In addition to all I have discussed above, he believed that the warm-up time was also a time when you say "Hello" to the band. As you conduct, you're looking around and saying with your eyes and face, "Susie, it's good to see you; I hope your Dad is feeling better." "Charlie, I see you decided not to quit the band." It gives you a chance for the little smile, wink, or some sort of acknowledgment to everybody in the room. There are so few opportunities in a rehearsal where you can say, "Thanks for coming again. I'm glad you're here."[8] While the reason for music is inherent in the musical experience, it is important for us to develop appropriate relationships with our players, to engender the common respect and personal trust between us as human beings which will foster the creation of quality musical performances.

Notes

1. Nicolai Malko. *The Conductor and His Baton.* (Copenhagen: Wilhelm Hansen, 1950), 27.

2. Ibid, 28.

3. John Paynter. "A Daily Warm-Up Routine," *Band* 1, no. 1 (September/October 1984), 6.

4. Joseph L. Casey. *Teaching Techniques and Insights for Instrumental Music Educators,* revised edition. (Chicago: GIA Publications, Inc., 1993), 395.

5. James Middleton, Harry Haines, and Gary Garner. *The Symphonic Band Winds: A Quest for Perfection.* (San Antonio, TX: Southern Music Co., 1986), 57.

6. Paynter, 6.

7. *Sixteen Chorales by J. S. Bach,* compiled and arranged by Mayhew Lake. (New York: G. Schirmer, 1938).

8. Paynter, 9.

Dana Rothlisberger is director of bands at Towson State University in Towson, Maryland. This article originally appeared in the April/May 1996 issue of the Maryland Music Educator. *Reprinted by permission.*

How to Drive Your Band onto the Intonation Super Highway: Some Techniques to Help Young Bands Play in Tune

Michael Salzman

For most of us, the one aspect of teaching young bands that "hurts" the most is their intonation (or lack thereof). Sometimes we develop such incredible "selective hearing" (the ability to hear whatever you want to hear) that we don't even notice how out of tune our groups are. We hear their progress in other areas, and we ignore the pitch. But it doesn't have to be this way. Learning to play in tune is not a concept that is too difficult for young musicians to understand, and it does not have to be something that we just put up with "until they become more mature players." In actuality, putting it off just reinforces poor intonation. There are many ways to address this subject with beginning and young bands. While discussing the topic recently with a group of sixth-grade trumpet players, I stumbled onto the phrase "Intonation Super Highway" and it stuck. There are three "On Ramps" onto this Super Highway. They are: (1) a firm and well-formed embouchure; (2) a steady stream of air; and (3) the ability to listen and play at the same time. This article will look at each of these and describe some methods for making them work.

Embouchure

We teach our students how to form a correct embouchure on day one. But, do we continue to teach this on day two, three, four and on year three, day forty-seven? Constantly reinforce this concept with your students. Before a player can play a note in tune, he or she must first be able to hold the pitch steady. This will not happen until the player can form a firm and correct embouchure. This is a must for all wind players. Brass players should be encouraged to buzz their mouthpieces for a few minutes every day to develop the muscles necessary for a good embouchure. Show all your wind players pictures or videos of great players forming correct embouchures (stay away from Dizzy when you are on this subject) and encourage your students to practice in front of a mirror so that they can constantly check their embouchures.

Steady Air Stream

Teaching wind players to maintain a steady stream of air is also essential to their being able to sustain a steady pitch. Have your students think of the air as if it were "flowing" through their instruments. One exercise that works well is to have your band or lesson group pick a spot on the wall, perhaps the clock, and blow a steady stream of air onto that spot for ten seconds. Then have them do the same thing while playing a note on their instruments. This will help them to develop the "steady stream" concept.

Listening

This, of course, is the most important component to good intonation. What constantly amazes me is that students can subconsciously make the adjustments that are necessary to play in tune, even if they don't know if they are flat or sharp or even out of tune. When students listen to the players around them and try to match their pitches, if they are maintaining a good embouchure and a steady air stream, they will very often succeed. We don't always need to take the time to say "You're sharp" or "Push that slide in." Sometimes we can just say, "Listen, this note is out of tune" and that will be enough. There is, though, one thing that is necessary before this will happen. The students must know what "in tune" and "out of tune" sound like. We must always point out examples of both good and poor intonation. The students must be aware of what is good and what "hurts." As an example, have two students adjust their instruments so that they will be significantly out of tune and have them play the "same" note together. Teach your students to listen for the beats produced by out-of-tune notes. Then have them gradually adjust their instruments so that they are more and more in tune with each other and point out how the beats get slower and then finally disappear. Once they can hear this, the subconscious

part will take over—as long as they are continuously encouraged to listen to each other and as long as we continue to point out both good and poor examples of intonation.

Electronic Tuners

Now that the prices of electronic tuners have come down so much, there is no excuse not to have one with you whenever you are teaching. Use an electronic tuner in lessons and, whenever possible, in rehearsals. Students will learn how to adjust both their instruments and their embouchures by working with a tuner. It is, though, very important to emphasize that tuning only gives us a starting point. When you tune a concert B-flat, you have only tuned that one note. After tuning that one note, have a student play a scale into the tuner to show them which notes are still out of tune. They need to learn that they cannot just set the tuning slide and forget about intonation now that they are "in tune." They are only close and must always listen and adjust in order to stay in tune.

The concept of intonation should and must be taught right from the start. Beginning bands can play in tune. Constantly reinforce the concepts of embouchure, air stream, and the importance of listening, and you will soon be driving your young band down the "Intonation Super Highway."

Michael Salzman is a band director in the Syosset Central School District in New York and adjunct professor of music at Hofstra University where he is the tuba and euphonium instructor. This article originally appeared in the December 1998 issue of New York's The School Music News. *Reprinted by permission.*

Eight Tips on Teaching Rhythm

by Constance Sanders

While this article targets beginning band students, most of the ideas can be used in any music class. In fact, some of them stemmed from experiences in general music.

Rhythm reading is one of the most important things we teach because it is the most difficult aspect of music for students to learn on their own. Once shown a fingering chart, or how to produce a few sounds, students often can figure out things from there.

Rhythm reading, however, would be difficult to learn merely from reading a book; it must be taught by someone who understands it and can teach the kinesthetic feel of rhythm as well as the theoretical aspects. Below are some ideas that have worked for me.

Steady Beat

Before working with instruments, spend time establishing some basic rhythmic concepts. Work with the down-up motion of the feet to establish the idea of a steady beat. Make sure the feet are going up and down evenly. Have students "tah" on the beat as they tap their feet. They need to understand that the "tah" should last from one downbeat to the next, and not just for the moment when their feet hit the floor on the downbeat. This will keep the tempo from accelerating.

Many method books now have accompanying CDs. These guarantee a steady beat and force students to play the piece up to tempo. A good analogy is the idea of jumping rope: just as putting the little bounce between jumps helps to steady the jumper, so the feeling of down and up of the beat keeps the tempo steady.

Tempo

Some teachers will tell students that certain notes are fast or slow, such as "eighth notes are faster than quarter notes." This simply is not true. Notes are not fast or slow; tempos are fast or slow, and the notes fit on the beat accordingly.

Practice the same exercises at different tempos to illustrate and help students get used to this concept. This also holds true for staccato notes; they are not fast, they are about half value. A staccato quarter note equals an eighth note and eighth rest; playing on the down of the foot and being silent on the up ensures that the notes do not become closer together, thus speeding the tempo.

Exercises

Use flash cards and other nonrepetitive exercises. Make sets of flash cards with many combinations of rhythms in various meters on 5 x 8 index cards and have them laminated. They will last for years.

The advantage of flash cards is that students must actually read the music, because it is not a pattern they have memorized. Also, this helps them begin to read rhythm patterns ahead, like words or syllables.

Most current method books have rhythm charts in the back that are very useful. Have the students "tah" the rhythms, then count and clap them (or the reverse), then play them. Stress that they should always "tah" or clap at the beginning of a new sound (not note, because there will be a new note in a tie, but not a new sound).

Rests

Rests are silences; they are just as important as notes, and they are performed exactly the same way—except they are not heard. Have students make a deliberate action to perform the rests. Ask them to "unclap" or "un-tah" (make a motion to close their mouths deliberately).

When to Introduce Rhythms

It is not necessary to wait until a rhythm appears in the method book to introduce it. Remember, students can learn the rhythms before they are physically able to play them on their instruments. Introducing rhythms in advance is helpful to students who want to work ahead in the book.

If the percussionists have new rhythms in their books, go ahead and teach these to the other students at the same time. Using the flash cards, they can learn the rhythms without worrying about fingering an exercise and will be more comfortable when the rhythm is introduced in the book.

Before teaching a new rhythm, try warm-ups on that rhythm on a five-tone exercise or scale. Do not show students the notation, and try to have them figure out rhythms without demonstrating them first.

For instance, in introducing eighth notes, one might ask, "Who can 'tah' a rhythm that has a new sound starting on both the down of the foot (or beat) and the up of the foot?" It might take a few minutes longer than an immediate demonstration, but eventually someone will figure it out. Further, the students will understand the concept better. Try these warm-ups daily for a week or two prior to the introduction of the rhythmic notation.

Rhythmic Hierarchy

Somewhere, in your room or a method book, you will have a chart that has a whole note divided into two half notes, four quarters, and so on. It is important for students to understand that the notes have the same relationship to each other, regardless of what note gets the beat. Remind students that the notes get their names from their relationship to the whole note, not because of how many beats they receive. (How many times have you heard that a half note gets half a beat?) Understanding of this chart will help considerably when it comes to teaching different meters, especially cut time.

Dotted Quarter Note

This is probably the most difficult pattern for young students because it requires conceptualizing a "mixed fraction" that is hard to feel. It is much easier to divide a beat evenly into halves, thirds, or fourths than to count one and one-half beats. The down-up-down of the foot is extremely helpful in teaching this pattern: "Play a sound that lasts for one and one-half beats—down-up-down—and another sound on the last upbeat." It is particularly good to use this pattern in those advanced warm-ups.

Anomalies

For some reason, the slur is a problem. In listening to both my own students in class and other students sight-reading during auditions, I have noticed that they do well until they reach two quarter notes slurred together. Almost invariably students play these quickly, usually as two eighths. This seems to be a common problem. Be sure to distinguish clearly between ties, slurs, and note beams, and give frequent reminders.

Another thing that plays havoc with rhythm reading is playing pieces with which the students are familiar. When "Jingle Bells" is printed in all quarter notes, but you hear that dotted quarter pattern (that you haven't taught yet) on "all the way" all quarter notes, you know that rhythm reading is not taking place. Point out from the very first instance of this that students should play what is actually printed on the page, not what they think it is supposed to be.

Constance Sanders is band director at R. A. Jones Middle School in Florence, Kentucky. This article is reprinted from the March 2000 issue of Kentucky's Bluegrass Music News *(it originally appeared in the September 1999 issue of the* Kentucky Collegiate MENC Journal). *Reprinted by permission.*

Sousa's Secret Formula
Thomas J. Trimborn

It was thought you could never hear our country all at once. But a man by the name of John Philip Sousa proved it could be done because he listened and heard the heartbeat of the American people, caught it in a trumpet, clarinet, oboe, and drum, and his music marched forth alive and bright as a silver dollar—brisk, beautiful, and strong. And thanks to recent scholarship and new editions of the marches he gave us, as fast as you could say Uncle Sam and the U.S.A., authentic performances will be with us for many years to come.

Once upon a Time

As this century draws to a close, we can look back on the history of bands and the music written for them and recall a love affair. Yes, a love affair America had with a portly little gentleman by the name of John Philip Sousa—composer, conductor, author, patriot. Although some have attempted to deny the heritage of the band by suggesting other genealogical lines, it is his artistic seed that lives on to this day. At the turn of the last century, America's Sousa had become the most famous and prolific musician in the world. His 136 marches, for which he earned the title of the "March King," were published and played by bands and orchestras, and on everything from the parlor piano to mandolin, guitar, banjo, and zither. Walking down residential city streets, one could hear Sousa marches coming from countless homes, as people played, danced, hummed and listened to them. Sousa was everywhere.

Hearing the Sousa Band

Of course, the ultimate treat was to hear a live performance of a Sousa march played by the Sousa Band. Although the marches were available on beeswax cylinder recordings, the scratchy, thin sound simply was not satisfying by comparison to the real thing. Huge crowds attended Sousa performances and were never disappointed because liberal quantities of his marches were always included in every concert. And people knew, or seemed to sense, that what they were hearing was somehow different, unique, and sounded like no other band playing the very same music. It was true. Could the difference be the unparalleled musicianship of the musicians—people like Herbert L. Clarke, Arthur Pryor, and a host of others? Yes, maybe so. Or could it be because the composer himself was conducting his own music? Yes, maybe that too. Or was it something more? People back then really never knew, and Sousa never revealed how he did it. After his death, and for many, many years, Sousa marches were performed, enjoyed and treasured as essential musical Americana, but there were those who always remembered the authentic Sousa sound in their own mind's ear and it never matched current practice. The performances always seemed a bit flat.

The Mid-20th Century About-Face

As this century wore on, those involved with the band, especially those with programming its repertoire, grew increasingly dissatisfied with the march form as a staple. Through the efforts of prominent educators, conductors, composers, organizations, associations, and foundations, contemporary composers were enticed to compose serious music for the wind band medium. This resulted in the creation of numerous wonderful works, many of which have become cornerstones of the literature. In the meantime, bands turned away from playing the time-honored marches so beloved a few generations earlier.

Fate and Knowledge Step In

While the trend on the part of some was not to perform marches (Sousa's or anyone else's), our great American military bands and community groups continued playing them. Then as fate would have it, along came author Paul Bierley to write the authoritative and acclaimed Sousa biography. This book, together with several others he wrote, included enough information about authentic performance practice to interest and attract prominent band directors to again champion this music. What Bierley and others learned, was that indeed Sousa had a kind of secret performance formula. Pieces of the puzzle were assembled by conducting interviews with surviving Sousa Band members, listening to original recordings, and examining the manuscript and the parts, some with markings inserted by Sousa musicians. The code was cracked.

Problematic First Editions

The original Sousa marches were published between 1873 and 1931, and since then, literally hundreds of arrangements have been made available. The first step for conductors is to determine if the march is indeed a first edition or a later arrangement. That information is clearly included on the score and parts. Original first editions are march size, published by any one of a host of publishers, and usually have an octavo-sized condensed score, although for some there is no score of any kind save the solo cornet part. Playing the original music presents numerous problems. Experts have found mistakes and inconsistent markings in many of the parts. The small size makes reading difficult and can cause mistakes in playing as a result. Rehearsal letters and numbers are absent, which makes efficient rehearsing problematic. If the choice is made to use original music, it is important for all of the above concerns to be addressed. Make photocopy enlargements of all the parts and insert rehearsal letters/numbers. Discrepancies in pitch and note values must be clarified via comparison with the score, or to agree with the majority of parts. Carefully examine all of the parts and score to ensure that rhythmically identical lines are articulated alike. Dynamic changes should occur simultaneously unless altered to achieve an expressive effect. There will be no short cut to avoid doing this prerehearsal preparation. In the end, conductors will be reading from a condensed score which often offers little indication as to what is being played by which instruments. Adding detailed score cues may help that situation, although conductors inevitably will be in the dark, needing to ask players about details.

Recent Concert-Sized Editions

Recent editions by Wingert-Jones and others have provided a viable choice when deciding whether or not to perform a first edition. They are concert-sized and easy to read, many having full or detailed, readable condensed scores. Comparison of one of these versions with a first edition will settle any question about whether it has been arranged (changed), or if it is essentially original. Of all the editions available, perhaps the purest and most historically informed are those edited by Frank Byrne and Col. John Bourgeois.

Sousa Performance Practices

With Sousa on the podium, his marches had a driving lift and pulsation which electrified his audiences. His interpretations were distinctly his

Overview of Sousa Performance Practices

- Introduction and first strain usually played as written.
- Second strain: first time, dynamic—piano. Cornets and trombones tacet; piccolo and upper clarinets (including E-flat clarinet) dropped an octave. On repeat all instruments back in as written, dynamic—fortissimo.
- Trio: cornets and trombones again tacet; piccolo and upper clarinets down an octave; snare, bass drum, and cymbals most often eliminated; bells double the melody; dynamic—piano. If trio is repeated, second time dynamic is pianissimo.
- Dog-fight/break strains played as written, all instruments in at written pitch.
- Last strain usually played twice, separated by the break strain. First time, piccolo, E-flat clarinet, cornets and trombones tacet; upper clarinets down an octave; dynamic—piano. On repeat, all instruments back in at break strain playing fortissimo and as written to the end. Climactic accents are commonly added here.

own and amounted to a secret formula which he kept to himself. He would deviate from the printed parts and score, mostly by adding accents, changing dynamics, and an occasional special effect. His tempos were always played with no variation, slightly faster than normal military tempos. The playing style he demanded could be referred to as "marcato style," which meant emphasizing the rhythm and accents, and also playing in a separated or detached manner for the sake of clarity. Except for lyrical passages, the Sousa Band played notes crisper and shorter to enhance the precision of rhythmic patterns. Special mention must be made of the all-important bass drum part. Accents were clearly heard to highlight the pulsation effect, but otherwise the beat was felt rather than heard. Recordings by the eminent Frederick Fennell certainly convey the spirit and importance of the percussion section, and should be listened to and studied as a matter of course.

Happily Ever After

In many ways Sousa marches are difficult pieces to play well, needing much more rehearsal time than one would imagine at first glance. However, when today's conductor applies Sousa's now not-so-secret formula in a sincere effort to re-create them authentically, the results can be spectacular. So many of the marches are masterpieces, acclaimed by the experts, and beloved by the masses the world over. In these compositions, Sousa not only defined and inspired the principal métier of the band's heritage—the march—but continues to reflect the essence of the American Spirit—originality, directness, energy, power, and hope. Sousa's secret formula isn't so secret anymore, because most, if not all, of it has been decoded. And because of that, America's love affair with the spirit of the March King can continue well into the next century and beyond. The year 1996 marked the centennial of "The Stars and Stripes Forever." For years to come, bands may observe similar anniversaries—1998, "Hands Across the Sea;" 2000, "Hail to the Spirit of Liberty;" 2001, "The Invincible Eagle." And so, on into the future, the bands that play them, and the audiences that hear them will learn that once upon a time there was a man known as the March King and that his marches indeed live happily ever after.

References

Bierley, Paul E. (1973). *John Philip Sousa: A Descriptive Catalog of His Works.* Urbana: University of Illinois Press.

Bierley, Paul E. (1973). *John Philip Sousa: American Phenomenon.* Englewood Cliffs, NJ: Prentice Hall.

Bierley, Paul E. (1986, April). "The Hero of the Band—John Philip Sousa." *The Instrumentalist,* 18–20.

Fennell, Frederick. (1954). *Time and the Winds: A Short History of the Use of Wind Instruments in the Orchestra, Band, and the Wind Ensemble.* Kenosha, WI: G. Leblanc.

Newsom, Jon (Ed.). (1983). *Perspectives on John Philip Sousa.* Washington, DC: Library of Congress Music Division.

Schwartz, H. W. (1957). *Bands of America: A Nostalgic, Illustrated History of the Golden Age of Band Music.* Garden City, NY: Double Day.

Sousa, John Philip. *Marching Along: Recollections of Men, Women, and Music* (Paul E. Bierley, Ed.). Westerville, OH: Integrity Press.

Whitwell, David. (1980). *A New History of Wind Music.* Evanston, IL: The Instrumentalist Publishing Co.

Thomas J. Trimborn is associate professor of music at Truman State University in Kirksville, Missouri. This article originally appeared in the Fall 1998 issue of Missouri School Music. *Reprinted by permission.*

Tackling the Monster
by Scott Watson (with Nancy Beitler, Kay Mancke, and Richard Steltz)

When renowned trumpeter Wynton Marsalis put together his music education series for PBS *(Marsalis on Music)*, the segment on practicing was entitled, "Tackling the Monster." No mom, dad, or instructor of an elementary instrumentalist would disagree—getting most kids to practice consistently is a monster!

The struggles parents go through each day to get their son or daughter to practice are legendary. This is especially true after the initial few months of playing. A few years ago, an interesting *Dear Abby* column appeared that enlightened us all. A concerned mother wrote to express her exasperation with having to nag her child to practice his instrument. She wondered whether she should force her child to practice. More memorable than Abby's reply were the responses printed in the weeks to follow. Letters poured in from professional musicians—soloists and members of major symphonies—all of whom indicated their distaste for practicing when they were younger (some even now!). The revelation here for parents is both sobering and comforting: practice, for many, is a necessary evil. It's probably normal that children don't *enjoy* working out a tough passage or technique. But if children and their parents can learn to deal with this part of instrument study, the rewards will make the sacrifice worth it.

Most parents don't write *Dear Abby* when they get to the end of their rope. They call the band director. What can the elementary band director who knows how hard and how important it is to get young players to develop a habit of daily home practice do to help? Over the years, the members of our department regard the following methods to encourage home practice as our favorites. They are geared to the beginner to intermediate level player.

Practice Calendar
A good place to start is with a method that both encourages and charts home practice. At the start of each month, students are given a blank practice calendar. This can be spiced up with cool, musical clip-art, etc. Since parents will see it weekly, it can include timely messages to parents, as well. Each day, after their home practice session, students fill in the number of minutes they have practiced. If students don't practice, they need to write "0." There is a space for mom or dad to initial the calendar at week's end, just to confirm that they've

reviewed their child's efforts. Each week at the start of any in-school lesson or sectional, we take a minute or two to check each student's calendar. Practice goals can be for total number of minutes played or number of days played. Praise for a good practice week comes in the form of cool, colorful music stickers placed on the calendar that week and lots of verbal encouragement.

Achievement Chart
At some point in the fall, a chart goes up on my wall with each band member's name on it. After a while, first-year players begin asking what the chart is for. Older players already know: I'm recording students' progress on things like concert selections and scales. Throughout the year, as students perform items on the chart, I check them off. To me, this means they played a song or scale approximately (subjectively) 90 percent or better. This is a great way to use competition in a positive and healthy way. For the most part, when members of a lesson group see others getting songs crossed-off, they don't want to be left out. They'll practice more and will even come in for extra help just to catch up. When the chart is completely filled with checks, we all know that we're ready for the concert! A couple of things to keep in mind: (1) Some students need to get checked off for doing their best, even if it's not quite 90 percent. Near concert time, if there's an area of concern in a song, bracket it and ask the student not to play the troublesome part. (2) Try to hear students play in pairs or small groups so no one is put on the spot. (3) Try to hold "help sessions" during recess, etc., to help a weak or timid student. See figure 1 for an example of an achievement chart.

Concert Music Cassettes
One in our department requires band members to tape-record themselves performing several concert selections. The tape is recorded at home or in school during recess, and the instructor offers helpful and encouraging comments when returning it. Students' eyes are opened to concepts of tone and rhythm as they are encouraged to listen to their own tapes. A "Make Your Own Sundae" incentive party is held—with help from the PTO, of course—for all band members who submit a tape. Needless to say, participation is high!

Practice Partners
I'm always asking my students if there are kids in their neighborhood with whom they can occa-

Student	Scale 1	Scale 2	"Ode to Joy"	"Hey, Jude"	"Do, Re, Mi"	"Thunder Drum"	"Irish Folk Dance"	"Japanese Folk Trilogy"	"Grand Old Flag"	"The Moldau"	Return Music

Figure 1. Fifth/Sixth Grade Band Spring Music

sionally get together and practice. An older brother or sister who plays, a friend from their grade or older, or even a parent can make taking out their instrument something to look forward to. Fifth- and sixth-grade band members love showing fourth graders the ropes. Check it out—I'll bet quite a few of your students' parents play a band instrument or piano. It seems that many families have what amounts to small instrumental dynasties that have been handed down from generation to generation! Take advantage of this as much as you can. Send a flute part home even if the student is a clarinetist. They'll have a ball playing together!

Accompaniment Tapes

Some method books offer companion cassette tapes or CDs with selected exercises or songs. You may want to make these available to students to buy or have the school purchase multiple copies to sign out.

If your district has the equipment, you can also use software sequencers (such as *Master Tracks Pro* or *Performer*) with a computer MIDI setup to create your own accompaniments. These can be either functional accompaniments to method book exercises or realizations of concert selections. With the help of a few stereo (RCA) patch cords, you can record the sequences to your tape deck. Since it's so easy to change tempos with the sequencing programs, I usually record two versions of each selection—a slow version for early in

the learning process and one at concert tempo for later when students have learned the notes. I make these recordings available for sign-out, assigning them to students who need extra encouragement, and I also use them during group lessons.

A less technical application of this same principal is to make a cassette recording of yourself playing a student's music. Use piano, or better yet, the same instrument the student plays. Violá!—now you are the student's practice partner!

Supplemental Music

Sometimes students in a lesson group just get in a funk; they seem apathetic and close to bailing out. Or maybe it's in the weeks following a concert when everyone just shuts down and stops practicing. At times like these, the introduction of some fun, but challenging, supplemental music is just what the doctor ordered. Some guidelines for choosing this music for your program include the following:

1. Pick music that doesn't sound too dated.
2. Try to avoid advanced, syncopated "Top 40" rhythms.
3. Be sure the key signatures aren't out of reach.
4. Look for concepts you want to reinforce anyway.

My favorite set to use is Hal Leonard's *Disney Solo Trax,* a collection of well-crafted arrangements of Disney classics the kids all know. What I really like about this set is its usefulness in introducing or reinforcing musical concepts that stretch young players in a painless way. I always look forward to using these in lessons at the end of the year to work on things like the dotted-eighth/sixteenth rhythm, upper range, or cut-time. Last year, after a lesson spent with the *Solo Trax* book, I overheard one of my young alto sax players remark, "Wow! I'm actually gonna practice this stuff!"

Incentives

OK, they're bribes, but the word "incentive" sounds more noble! Anyway, when I can tell a lesson group is up against the wall in frustration over something that requires extra time and effort to master but is within their grasp if they want it, I introduce a little chocolate into the equation. Pencils or stickers work well, too. See if your PTO will pick up the tab.

Teacher-Parent Communication

Many districts kick-off the year with a meeting for parents of beginning instrumentalists. Usually good practice habits are discussed, such as the following:

1. Play 20–30 minutes a day.
2. Try to have a routine practice time.
3. Use a music stand (not a sofa).
4. Isolate trouble spots and drill them separately.

Making these and other expectations known from the very beginning is wise. However, during the year and in subsequent years, phone calls home to see how a student is doing is equally as wise. Maybe you've noticed that a student has suddenly stopped progressing. Or maybe you'd like to suggest private lessons or extra material for someone who is no longer challenged. At the very least, you can provide a warning when your clar-inet group will be going over the break to those shrill "high notes!" I remember reading how band legend William Revels, when he was teaching in the schools, would actually drive out to visit the family of a student who was struggling or had quit just to see if there was anything he might do to turn things around. That sort of personal care had to make an impact.

Encourage Private Lessons

Many parents take the initiative themselves, getting recommendations from the band director and contacting the specialist. However, some parents who may be open to the idea just haven't considered getting private lessons to supplement their child's school study. Maybe the student is advanced and needs the challenge or is struggling and needs additional help. Either way, private study is a way to work through either situation and get a student playing regularly.

As the school year winds down, it is a good idea to send home a list of area private teachers, gently encouraging parents to consider the benefits to their child of keeping up their musical study during the summer.

Scott Watson is elementary band coordinator for the Parkland School District and band director at Kratzer and Cetronia Elementary Schools in Allentown, Pennsylvania. Nancy Beitler is band director at Southern Lehigh Middle School in the Southern Lehigh School District in Coopersburg, Pennsylvania. Kay Mancke is band director at Kernsville and Ironton Elementary Schools in the Parkland School District in Allentown, Pennsylvania. Richard Steltz is a retired band director from Fogelsville Elementary School in the Parkland School District in Allentown, Pennsylvania. This article originally appeared in the Fall 1998 issue of Pennsylvania's PMEA News. *Reprinted by permission.*

Building Ensemble Musicianship for Your Concert Band

by Patrick Winters

In no way does this article attempt to address all of the many facets of producing a quality band sound. Instead, I would like to address a few fundamental concepts that I have found to be successful for me in working with younger bands. For many of you these ideas will be remedial, and for others a refresher. Perhaps there will be an old idea or two that are put forth in a slightly different manner.

Balance and Blend

The "Pyramid" Sound

It is safe to say that most of us want our ensembles to have a rich, warm, resonant quality. One way to achieve this is to balance the group by asking for more sound from the lower voices and less sound from the upper ones. Try playing a fully voiced chord that lies comfortably within the players' range as an example. By having students visualize the shape of a pyramid, they should strive to "fit" their own instrumental voice into that context. Once you've created the desired "warmth" from the group, I find it useful to have students play with the opposite (wrong) balance. Ask them to invert the pyramid in order to hear what is not desired. They will immediately hear the "bright" quality that you are trying to avoid. Identify that "wrong" sound using words like "harsh," "top-heavy," "strident," etc. Reinforce this point by having your group play with the correct balance. Refer to this blend/balance with words such as "rich," "dark" and "resonant." Don't forget to include the percussionists. Insist that they listen to the overall sound and adjust their volume tastefully. They need to be aware of how the many tone colors they create affect the ensemble's overall balance. For example, cymbals, triangle, and tambourine tend to create a "bright" color, and therefore should be balanced accordingly.

The "Long Note Rule"

When holding notes of four counts or more, it is likely that others have a more important part. Listen. Determine the musical function of your note(s), and balance within that musical context. Create "shape" and "interest" to long notes— slight crescendo, diminuendo, *fp* with slight crescendo, etc. Listen to the melodic line for guidance.

The "Short Note Rule"

When playing short tutti notes (as in stingers, buttons, etc.), be sure to have players play long enough so that notes have a chance to "speak." Practice holding out short notes as fermatas to examine all parts of the chord. Then play a "slice" of the sound to the desired length. Generally, try to avoid using the tongue to "stop" the sound, which can prevent the sound from resonating.

Ensemble Crescendo

Lower voices should crescendo first and upper voices last. The reverse is true on diminuendo.

Saxophone Blend

When saxophones double brass parts, as they often do in "young band" arrangements (i.e., alto saxophones and horns, tenor saxophones and baritones, etc.), try having saxes play about half the volume of brasses. Have saxophonists strive to play "inside" of their brass doubling partners.

Dark Releases

At cutoffs, have lower voices release slightly late, upper voices slightly early, etc. This will help to "darken" the sound of the group.

Inner Parts

Are the "inner" parts being heard (3rd clarinet, 2nd trombone, etc.)? As conductors, do we tend to follow (and therefore listen) primarily to the melodic line? Keep your ears "searching" to hear all parts. You might try rehearsing your group leaving out the melody altogether at times. This will help students to be aware of chordal complexities and should improve intonation.

Percussion

Less is usually more! Too often, overpowering percussion volume flaws otherwise good band performances. Allow your percussionists to experience the excitement of creating soft intensity. Encourage your players to explore all dynamic ranges.

In unfamiliar performance venues, encourage the percussionists to assess the hall. Percussionists can and should "tune" to the room. This may mean bringing carpet squares to place on the floor under instruments, changing mallets, etc. I have found that wearing an oven mitt on the free hand of the bass drummer can help to dampen the sound in a very "live" room. The possibilities are endless!

Phrasing

Crescendo

Encourage your students at an early age to follow the natural tendency to crescendo when the melodic line ascends and visa versa. Train students to search for ways to create "nuance" within phrases. Allow them to get involved with "going beyond the printed notes." I sometimes find it helpful to sing a particular part for students from the podium. Hopefully this encourages expressive playing!

Fermatas

Often times in performances, fermatas are not held long enough. Be sure to give fermatas the proper length dictated by the music. Again, sustained notes usually require "shaping." Often it is appropriate to ritard leading into fermatas, even if it is not marked.

Breathing

Clearly define when players should take their breaths together, stagger breathe, or sustain notes in a phrase. Because younger players typically have difficulty holding notes the full value, have students mark their parts accordingly (i.e., -4, -2+, etc.). Remember, "It's better to leave out a note to take a breath than to chop one in half."

Articulation

Tonguing

I find that many young players tend to over-articulate using too much tongue, or the tongue is arched too high causing a very bright or harsh attack. This is especially true if they see ff in the part. Several players attacking together require a "lightness" of attack and articulations. Try having brass players use a softer syllable such as "doo" or "dah." "Tam" and "teh" should be reserved for a very aggressive style. The word "attack" itself implies a harsh approach to sound. You may want to use the term "fronting the sound" to describe the amount and style of attack. Try playing an entire passage without using any tongue at all. Gradually add the tongue for the desired sound. Some directors of young players use a numbering system (scale of 1 through 10) to indicate the amount of tongue to be used. I find it helpful to use descriptive words along with musical terms to describe the kind of attack, or fronting, sound I want. For example, staccato = "pin prick" or "dot," marcato = "buoyant" or "bouncing," etc. Try creating a vocabulary of your own that will work well with your students.

Legato Style

Very often young ensembles lack rhythmic clarity when playing legato. Notes tend to lose punctuation due to a lack of focus at the attack. You may want to try having students begin by playing a passage completely slurred. Then, have them use a slight tonguing stroke, as the air continues to flow. I like saying, "gently dent the air stream." The concept is much like a pulsating lawn sprinkler.

Releases

Unless an abrupt cutoff is desired, don't use the tongue to release long tones or on chorale-type playing. In an attempt to be very exact, sometimes students will articulate at the release point. Try having the players inhale at the precise point of release. This will ensure that they don't involve the tongue, thus making a more resonant cutoff. Be careful, however, that players use good breath support through to the end. The tendency will be for them to lose support of the sound just before the release, causing a "sag" in the tone quality and/or pitch. In addition, insist that the players stay completely still and silent after the release of the last note of a piece or movement. Encourage students to focus in on the resonance of the final note and the silence that follows. Don't allow there to be any distractions from creating this powerful effect.

Dynamics

Dynamic Ranges

Younger students relate well to a numbering system of dynamics, 1 being the softest … 10 being the loudest. It may be helpful (or even necessary) to equate a numbering system to the traditional dynamic markings (5 = mf, etc.). Have students strive to use more air (breath support) when playing softer.

Volume

Are you allowing your group to consistently play too loud? (ugghhh!) Here are a few admonitions borrowed from Ed Solomon: "Don't play any louder than lovely," "Don't take a breath during a crescendo or a decrescendo," "Listen. Does the musical line call for more or less volume?" "Whole notes don't sit there; they grow or swell," "Support the long notes and go the full value—go to the beat or the bar line."

Crescendo

At the crescendo sign, try having your ensemble drop down one dynamic before the swell. This helps create the effect of a larger dynamic contrast and helps to avoid overblowing. Remember, lower voices should crescendo first and upper voices last.

Tempo/Time
Maintaining Time
Holding a steady pulse and counting is every band member's responsibility! Silent counting games help to make this point and will increase the concentration and focus of the group. Try this one: With instruments held on laps, ask your students to vocalize a short sound (try using "dot") on a predetermined count. (Start off using count 10 or 12). Begin by counting off aloud for them at a moderate tempo, then gradually fade out your voice. Students should continue counting silently in their heads until it's time to say "dot." You will immediately discover who is and who is not counting to themselves. Try it again, this time make the count higher (count 24, for example). Obviously, the higher the number, the more room for error and the more the group will need to concentrate. Don't allow anyone to tap his or her feet. Repeat the game at varied tempos. It's fun and it encourages students to be proactive and independent counters!

Entrances
Do your players miss making entrances with good tempo after extended rests? This is a common problem unless students are trained to internalize the pulse. I like the analogy of "jumping on a moving train"—one cannot stand flat-footed and expect to be able to hop up on the moving train without injury. In order for players to enter with proper timing, they must prepare by feeling the tempo before they take the breath to enter.

Dynamics and Tempo
Do your players rush forte passages and drag softer ones? Volume should not affect tempo, but we know that there is a strong tendency for that to happen. This occurs because young players exert more energy as they play stronger and vice versa. Making students keenly aware that this tendency exists is part of the solution. Of course, players should play with energy regardless of the dynamic level. Training players to use strong breath support at all dynamic levels should help to counter tempo fluctuations.

Patrick Winters is director of bands and professor of music at Eastern Washington University in Cheney. This article originally appeared in the January 1999 issue of Washington's Voice. *Reprinted by permission.*

The Perils of Directing a Small Band: A New Paradigm
by Phillip C. Wise

A few weeks ago I received a call from a band director who teaches at a small private high school. It was obvious he was distraught; his quivering voice elevated in pitch, and the pace of his run-on sentences could mean only one thing … injustice. He desperately attempted to explain the incongruity of the judges' comments—the critiques that had earned his twenty-three piece ensemble a III rating at large group contest. He read from the adjudicating form: you need to balance instrumentation; too bad you only have one trombone; your rendition is not appropriate or authentic; the oboe solo would have sounded better than the muted trumpet. "Why these types of comments?" he pleaded.

Why? Because you're the director of a small band (15–30 members), and although there are literally thousands of small bands in this country, it seems this ensemble has become a social pariah. Adjudicators don't really know how to objectively appraise this ensemble, and human nature is such that when one is uncertain, the tendency is to become disapproving and discrediting. Who is to blame for the capricious evaluations so often registered to the small band? Let's delve into the plight of the small school band director as well as the difficulties associated with adjudicating the *small* band within the *large* group structure.

First, how does a director respond to these comments? *Needs balanced instrumentation.* A most prolific and astute observation! Directors of small bands are quite aware of their inherent balance problems. Can this be resolved? Does the director have enough instrumentation in the other sections to switch students in an attempt to correct the imbalance? Is the director able to immediately start the correct number of high school students on the needed instruments and prepare them for a proficient performance? *Too bad you only have one trombone.* No kidding! Is this remark relative to the musical performance given by the students? Can this be corrected in a rehearsal situation? Could there be alternative reasons why there is one trombone in the band (two trombones moved last semester and the director switched the only other trombonist to tuba so there would be a tuba section)? Tough to fault that logic! *Your rendition is not appropriate or authentic.* Translation: your ensemble is too small to make this band piece sound genuine. What is authenticity to a traditionalist anyway? *The oboe solo would have sounded better than the muted trumpet.* Of course it would have; however, there is no oboist in the band. By the way, no critique was offered to the student who *performed* the solo part. Are you starting to get the picture? This type of commentary speaks more about the judge than the band.

Teaching in a small school district with a limited number of students to draw from and directing a small ensemble is a phenomenon one can only identify with by experiencing the challenge. When adjudicators make these types of nebulous comments regarding external factors rather than basing their evaluation on the musical performance, it seems the small band hasn't a fighting chance. The results of these frustrating experiences have left many programs out in the cold—fearful to perform at adjudicated large group contests/festivals.

Both adjudicator and director must not only be willing to examine the small band in a different light but also to redefine its existence. This paradigm shift should not be a *watering down* of high musical standards (proper balance, blend, intonation, tone, rhythm, phrasing, dynamics and interpretation) but rather an awareness that the small band (15–30 members) has divergent musical characteristics. As music educators we have the unique opportunity, and obligation, to define the standards, structure and evaluative guidelines for this manifestation. Only then will the thousands of students who are members of small bands reap the musical and personal benefits of our alliance.

We could begin by evaluating the small band on the basis of aural performance rather than conceptualization. Let's be honest, even the most astute judge creates a perception when a one-hundred-fifty-piece band enters the stage in pressed black and white tuxedos—it's human nature. Myth debunked: bigger isn't always better! Each band must be reviewed based upon its own merits. Of course, some will argue that adjudication of the band must be governed to one standard (the consummate and traditional band

sound); however, this argument is only valid if you are comparing homogeneous groups. Let's widen the scope of our perception to include a new definition for this ensemble. Let's consider this anomalous group: *mixed chamber winds.*

Until a curriculum is developed to better define this new archetype, directors must stop shooting themselves in the foot and then frantically looking around for the guilty party. The conductor of the small band must accept part of the blame for the comparing standards they currently face. Most small bands suffer from instrumentation imbalances yet perform stock concert band arrangements. Composers write for the perfectly balanced band and then expect you, the director, to make needed interpretation and instrumentation/balance adjustments. If your band is not balanced, you must become empowered to *rearrange the composition* by analyzing the texture of the piece, ensemble strengths and weaknesses and availability of instrumentation (at contest, simply notate these alterations on the judges' scores).

Select literature that is consistent with your ensemble. If you have a high school band of twenty, should you attempt to perform a Mahler orchestral transcription? Your band would most likely be better suited for a Mozart transcription of *Eine Kleine Nachtmusik* (rearranged, of course). Directors must work hard to find exemplary literature that exalts the strengths of their ensembles. Many have found a safe-haven through smaller publishing houses such as the flexible-part band literature published by Big Hill Music Press in Grand Coteau, Louisiana. These creative arrangements can be mixed and matched to fit your ensemble. Although not abundant, valuable chamber, small band, and part literature is available, and more will be published if educators demand it. Remember, traditional orchestrations can still be performed with appropriate modification.

Directors often believe they must work to fill the performance hall, doing everything imaginable to sound like a big band. However, it is futile to attempt to recreate the robust sound of a one-hundred-piece symphonic band. In their zeal to emulate the larger ensemble, overblowing occurs, systemically creaking intonation problems. Even the least discerning listener will take note of these transgressions. Small ensemble characteristics often overlooked include the impressively clean articulation that can be obtained and the unique transparent sound that cannot be duplicated by the traditional symphonic band. Taste is much more important than volume!

The music education community must begin to re-evaluate the significance of the small band by creating a new paradigm—the *mixed chamber winds*. A sanctioned ensemble without constraints of preconceived instrumentation requirements, size or repertoire. Defined by its strengths: unique textures, mixed instrumentation, flexible timbre, creativity, transparent sound and alternative literature. The *mixed chamber winds,* an ensemble that promotes *inclusion* and *opportunity* regardless of school size or student population—an ensemble that allows students and directors to succeed!

Phillip C. Wise is associate professor of music education at Missouri Southern State College in Joplin. This article was originally published in the December 1998 issue of the National Band Association Journal. *Reprinted by permission.*

Section 2

 # Repertoire

If music is the destination, repertoire is the vehicle. With the vast amount of music available, how do band directors separate the quality pieces from the run-of-the-mill ones and select music that will inspire and serve as a learning tool for their students? The articles in this section shed light on the subject of repertoire.

 Section 2

Repertoire

Finding Quality Music for Our Bands
by Lynn D. Cooper

The start of another school year brings us all back to the quest for fine literature for our ensembles. The selection of appropriate music for our ensembles is one of the most important responsibilities of any ensemble director, and it is a task which can consume an enormous amount of time. It is, however, time well-spent, because one of our primary responsibilities as music educators is to find good music of the highest caliber to rehearse and perform.

Our search for outstanding music for our ensembles may be aided by establishing criteria to help us more easily identify "quality music." Many KMEA members will recall the CBDNA-sponsored session at the 1995 In-Service which dealt with "Quality Music for Quality Bands." As part of that presentation, Dr. Ben Hawkins, from Transylvania University, discussed ten points which we may want to consider when we evaluate a piece of music for possible performance. He noted that few pieces will meet all the criteria.

1. Does it have good melodies?
2. Are there interesting harmonies?
3. Is there variety of texture?
4. Are there opportunities for student problem-solving?
5. Is there potential for stimulating student imagination?
6. Is there potential to refine student emotional response?
7. Does it provide potential to expand student understanding of the nature of "music"?
8. Will it contribute to creating a satisfying concert program?
9. Is it developmentally appropriate?
10. Is it by an acknowledged master?

Dr. James Nielson listed several components of what he considered to be "quality" music in a booklet first published by the Leblanc Corporation in the 1970s called "What Is Quality In Music?" Among them were: Rhythmic Vitality; Genuine Originality; Melody, which has the qualities of economy, logic, and inspiration; Harmony, which is consistent with and is suitable to the style; Craftsmanship; a Sense of Values (meaning that everything is in balance and proportion and that there is a sense of continuity); what he calls "Justified Emotion"; and the Test of Time.

I like to define "good" or quality music as music which has the qualities of excellent construction and genuine expressiveness. Whatever the criteria we choose to help us select music for rehearsal and performance, it is also essential that the chosen music be appropriate for our ensemble. Many conductors find it helpful to take a dispassionate look at the strengths and weaknesses of their ensembles, and to use that evaluation to guide their music selection. While a band which has difficulty playing sustained and well-shaped musical phrases should work to develop that essential skill in rehearsal, it may not be wise to program music which relies heavily on that skill for a major portion of the work.

It also seems that most of the literature we perform should be sight-readable by our ensembles in some recognizable form. Since the ensemble would not be spending most of their time overcoming technical problems, they could concentrate on tone, intonation, balance, blend, phrasing, etc. Certainly, we want to challenge our ensembles with some pieces, both technically and musically, but we must ensure that it is a reasonable and conquerable challenge. Most conductors have a tendency to "over-program" for their ensembles at times, but in so doing, we may set ourselves and our students up for great frustration when we make unreasonable musical or technical demands.

Where do we find "quality music" for our ensembles? We are all inundated with recordings for new music publications and some of that music is very fine, but it is a giant "sifting" process to find the few "grains of wheat." New music reviews in our professional journals are helpful, but be careful that the reviewers are evaluating the music by the same standards which you use. Referring to music lists published by national and state associations is often helpful, and there are now several excellent books which have recently been published listing recommended music.

Students will respond to good music. We do not have to give them only what they think they want. That is not to say that we should only play heavier "concert" music all the time. Some lighter music is of excellent construction and has genuine expressiveness. What we should avoid is what I call "pop trash"—light, poorly arranged, popular music which is often not even a good representation of the original version and which possesses absolutely no musical integrity. Actually, much of the new "concert" music published in the past few years has a certain "pop" quality to it. We have so little time to rehearse and perform music with our students—why not use our limited time working on music of lasting value?

The selection of good music for our ensembles is an extremely important responsibility. There is a lot of truly outstanding good music, but there is also a lot of music which should never be played. If we want our bands and orchestras to be taken seriously as a worthy performing ensemble and as a curricular subject, then we had better be sure that the literature we select for them is of the highest, most worthy caliber.

As part of the session at the 1995 KMEA In-Service mentioned earlier in this article, a list of outstanding Grade 3 and Grade 4 band music was prepared from the recommendations of college band directors and several district band chairs. The music which received the highest number of recommendations can be found in figure 1. It is music of high caliber which will enrich the lives of your students.

Lynn G. Cooper is director of bands, professor of music, and chair of the music department at Asbury College in Wilmore, Kentucky. This article originally appeared in the October 1995 issue of Kentucky's Bluegrass Music News. *Reprinted by permission.*

Figure 1. Quality Music for Quality Bands (Grades 3 and 4)

Developed by CBDNA-KY for a Clinic presented at the KMEA In-Service on February 10, 1995.

Grade 3

Title	Composer/Arranger	Publisher
Cajun Folk Songs	Frank Ticheli	Manhattan Beach
Court Festival	William Latham	Summy-Birchard
Fanfare, Ode and Festival	Bob Margolis	Manhattan Beach
Festivo	Vaclav Nelhybel	Belwin
Kentucky - 1800	Clare Grundman	Boosey & Hawkes
Overture for Winds	Charles Carter	Bourne
Polly Oliver	Thomas Root	Kjos
Prelude and Fugue in B-flat	J. S. Bach/R. L. Moehlman	Warner/MPH
The Battle Pavane	Tielman Susato/Bob Margolis	Manhattan Beach
Three Ayres from Gloucester	Hugh Stuart	Shawnee
Variation Overture	Clifton Williams	Ludwig

Grade 4

Title	Composer/Arranger	Publisher
A Festival Prelude	Alfred Reed	Marks/Belwin
Blessed Are They	Johannes Brahms/Barbara Buehlman	Ludwig
Chorale and Alleluia	Howard Hanson	C. Fischer
Chorale and Shaker Dance	John Zdechlik	Kjos
Dedicatory Overture	Clifton Williams	Piedmont Music
Emperata Overture	Claude T. Smith	Wingert Jones
English Folk Song Suite	Ralph Vaughan Williams	Boosey & Hawkes
First Suite in E-flat	Gustav Holst	Boosey & Hawkes
Irish Tune from County Derry	Percy A. Grainger	Carl Fischer (TRN)
Salvation is Created	Pavel Tschnesokoff/Bruce Houseknecht	Kjos
Second Suite in F	Gustav Holst	Boosey & Hawkes
Three Chorale Preludes	William Latham	Summy-Birchard
Toccata	Girolamo Frescobaldi/Earl Slocum	CPP-Belwin
Ye Banks & Braes o' Bonnie Doon	Percy A. Grainger	Schirmer

Women Composers for Band

*by John Culvahouse and
Dwight W. Satterwhite*

Many women composers have published works for band or various combinations of band instruments. We have chosen to highlight three of the most prominent and most prolific of these fine composers. Their works range in difficulty from pieces suitable for elementary bands to compositions that offer a challenge to university-level ensembles. All, however, are interesting and well worth examining.

Cindy McTee (b. 1953) holds the B. Mus. from Pacific Lutheran University, the M.M. from Yale, and the Ph.D. from the University of Iowa. She also completed a year of study in Poland with Krzysztof Penderecki at the Academy of Music in Cracow. She is professor of composition at the University of North Texas.

A versatile composer, McTee has written commissioned works for the Dallas Symphony, Northern Arizona University, the Barlow Endowment, the American Guild of Organists, and the College Band Directors Association. She has received awards from the National Endowment for the Arts, the American Academy of Arts and Letters, the Fulbright Program, and the Big Eight Band Directors Association, among others.

Her compositions have been performed by the London Philharmonic, the National Symphony Orchestra, the Cleveland Orchestra, the Buffalo Philharmonic, the St. Louis Symphony, the Honolulu Symphony, the Pittsburgh New Music Ensemble, and more than 60 wind ensembles throughout the U.S. Some of her most notable works are *Soundings, Circuits,* and *California Counterpoint.* The University of Georgia Bands have joined a consortium with nine other institutions to commission a new work by McTee, which will be premiered in the winter of 2001.

Anne McGinty is the most prolific woman composer in the field of concert band literature. Her many compositions and arrangements (she has published over 150 titles) extend from ele-

mentary through college level. She and her husband, John Edmondson, are co-owners of Queenwood Publications and are responsible for the creation, production, and international sales and distribution of Queenwood's catalog of concert band music.

McGinty, who earned her bachelor's and master's degrees in music from Duquesne University, is also active as a guest conductor, clinician, and speaker. Of the composers discussed here, McGinty's works are most accessible for school bands.

Drawing on her multicultural background, **Alice Gomez** is rapidly gaining international acclaim for her Latino- and Mexican Indian-influenced compositions. She grew up in San Antonio, Texas, playing the drums in her father's Latino dance band. During her tenure as composer-in-residence with the San Antonio Symphony, she created 21 new works. Since 1990 she has also worked as an arranger of Hispanic and popular music for the San Antonio Symphony. Although she is chiefly an orchestral composer, many of her works for smaller ensembles feature interesting parts for band instruments, particularly percussion.

Gomez is an instructor of music at San Antonio College, where she teaches basic composition, percussion, world music, and jazz ensemble. As a percussionist she performs with the San Antonio Early Music Ensemble and the San Quilmas Consort.

Various political and social struggles have influenced Gomez's compositions. Her "Mass for Justice and Peace" is a plea for universal peace and understanding, inspired by the devastation and starvation in Somalia. Her chamber work for viola, percussion, and piano, "Number 9," depicts the Bosnian struggle.

Dwight Satterwhite is director of bands and John Culvahouse is associate director of bands at the University of Georgia in Athens. This article originally appeared in the Spring 2000 issue of Georgia Music News. Reprinted by permission.

Teaching Multicultural Band Music
by Robert J. Garofalo

Peoples of the world have always expressed themselves through music. And most music has been transmitted from one generation to the next by rote learning (by ear without notation). Discovering the rich diversity of the world's music is stimulating. For example, music and dance are vital elements in nearly all phases of African life—birth, marriage, puberty initiation, hunting, farming, and entertainment. Probably the most outstanding feature of African music is rhythmic complexity. The music is performed on a variety of musical instruments, especially drums, although xylophones are widely used and frequently played in ensembles. Elements of African music can be heard in the music of both Latin America (calypso) and the United States (blues and jazz).

Many non-Western societies around the world, especially African, Asian, Polynesian, and American Indian, base their music on the pentatonic (five-tone) scale. Although there are many forms of the pentatonic scale, they all have one characteristic in common—there are no half steps in the note series. You can teach band students to play pentatonic melodies by practicing the scale patterns in figure 1 and by showing them how to produce a pentatonic scale at the piano using only the black keys.

Teaching Strategies and Activities

When teaching band students how to play multicultural music, be sure to include both in- and out-of-class listening (see the Resources sidebar). Students need to have good aural models to emulate. Here are a few listening activities that you may want to consider using:

1. Listen to two different recordings of the multicultural piece you are playing and compare the performances.
2. Listen to and compare multicultural band pieces arranged by good composers such as "Variations on a Korean Folk Song" by John Barnes

Chance, "La Fiesta Mexicana" by H. Owen Reed, and "Amazing Grace" by Frank Ticheli.

3. Compare differences between folk music ensembles and instruments from various countries around the world. For example, compare the Caribbean steel drum band to the Indonesian gamelan orchestra.
4. If appropriate, compare different interpretations of the American spiritual "Amazing Grace" (see figure 2). There are many recordings of this piece in almost every conceivable performance medium.

To enhance your band's experience in performing a multicultural piece:

1. Invite students with different cultural and ethnic backgrounds to explain and demonstrate the music and instruments of their countries. As an alternate, view a videocassette about ethnic music (see the Resources sidebar).
2. Plan a multicultural concert with your school's choral director and invite local ethnic musicians or ensembles to join the performance. If possible, include costumed folk dancing in the presentation.
3. Attend an ethnic folk life festival and experience the cultural diversity of different people.

Multicultural music offers many opportunities for interdisciplinary study. For example, related study topics could include ethnic folk life and cultures (food, dress, customs, and so on), folk art and dancing, and world geography.

To augment student knowledge when performing multicultural music, distribute a list of related terms with brief definitions. Sample terms could include: *pentatonic scale, spiritual, folk instrument* (such as *steel drum, zither, shawm, gamelan*), and *heterophony*. Heterophony, for example, is a type of music texture or sound that occurs when two or more musicians perform a melody simultaneously but with slightly different interpretations. Heterophony is prevalent in many types of primitive, folk, and non-Western art music (such as Chinese or Japanese) where melody and not har-

---

Figure 1. B-flat and E-flat Pentatonic Scales

Pentatonic Scales	On B-flat					On E-flat				
Concert Pitch Instruments:	B-flat	C	E-flat	F	G	E-flat	F	A-flat	B-flat	C
B-flat Transposing Instruments:	C	D	F	G	A	F	G	B-flat	C	D
E-flat Transposing Instruments:	G	A	C	D	E	C	D	F	G	A
F Transposing Instruments:	F	G	B-flat	C	D	B-flat	C	E-flat	F	G

Resources

Audio Recordings

The best sources for recordings of multicultural music for middle school band are the publishers. For recordings of advanced works, consult the Catalog of Band Recordings which is available at no cost from the West Coast Music Service, PO Box 3501, North Ft. Myers, FL 33918 (813/731-0565). A few recommended recordings for correlated listening are listed below.

The Audio-Forum has an extensive catalog of recordings of authentic music from around the world (with indexes to ethnic musical instruments and folk music). Order the catalog by phone (toll free: 800/243-1234), fax (203/453-9774), or mail (Audio-Forum, Suite M20A, 96 Broad St., Guilford, CT 06437).

MENC has five audiocassettes—Sounds of the World (East Asia, Eastern Europe, Latin America, Middle East, and Southeast Asia) available for purchase. Order by phone (toll free: 800/828-0229), fax (703/860-1531) or mail (MENC Publications Sales, 1806 Robert Fulton Drive, Reston, VA 20191).

The Library of Congress has an extensive catalog of recordings available from The Archive of Folk Culture. This source is especially rich in the music of North and South America, especially Indian, Afro-American, Hispanic, and Anglo-American. Order a catalog from The Motion Picture, Broadcasting and Recorded Sound Division of The Library of Congress, Washington, DC 20540 (202/707-5510). Another invaluable government resource of recordings of ethnic and folk music from around the world is Smithsonian Folkways Recordings, 750 9th Street NW, Suite 4100, Washington DC 20560 (800/410-9815). Their free catalog includes over 2,100 historic recordings listed by performer, geographic area, and subject matter.

- "Amazing Grace" has been recorded on compact disc by Aretha Franklin (Rhino 906), Judy Collins (Electra 75030-2), and Jessye Norman (Philips 432 5462).
- Dallas Wind Symphony, Howard Dunn. Reference Recordings RR-38CD. Titled *Fiesta,* this superb recording features Hispanic-influenced music including H. Owen Reed's "La Fiesta Mexicana," Morton Gould's *Santa Fe Saga,* and Clifton Williams' *Symphonic Dance No. 3,* "Fiesta."
- Tokyo Kosei Wind Orchestra, Frederick Fennell. KOCD 3503. Includes *Variations on a Korean Folk Song* by John Barnes Chance.
- *Pan All Night:* Steelbands of Trinidad and Tobago. Delos DE 4022.

Video Recordings

MENC has four videocassettes on the teaching of music of African Americans (#3070), Hispanic Americans (#3071), the American Indian (#3072), and Asian Americans (#3073). Order by phone (toll free: 800/828-0229), fax (703/860-1531), or mail (MENC Publications Sales, 1806 Robert Fulton Drive, Reston, VA 20191). Insight Media has an extensive catalog of videotapes about ethnic and folk music from around the world—Africa, American Indian, Latin America, India, Japan, Middle East, and Russia. For information, write to Insight Media, 2162 Broadway, NY, NY 10024, phone (212/721-6316), or fax (212/799-5309).

- *Bringing Multicultural Music to Children.* MENC (1992) Video resource #3075. Innovative ways to teach the music of other cultures. Includes songs and chants from Africa, China, and Jamaica; and music from Native Americans, African Americans, and so on.
- *Chinese Instruments and Music.* Video cassette #V72185. The history of China is interwoven with the development of music. Available from Audio-Forum (see under Audio Recordings above).
- *Amazing Grace* with Bill Moyers, A Video Journey. Videocassette #V72337. Available for purchase from Audio-Forum (see under Audio Recordings above), or for rental (check your local video store).

CD-ROM

Microsoft Musical Instruments. Explore musical instruments from around the world. Microsoft Home Exploration Series.

Books & Articles

Haywood, Charles. *Folk Songs of the World.* John Day Company, 1966. Folk songs gathered from more than 100 countries, with commentary on their musical cultures and descriptive notes on each song. Texts are in the original languages with English translations. Includes chord suggestions for instrumental accompaniment.

O'Connor, Al. "So You Want To Start A Steel Band …" *Percussive Notes* (Spring/Summer 1981).

Schmid, Will. "World Music in the Instrumental Program." *Music Educators Journal* (May 1992).

Sorrell, Neil. *A Guide to the Gamelan.* Faber and Faber Limited, 1990.

Svaline, J. Marc. "Why Not Start A Steel Band?" *Music Educators Journal* (November 1995).

Figure 2. Amazing Grace

This spiritual has endured across time, oceans, and cultures to become one of the most beloved of all American songs. The words, expressing love, hope, and redemption, were written by John Newton, an 18th century English slave ship captain who later reformed and worked to abolish slavery. The melody, of unknown origin, has been interpreted by countless singers and musicians, ranging from pop singer Aretha Franklin to opera star Jessye Norman.

Learn to play and sing this song in your own style. If you perform it in unison with a friend who sings or plays it in his or her own style, the result should be heterophony.

Used with permission of Meredith Music Publications.

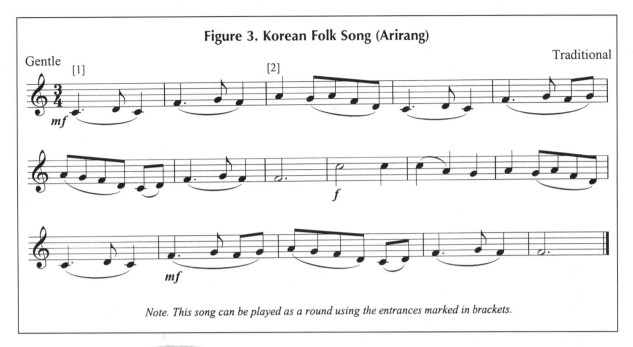

Figure 3. Korean Folk Song (Arirang)

Traditional

Gentle

Note. This song can be played as a round using the entrances marked in brackets.

mony is predominant. Heterophony often occurs in American dixieland jazz when the musicians play the melody together in their own individual styles.

Gamelan music of the Indonesian Islands of Java and Bali is largely based on a complex form of heterophony. *Gamelan* is a general term for an Indonesian orchestra or ensemble of mostly pitched percussion instruments employing different types of gongs and mallet keyboard instruments that are somewhat like the xylophone and orchestral bells. Gamelans perform for ceremonial functions and puppet plays, and they often accompany dancing. Gamelan music is highly developed and unique in the world, having evolved over centuries of practice and use. The gamelan instrument consists of a double row of tuned bronze kettles resting on a horizontal frame. The instrument is played with two long sticks wrapped with red cord at the striking end.

You may also want to stimulate a class discussion around the question: How do folk instruments and music reflect the social, economic, and geographic circumstances of a people? A follow-up question might be: Why do the people of the Carribean perform on steel drums while the highlanders of Scotland play bagpipes?

Creative Projects for Students

While teaching students how to perform a multi-cultural composition, require them to complete a creative project on their own. You'll be amazed at what students can accomplish when motivated to do a little creative work outside of class.

- Learn to play an ethnic folk melody on your instrument. For example, the Korean folk song shown in figure 3 is relatively easy to play on any band instrument and on the piano (start on D-flat, and use the black keys only).
- Create a pentatonic melody that you can play on your instrument.
- Attend an ethnic music concert and write a report that can be shared with the band.
- Investigate and report on an ethnic folk music ensemble (such as the Mexican mariachi band, Indonesian gamelan orchestra, Caribbean steel, and so on).
- Investigate and report on an ethnic folk instrument (such as the Indian sitar, Japanese koto, African slit drum, American Indian flute, Appalachian hammered dulcimer, Russian balalaika, Turkish shawm, Scottish bagpipes, and so on).
- Investigate and report on the ways in which music is part of the life of an ethnic group in your community.
- Learn to play a melody on an ethnic folk instrument.
- Determine your own project with the approval of your teacher.

Before selecting a multicultural performance composition from the Recommended Multi-cultural Music sidebar, survey the ethnic diversity in your band, school, and community so that you can more effectively plan to meet the needs of students. The list does not include ethnic music of Western or Eastern European countries because

Recommended Multicultural Music

African & African-American
For Middle/Junior High School Bands:
Curnow — *African Sketches* (Hal Leonard) 2 [African folk songs]
Davis — *Songs of Nyasaland* (Ludwig) 3 [African folk songs]
Edmondson — *Amazing Grace* (Hansen) 2 [Spiritual]
Grisman — *Uganda Lullaby* (Elkan-Vogel) 3
Handy/Balent — *St. Louis Blues* (Carl Fischer) 2
Hilliard — *Essays on an American Hymn* (Carl Fischer) 2 [Spiritual]
Holmes — *Amazing Grace* (TRN) 3
Joplin/Erickson — *The Crush Collision March* (Belwin) 2+ [Afro-American composer]
LaPlante — *Every Time I Feel the Spirit* (Shawnee) 2+
Stuart — *Three American Folksongs* (TRN) 3 [Negro folk songs and dances]

For High School Bands:
Hilliard — *Requiem* (TRN) 4 [Afro-American composer]
Hilliard — *Variations on an African Hymnsong* (Barnhouse) 4 [Nigerian folk song]
Still — *Folk Suite* (Bourne) 5 [Afro-American composer]
Ticheli — *Amazing Grace* (Manhattan Beach) 4 [Spiritual]

Asian
For Middle/Junior High School Bands:
Cramer — *Fantasy on Sakura Sakura* (TRN) 2 [Japanese folk song]
Cummings — *Gamelan* (Grand Mesa Music) 2+ [Inspired by the gamelan orchestras of Indonesia]
Curnow — *An Oriental Portrait* (Hal Leonard) 2
Curnow — *Korean Folk Rhapsody* (Jenson) 2 [Ahrirang]
Erickson — *Japanese Fantasy* (Belwin) 2 [Based on Japanese folk songs]
Foster — *Variations on a Chinese Folksong* (Wingert-Jones) 2
Garofalo — *Chinese Folk Song Medley* (Grand Mesa Music) 2 [Chinese folk songs]
Garofalo & Whaley — *Ahrirang* (Meredith) 2 [Korean folk song with optional chorus]
Gingery — *Korean Folk Song* (William Allen) 2 [Ahrirang]
Glazer — *A Japanese Fantasia* (Bourne) 2 [Japanese folk songs]
Grundman — *Japanese Rhapsody* (Boosey & Hawkes) 3
Hilliard — *Korean Festival* (Boosey & Hawkes) 2 [Variations on a different Korean folk song]
McBeth — *Canto* (Southern) 2 [Pentatonic with hand clapping]
McGinty — *The Great Wall* (Queenwood) 3 [Songs of China]
Nowak — *Asian Song* (William Allen) 2
Ployhar — *Korean Folk Song Medley* (Belwin) 2

For High School Bands:
Chance — *Variations on a Korean Folk Song* (Boosey & Hawkes) 4
Jager — *Japanese prints* (Belwin) 4
Konagaya — *Japanese Tune* (Molenaar) 4
Kirby — *San Pei Folk Song March* (TRN) 4
Kaneda — *Japanese Folk Song Suite* (Concert Works) 4
Rogers — *Three Japanese Dances* (Presser) 5

Hispanic
For Middle/Junior High School Bands:
Christensen — *Jalisco Olé* (Rendor) 3 [Tribute to mariachi music of Mexico]
Codina/Balent — *Zacatecas* (Carl Fischer) 2 [Mexican march]
Erickson — *Mexican Folk Fantasy* (Summy-Birchard) 3
Gates — *Two Mexican Songs of Chiapas* (Southern) 3
LaPlante — *Monterey March* (Daehn) 2 [Mexican folk song]
Padilla/Hubbell— *El Relicario* (Carl Fischer) 2
Rhoads — *Brazilian Folk Dance* Suite (Kjos) 3
Sosnik — *Las Pinatas* (Bourne) 2 [Optional mariachi band]

For High School Bands:
Gould — *Santa Fe Saga* (G. Schirmer) 6
Nixon — *Fiesta Del Pacifico* (Boosey & Hawkes) 5
Reed, H. Owen — *La Fiesta Mexicana* (Belwin) 6
Williams — *Symphonic Dance No. 3* "Fiesta" (Sam Fox) 5

North American (Including Native American Indian)
For Middle/Junior High School Bands:
Hilliard — *Acadian Festival* (Carl Fischer) 2 [Cajun folk songs]
Barnes — "Trail of Tears" (Southern) 4 [Tone Poem describing the trek of the "Five Civilized Indian Tribes" (Cherokees, Choctaws, Creeks, Chickasaws, the Seminoles) who were forced to march with great suffering to a reservation in Oklahoma in 1838–39]
Chattaway — *Mazama* (William Allen) 4 [Ancient Indian legends of the Pacific Northwest]
Hilliard — *Ghost Dance* (Boosey & Hawkes) 5 [Inspired by the powerfully moving events surrounding the tragedy of the Lakota (Sioux) Indians who were massacred by Federal soldiers on December 29, 1890]
Ployhar — *Variations on a Sioux Melody* (Belwin) 4
Ticheli — *Cajun Folk Songs* (Manhattan Beach) 4

---

there are many published folk song settings and arrangements of such music for bands by Grainger, Holst, Vaughan Williams, Milhaud, Grundman, Erickson, Ployhar, Kinyon, Davis, and many others.

The music has been graded on a scale from 1 to 6. Generally, grade 2 music is appropriate for middle school bands, grade 3 for junior high school bands, and grade 4 and higher for high school bands.

Robert J. Garofalo is professor of music education at the Catholic University of America. This article is adapted from his book Instructional Designs for Middle/Junior High School Band *(Vol. 2 of* Guides to Band Masterworks), *published by Meredith Music Publications in 1995. This article originally appeared in the January/February 1997 issue of the* Maryland Music Educator. *Reprinted by permission.*

Assessing Difficulty Level in Band Music

by John E. Owen

The assessment of difficulty and suitability of any work requires the thoughtful consideration of many elements, both individually and collectively. This can be especially difficult for a young conductor, or one new to conducting an ensemble. While a publisher's rating on the I–IV scale of difficulty can serve as a broad guide, it falls to the individual conductor to assess the level of his or her own ensemble in comparison with these established standards. Complicating the job is the fact that each piece of music might have its own intrinsic difficulties, quite separate from broad categories.

As a starting point I suggest considering the following twelve items in formulating initial judgments of difficulty:

1. Instrumentation: required instruments and level of exposure given various instruments
2. Scoring, doubling, and editing
3. Length of composition and use of repetition
4. Use of accidentals
5. Tempos
6. Historical period of the composition and harmonic background
7. Technical demands for individuals and sections of the band
8. Meters: type, number, sequence, and frequency of changes
9. Key relationships: key areas and changes within and between keys
10. Interval structure and shape of the musical line
11. Rhythmic characteristics: types of rhythmic elements, frequency and distribution of the elements within the work
12. Range and tessitura

Some of these items (chiefly numbers 1 through 3) are subject to manipulation and even change by the conductor. Others (numbers 4 through 8) might yield to careful practice and rehearsal; and some (numbers 9 through 12) probably cannot be changed very much and might present insurmountable obstacles.

Looking for Changes

It is possible to make changes in each of the items numbered 1 through 3, affecting the difficulty level of the work, and to do so without seriously altering the intent of the composer. It is obvious that such changes must be made with musical discretion and in keeping with the original nature of the composition.

1. Instrumentation

This might well be the first consideration of the conductor when examining a new score. When a score calls for instrumentation not available to an ensemble, the conductor must decide whether appropriate substitutions can be made. In compositions for younger bands and in many older transcriptions for band, cues and alternate instrumentations often are provided. In newer works, however, the composer's intentions are much more clearly specified, and changes still might be entirely unsuitable. Still, there are many times when a substitution will not damage the musical integrity of a composition, and might make particular works available to performers who otherwise would not be familiar with them.

2. Scoring, Editing, and Doubling

There is no doubt that doubling of lines can present challenges in performance, including pitch problems, clarity of the line, consistency of articulation, and balance. The conductor must decide whether adding or removing a doubled line is a viable solution. For younger players, doubling can provide a valuable security in performing. As players advance, however, the doubling can also have a limiting effect on clarity and instrumental color. Too much doubling can rob the ensemble of contrast.

Problems in doubling can sometimes be lessened by changing the voicing of a chord, the written octave, or the distribution of voices between sections. Parts can be rhythmically edited, or even revised slightly, without undue change to the piece.

3. Repetition and Length

Length of a work can be an important consideration when assigning a difficulty rating and must also be considered relative to the other works planned for a concert or program. When considering repetition, remember that not only can some repeats be omitted within the music but also to look for repetition within the piece as a clue about the preparation time required. Repetition and variation are, of course, central techniques in composition, and can be useful in determining the difficulty of any work.

Yielding to Rehearsal

Items within this category are most likely to yield to change through rehearsal and practice. While presenting problems, these ordinarily can be improved or corrected through careful teaching and appropriate effort. These are generally more complex problems than those in Category 1, and will result in a greater degree of difficulty for most ensembles.

4. Accidentals

While the incidence of accidentals in a composition affects reading difficulty, it can also serve as a valuable clue about the harmonic organization of the piece. In assessing the use of accidentals, it is important to determine how frequently they are used, what types of accidentals are used, and where they occur. In slow tempos, accidentals might present few challenges. Rapid passages with frequent accidental use, however, often indicate a high level of difficulty. One of the chief purposes of practicing scales is to learn patterns which are frequently used and to construct motor chains to allow them to be played easily. The use of accidentals often signals the use of patterns which are less easily recognized and, therefore, less easily played.

5. Tempos

Tempos can be a concern because of technical proficiency, but also must be considered relative to musical intent and possible variations in indicated tempos. Elizabeth Green recommends the following process in determining tempo:

> 1. Check the composer's requested tempo indications: Presto, Lento, etc. 2. Study the melodic line. Try several slight variations of tempo within the composer's designation. Choose what you deem best. 3. Glance through the composition, noting especially the faster notes and making sure that they are playable at your chosen tempo. (*The Modern Conductor,* Fifth Edition, p. 287.)

6. The Historical Period of Composition and the Accompanying Harmonic Tendencies of It

Works from historic and stylistic traditions with which performers are less familiar are likely to cause difficulty in learning, as well as performance problems. This is as true for an ensemble attempting a Mozart transcription for the first time as for one tackling a piece by Joseph Schwantner. In choosing a work of this type, the conductor must allot ample rehearsal time for developing the ensemble's knowledge of the harmonic, melodic, and rhythmic characteristics of the period. If the ensemble is not accustomed to playing music from

many different styles and periods, the level of difficulty must be adjusted upward.

7. Technique

In assessing difficulty, one of the primary concerns of many young conductors is the level of technical expertise required. This includes fingering skills, articulations, length of extended passages, or anything requiring good motor coordination. Technique is not limited to how many notes are written and how fast they are, but it also connects with several of our other items. These could include melodic and rhythmic patterns, range, instrumentation, and whether there is a relationship to a previously learned scale or pattern. Most articles and texts that refer to assessment of difficulty concern themselves primarily with technical challenges. The acquisition of performance technique is a combination of time spent in practice, instructional strategies, and individual ability. The assessment of technical difficulty often comes down to a simple question: "Can this material be learned in the time allotted to it?"

8. Meters and Changes in Meter

While a relatively advanced ensemble might be able to play virtually all common meters competently, a work which utilizes changing meters, especially in patterns which are not easily predicted, might be very difficult. For a younger band, changes from 3/4 to 6/8 might be confusing; for more advanced groups asymmetrical patterns are less likely to be familiar. Because these changes are probably less intuitive for the musicians, extra concentration and effort and extra rehearsal time are required to perform them.

Fixed Difficulty

Items in this category could be thought of as "fixed"; that is, they are not easily changed by the conductor, nor are they easily solved through rehearsal. Each might increase the degree of difficulty; in various combinations they can increase difficulty level dramatically.

9. Key Relationships

Individual key centers might cause less difficulty than the relationship between keys, and the number and direction of key changes. Given sufficient time and adequate instruction, a sequence of keys can be learned, and the performer's ability to successfully play the sequence can be improved through practice and rehearsal. However, the relationship of the key centers to the overall tonality of a musical composition can greatly increase the difficulty of learning and performance. For younger ensembles, it might be difficult to learn how many flats or sharps are in the key signature; for more advanced performers, the relationship of the key centers, or whether the work has a definite tonal center might be determinants in assessing difficulty. Gordon lists a helpful taxonomy of key relationships ranging from major to multitonal in *Learning Sequences and Patterns in Music.*

10. Interval and Shape or Line

The size and type of intervals found in a work share some characteristics with key relationships, because the interval structure can be related to the overall. Simpler pieces often contain intervals which are smaller, simpler, and easier to perform. In *Music for Sight Singing,* Ottman uses a progression from step-wise movement, to intervals of the tonic triad, to modal melodies, and to modulations to remote keys. While instrumental music is not strictly analogous to sight-singing, this pattern could serve as a useful guide when considering difficulty in interval. Accurate assessment of the difficulty requires an examination of the interval content both of melodic and supporting lines. It is particularly important to examine the sequence of intervals, and the amount of variance between intervals for particular instruments.

11. Rhythmic Characteristics

Like technical aspects of music, rhythm receives a great deal of attention. Rhythms can sometimes be simplified, but the overall rhythmic nature of the piece is a strong determinant in assessing playability and difficulty. Like the study of intervals, Ottman develops the study of rhythmic characteristics in a progressive order; this same order is adopted by Duane Wareham in his unpublished doctoral dissertation, "The Development and Evaluation of Objective Criteria for Grading Band Music into Six Levels of Difficulty." Rhythmic patterns which contribute to an advanced level of difficulty include syncopations, entrances off of the beat, unusual rhythmic groupings, rhythms which superimpose different patterns, and any rhythm which is unfamiliar to the ensemble. In particular, rhythms which come from less familiar idioms such as jazz, various ethnic traditions, and from contemporary practice might prove more difficult.

12. Range and Tessitura

For some compositions, the range and tessitura might not be a significant concern when assessing difficulty. Composers writing for the educational market are generally very aware of range limitations, and carefully avoid exceeding suggested limits. If the overall tessitura is too high for a performer to play comfortably, however, few alternatives exist. Changing octaves might significantly change the piece; performers trying to play outside their comfortable range are far more likely to utilize poor playing technique to achieve the extreme pitches.

While most obvious for brass players, woodwinds also have difficulties, which must not be ignored, in extreme registers. It is possible for a composition to be playable in all regards, except for the range. Particularly noteworthy are the works of baroque composers who wrote high brass parts in order to utilize the greater number of scale tones available in the upper partials of the instrument. Likewise, many contemporary compositions make use of extended ranges for all instruments, in both the higher and lower registers.

Charting the Level of Difficulty

Even though the teacher might have made decisions about difficulty level in each of the twelve ideas listed here, the final decision about the playability of a particular piece can be clarified by using a chart like the one in figure 1. Chart the difficulty level for each individual element, then link the boxes to form a graph, illustrating where the piece is most likely to present difficulties for the ensemble in question. After examining the shape of the graph, assign a difficulty level for the entire work, based not only on the piece itself, but on the ability level of the ensemble.

Summary

Twelve items may be considered when assessing the difficulty level of a piece of music. Each item is related to the others and thus should be considered both individually and collectively. A composition with difficulty in only one item might be relatively easy to perform; one with high degrees of difficulty in each of these items could be very difficult. In seeking to become more skillful when assessing difficulty level, the teacher-conductor must develop a clear and careful taxonomy, incorporating these ideas, his or her experiences, the recommendations of associates and written music reviews and a clear picture of the capabilities of the ensemble in question. When these things are done, the match between the performers and the music is likely to be smooth and accurate.

Figure 1. Level of Difficulty Chart

Title: _____   Composer: _____

Category	I: Easy	II: Medium Easy	III: Medium	IV: Medium Advanced	V: Advanced	VI: Very Advanced
Instrument						
Scoring						
Length						
Accidentals						
Tempos						
Period						
Technique						
Meters						
Keys						
Intervals						
Rhythms						
Ranges						
Overall Level						

Notes: _____

_____

_____

Bibliography

Gordon, Edwin E. *Learning Sequences and Patterns in Music.* Chicago: G.I.A. Publications, 1977.

Green, Elizabeth A. H. *The Modern Conductor.* Englewood Cliffs, NJ: Prentice-Hall, Inc., 1981, 1992.

Hoffer, Charles R. *Teaching Music in the Secondary Schools.* Belmont, CA: Wadsworth Publishing Co., 1983.

Hunsberger, Donald and Roy Ernst. *The Art of Conducting.* New York: Alfred A. Knopf, 1992.

Kohut, Daruel L. *Instrumental Music Pedagogy.* Englewood Cliffs, NJ: Prentice-Hall, Inc., 1973.

Liles, Jack N. "A Study of the Effectiveness of Rhythmic Drill Materials Students/Conductor-Teachers While Conducting Live Ensembles from a Full Score." *Dissertation Abstracts* 40, 4797A.

Ottman, Robert W. *Music for Sight Singing.* Englewood Cliffs, NJ: Prentice-Hall, Inc., 1967.

Prentice, Barbara. "Selecting Music for Young Band." *The Instrumentalist* 41 (September 1986): 55–58.

Wareham, Duane E. "The Development and Evaluation of Objective Criteria for Grading Band Music into Six Levels of Difficulty." *Dissertation Abstracts* 29, 926A.

John E. Owen is professor of trumpet and director of bands at Heidelberg College in Tiffin, Ohio. This article originally appeared in the May/June issue of Ohio's Triad. *Reprinted by permission.*

Music Repertoire as Curriculum?

by Laura K. Sindberg

Is it really valid to consider the music selected for study and performance as representing a curriculum? The answer is a qualified "yes." The qualification relates to how the music was selected and how it is used as a resource for teaching and learning. Just as the CMP Model for planning instruction identifies "music selection" as an important part of the process, for many music educators the music *is* the curriculum. Therefore, it is essential that careful consideration be given to music selection—regardless of the age or achievement level of the students.

If music is treated as curriculum, then it is valuable to create a list of repertoire for an entire year … or even for the entire length of time that a student could conceivably be in the same performing group. Creating a repertoire list gives everyone a chance to look at the broader, long-term view and will quickly make it clear if the repertoire list lacks balance, variety, or quality.

Figure 1 is an excerpt of the repertoire used for the Waukesha Central Middle School Bands. For each title, I've included skills, concepts or learning activities which are extracted from the music.

A repertoire list provides a good foundation for planning instruction in music performing groups. Many resources are available to assist in selecting high quality music. Repertoire receives a lot of attention because quality repertoire is essential to excellence in teaching and learning music.

Laura K. Sindberg is director of bands at Central Middle School in Waukesha, Wisconsin. This article originally appeared in the February 1999 issue of The Wisconsin School Musician. *Reprinted by permission.*

Figure 1. Suggested Repertoire

Titles & Outcomes	Composers	Date
All Ye Young Sailors • learn to perform in 6/8 • work of commissioned composer • example of folk song style	Pierre LaPlante	5/98
Fanfare, Ode and Festival • study Renaissance • musical elements: texture, expression	Claude Gervaise, Bob Margolis	5/98
Rhythm Machine • musical elements: form, expression • develop separated articulation • emphasize use of percussion	Timothy Broege	5/98
Londonderry Air • espressivo, phrasing • use of music to express text • affect: what is beautiful about this song	Traditional, arr. James Ployhar	3/98

Programming for the School Ensemble
by Christian Wilhjelm

Over the past several months a number of colleagues have asked questions regarding programming for high school band. Programming for any ensemble is at best a controversial and difficult task. Balancing the entertainment value with substance seems to be a key issue with many ensembles. Throw into the mix the limits on rehearsal time and space, the lack or overabundance of instrumentation, certain imposed criteria ("the superintendent really enjoys marches"), and you find yourself faced with a dilemma when choosing material to perform.

As educators, it seems the dilemma is even more knotty. Do we program selections that will be rather easy to perform with apparent mass audience appeal, or do we select works that will have a lasting educational value for our students? (Does the wording of this question suggest an opinion? ... so much for unbiased tests.) In fact, like most, I have strong opinions on this issue. It would take a powerful argument to get me to reconsider as these opinions have been developed and reinforced throughout my career. I've felt for a very long time that great music has its own value and, though not entertaining in the 15-second sound-bite sense, will be appreciated. I must concede that it has dawned on me somewhat late in life that, in many cases, music that is very entertaining can also be valuable as a teaching tool. I have always been able to use the marching-band season as an important time in the development of student musicians. At the same time, I have been careful to dedicate only the first four or five weeks of school for this purpose.

Every school district has different parameters and requirements. This is not a "one size fits all" issue. The needs and abilities of the teacher also play a major role in this. For this issue, I have sought the advice of some our respected colleagues. I have asked each of them to submit a recent program along with a statement regarding their philosophy of programming. I asked them specifically to define their concert programming in terms of meeting the educational needs of their students.

Perhaps there is an answer of sorts here. Rather than programming music whimsically and finding the educational language to justify what we are doing, decide first what it is that is important to teach and search for the literature that best enables us to teach "music" as we should. When required,

we can arrive at fairly elaborate explanations concerning the value of our curricula. We are careful to explain that we teach a broad spectrum of musical styles and that students learn to understand and appreciate music of different national backgrounds and generations. Harvey Phillips once stated his profound disappointment that many students now graduate high school never once playing a work by Bach, Wagner, or Tchaikowsky, his point being that we have a wealth of excellent transcriptions that would allow our students to experience this music firsthand. Unfortunately, we know all too well that many students are also graduating our high school programs without playing Holst and Grainger, the centerpieces of our repertoire. Certainly just as in math, science, English, U.S. History, etc., we must have a "basic" core of material that is universally taught. Granted this would have to be programmed with fairly wide latitude to cover the great range of scope of our ensembles, but there must be fundamental concepts and expectations which must be attained by all high school instrumental musicians.

Three of our colleagues have offered personal suggestions as well as samples of recent programs. These teachers have distinguished themselves as outstanding educators and contributors not only with the success of their own music programs, but to the health of music education in New Jersey and beyond. Curt Ebersole, band director at Northern Valley High School in Old Tappan teaches band, orchestra, and music theory. He maintains a consistently fine program and actively participates and contributes to All-County, Regional, and State activities, often working the long hours in the tabulating room. He has served as the host, the manager, and the conductor of these ensembles and is always picking up the slack by taking care of the last minute detail that needs to be done. He is a remarkably willing and hardworking individual. Curt was named Bergen County Teacher of the Year in 1994–1995. Jerry Risden, band director at Long Branch High School, has been one of the catalysts in Central Jersey. Year-in, year-out, Jerry plays a key role in the success of the regional operation. He is active as a professional trombonist playing regularly with the St. Peters by the Sea Orchestra, quickly becoming New Jersey's most popular orchestra. Jerry has impressed all who know him as a warm personal educator who works tirelessly in the best interests of the students. Bruce Yurko, is a musician and educator who has gained everyone's respect and admiration, most recently with the astounding performance he elicited from the All-State Symphonic Band (I would borrow some of the words of praise that he shared with the students, "excellent, superb" and add in the truest sense of the word "outstanding"). In addition to being a composer and a colleague of some of our nation's finest composers, arrangers, and conductors, Bruce also serves on many committees, etc., seeing to the educational needs of a great number of the musician/students in New Jersey.

Curt writes concerning programming:

Building a concert program is a lot like writing a musical composition. It needs a beginning, a climax, and an end. In addition, the selection of a program for a particular concert [requires] the balance of many factors:

- Purpose of the ensemble/occasion
- Talent pool and experience
- Endurance considerations
- Balance of repertoire for players, conductor, audience.

The parameters of the first four factors are usually given values that the conductor cannot alter. The last factor, however, allows for considerable creativity. In considering the repertoire in this way, I often use this old adage to help in my selection: "Something old, something new, something borrowed, something blue."

"Something old"—I like to include an old favorite, be it that of the audience, or of mine personally. This is also an opportunity to select something for which I know the score quite well. (See figure 1, Vaughan Williams, "Folk Song Suite"—a standard of the repertoire.)

"Something new"—I enjoy the challenge of selecting something brand new from a noted composer on each program. If I can, I try to select something which I have not heard in any way before, or that will be new for the players (de Meij, "Gandalf the Wizard").

"Something borrowed"—This could be a work "borrowed" from another medium (an arrangement of an orchestral work, etc.) or a work heard at a convention or recommended by a colleague you respect. When selecting an arrangement of a work, use only the best quality arrangements (Elgar, "Nimrod").

"Something blue"—This work should excite and move the players, audience, and the conductor. After all, the excitement of music is the core

basis of what we are as musicians. (Elgar, "Nimrod"; Fillmore, "Americans We").

These concepts, coupled with your purpose, feel for your talent pool, and limitations of timing and endurance should help to build an effective and musical concert program.

Gerald A. Risden has taught in the Long Branch school district for nearly twenty years. Long Branch is an urban high school with a student population of 900 characterized by its ethnic diversity. Jerry writes:

The selection of concert music to be performed is done with the goal of stretching the musical horizons of the student performer. Stylistic variation, worthwhile literature and appeal to the student body (and audience) are always in the mind when contemplating programming. Music of different cultures, varied time periods, and relevance to the students' experience is deliberately sought. In addition, it is good when concert programming reinforces other academic studies undertaken in the school.

Two practical factors are in view when selecting literature. One is that, at present, outside private instruction is just about nonexistent. This means that all technical difficulties must be dealt with during the rehearsal periods. The second factor is that not all band members are scheduled for band class during the same time frames which means that balance and blend are difficult to address during class time.

Approximately a quarter of the music planned for our concert band is chosen to give the students exposure to original works for the wind band. Composers such as Clare Grundman, Vaclav Nelhybel, John Barnes Chance, Ralph Vaughan

---

Figure 1. Sample Program from Orange County High School

Program
Orange County High School Music Festival Band
conducted by Curt Ebersole
English Folk Song Suite . . . Ralph Vaughan Williams
  1. March: Seventeen Come Sunday
  2. Intermezzo: My Bonny Boy
  3. Folksongs from Somerset
Nimrod from "Enigma Variations" . . . . Edward Elgar, arr. Alfred Reed
"Gandalf the Wizard" from
  "Lord of the Rings" . . . . Johan de Meij
Americans We . . . . Henry Fillmore

Williams, Frank Erickson, John Philip Sousa, and Henry Fillmore are represented on our programs. Students are made aware of the difference between original band works and arrangements and transcriptions.

Another quarter of the repertoire is chosen from the fine transcriptions available giving the students the opportunity to perform the works of Bach (Prelude and Fugue in B-flat), Grofe ("On The Trail"), Wagner (Overture to *Die Meistersinger),* Dvořák (Finale to *The New World Symphony),* Lecouna ("Malaguena"), Tchaikowsky (Finale, Symphony No. 2), Offenbach ("Ballet Parisien"), etc., etc. Without these arrangements our band members would be unable to experience a wealth of quality music.

A third quarter of our programming consists of music most likely to be heard by the students prior to rehearsal. This is the category of popular classics by Cole Porter, George Gershwin, Duke Ellington, The Beatles, etc. The familiarity pleases the performer and the listener. Trendy music is usually avoided for the concert band with deference given to selections with proven long-time appeal. Good music from the theater is included in this segment of programming.

The remainder of the literature is chosen to feature strong soloists and/or sections of the band. Recent selections include "Morceau Symphonique" by Guilmant for trombone and band, Concertino for clarinet and band by Weber, Sonata from *Die Bankelsangerlieder* for brass ensemble, movements from *Eine Kleine Nachtmusik* arranged for clarinet choir. The specialized skills needed for soloing and accompanying as well as small ensemble playing give an added dimension to the band members' performing perspective.

Every band has certain strengths and weaknesses. These factors will vary from year to year. Aesthetic goals with attention to these practical concerns will yield optimum results. The students will have a positive educational experience and the audience will be glad to be a part of it. (See figure 2 for a sample program.)

Figure 2. Sample Program from Long Branch High School

Music for a Spring Evening
Long Branch High School Symphonic Band and Stage Band
Gerald A. Risden

Program

Symphonic Band

Block M Concert March . . . . Jerry H. Bilik
Toccata for Band . . . . Frank Erickson
Fantasy on American Sailing Songs . . . . Clare Grundman
Malaguena . . . . Ernesto Lecuona

Clarinet Ensemble

Caprice for Clarinets . . . . Clare Grundman
Over the Rainbow . . . . Harold Aiken

Symphonic Band

Symphony Number 2, Finale . . . . P. I. Tchaikowsky

Intermission

Stage Band

Tiger of San Pedro . . . . John La Barbera
A Whole New World . . . . Alan Menken
Stompin' at the Savoy . . . . Benny Goodman
That's a Wrap . . . . Jeff Taylor

Symphonic Band

George Gershwin, A Symphonic Portrait . . . . Arr. B. Chase
Selections from "Cats" . . . . Andrew Lloyd Weber, arr. by John Edmondson
Original Dixieland Concerto . . . . John Warrington
A Tribute to Elvis . . . . arranged by James Christensen
Them Basses . . . . G. H. Huffine

Bruce submitted a number of past programs. Consistently, he programs not only works for his full ensemble (Wind Ensemble) but also several works for chamber groups. Figure 3 is a sample of the repertoire from his past several programs.

On several occasions, I have enjoyed extended conversations with Bruce regarding programming. He has a remarkably comprehensive view of the repertoire and is especially aware of that which is new and valuable. (Unfortunately, much of what's really "hot" doesn't get published). Every year at the All-State tryout, I find myself writing down a new list of material to discover. These conversations have assisted me tremendously in programming for the Ridgewood Concert Band (we recently played one of Bruce's compositions, "Incantations"), the Montclair State University Band, and the Pascack Hills High School Band, the point here being that some of this repertoire requires a very high level of technical proficiency whereas much of this music can be mastered by any talented group of musicians willing to work and prepare.

If I were to add one thought that Bruce conveyed to me in absolute terms, "I prepare." Bruce spends untold hours reviewing scores and planning strategies for teaching music to students. Granted he has a group of very talented students, but his success and the success of those students is the result, in large measure, of his dedication and preparation.

The same can be said for Curt and Jerry. We are fortunate to have in our number many talented and dedicated musician/teachers. These folks are an invaluable resource as we strive to develop ourselves and our "programs." It has been my experience that these teachers appreciate the opportunity to help make music and music teaching better and they will gladly assist you if you have any specific questions. It seems more and more that our colleagues are among our greatest resources.

Christian Wilhjelm is conductor of the Goldman Memorial Band in New York City and the Ridgewood Concert Band in Ridgewood, New Jersey; band director at Pascack Hill High School in Montvale, New Jersey; and an adjunct faculty member at Montclair State University and William Patterson University. This article originally appeared in the May 1995 issue of New Jersey's Tempo. *Reprinted by permission.*

Figure 3. Sample Program from Cherry Hill West and Cherry Hill East Wind Ensembles

Cherry Hill West Wind Ensemble
December, 1993
Bruce Yurko, Director

Program

Festive Overture, opus 96 . . . . . Dmitri Shostakovitch
Apocalypse . . . . Robert Jager
William Byrd Suite . . . . Gordon Jacob
  "John, Come Kiss Me Now"
  "The Bells"
Toccata Marziale . . . . Ralph Vaughan Williams
Pineapple Poll Suite . . . . Arthur Sullivan
  1. Opening Number
  2. Jasper's Dance
  3. Poll's Dance
  4. Finale
The Testament of Freedom . . . . . . Randall Thompson
  The God Who Gave Us Life
  I Shall Not Die without Hope

Cherry Hill East Wind Ensemble
May, 1994
Bruce Yurko, Director

Program

Handel in the Strand . . . . Percy Grainger
Prelude in E-flat Minor . . . . Dmitri Shostakovitch
William Byrd Suite . . . . Gordon Jacob
  "John, Come Kiss Me Now"
Symphonic Movement . . . . Vaclav Nelhybel
Commemoration Overture . . . . . . Elliot A. Del Borgo
Suite Francaise . . . . Darius Milhaud
Pineapple Poll . . . . Arthur Sullivan
  Opening Number
  Poll's Dance
  Finale

Section 3

Cross-Curricular Projects

The cross-curricular teaching techniques of the authors in this section show band directors how they can work with teachers in other disciplines to create meaningful experiences for all involved. When several disciplines combine forces, the results can be impressive.

 Section 3

Cross-Curricular Projects

Music Performance and More
by Sally Childs and James Loach

As school districts develop new graded courses of study based on *Ohio's Model Competency-Based Programs: Comprehensive Arts Education,* directors of performance groups seek new ways to make a performance more meaningful to students. The playing experience can go beyond the elements of tone, intonation, interpretation, and technique, and, though these must remain of primary importance, it is possible for students to experience music which has more relevance to all curriculum and society. These musical experiences can be life-centered and allow students to develop a broader understanding and appreciation of the role music can play in people's lives.

In the past two years, Jim Loach, the director of bands at Garfield High School (Akron Public Schools), has crossed this bridge between performance and meaning. In the spring of both years, Mr. Loach has chosen a band selection which lends itself to be explored in depth by the students. In 1998, Mr. Loach visited the Kennedy Space Center in Florida and this, in combination with the motion picture *Apollo 13* (the depiction of the harrowing experience of astronauts Jim Lovell, Fred Haise, and Jack Sweigert), inspired him to select the band arrangement of *Apollo 13* by James Horner, arranged by John Moss. He believed that "this was the vehicle to use to teach in an interdisciplinary manner and provide more meaning to the music."

After sight-reading the band arrangement of *Apollo 13,* the students watched the movie and were assigned to write a synopsis of the space program of the late 60s and early 70s in which they shared what the movie meant to them and how they were inspired by man's capabilities when forced to rely on his own resourcefulness. As rehearsals progressed, not only did technicality

improve, but the musicality seemed to improve more rapidly than usual, perhaps due to the effect of knowing the facts behind the music. Students critiqued their own performance throughout the rehearsals, commenting on how phrasing could effectively be done to interpret the music properly. Furthermore, the students began to comment on interpretation of mood, themes, or meanings of the music.

The next step was an audition with NASA's John Glenn Research Center in Cleveland, which resulted in the band being asked to perform at the Center's "Take Your Child to Work" Day. Ironically, the program at NASA was the celebration of the anniversary of Apollo 13 and the landing-on-the-moon project. The role of the band was to provide the background music to the NASA slide presentation of the manned space craft landing on the moon. Following the performance, the students toured the Research Center. During the first stop, the students were exposed to the principle of flight, theories of weather, and solutions to protect the population in case of catastrophic tornadoes or floods. Students also visited the zero-gravity facility, where they discovered that experiments in the medical field were performed which result in the cure of diseases. Not only did the tour introduce students to theories of aero-dynamics, physics, and medical research, but it also permitted students who were considering aeronautical and mechanical engineering to talk with NASA individuals about career opportunities.

The spring concert was the finale of the learning experience. All the numbers performed by the band were related to the space theme, with the final number being Moss's arrangement of *Apollo 13.* It was obvious that the experiences of the students over this eight-week period made connections in various ways. But what was most exciting was the musicality of *Apollo 13,* which resulted in a standing ovation from the audience!

Tragedies this last school year prompted Loach to look toward another connection between music and life's experiences. Besides the shooting in Littleton, Colorado, and war in Kosovo, a student from Garfield High School was killed. So this time, he selected *Reverence for Life* by Frank Erickson, which is based on the life of Albert Schweizer. Again, performance was only a part of the experience. The students researched the life of Albert Schweitzer and were required to write a short paper about him, as well as to express what they love about life and to interpret how *Reverence for Life* reflects what might have been Schweitzer's love of life. In addition, they were asked to talk with band members seated on either side of them and to find positive aspects about each. Finally, they were to write about how they intended to make a difference in the world. As students rehearsed, Loach reminded them to think how each is a member of the (band) community and everyone has a place and is connected to everyone else, thus encouraging the band members to look beyond the musical performance.

As music educators, we are all aware of the importance of music in children's lives and of the enormous amount of research that indicates the positive effects of music on student learning. Music cannot be considered frill, but a necessity in the education of all children. Jim Loach has successfully brought deeper meaning and relevance to the music performed by his band. He has integrated his curriculum with many areas, most importantly through writing, in which the students verbally express their thoughts, emotions, and interpretations.

Obviously, with all there is to teach students about music and to rehearse with performance groups, it is not possible to delve into each piece in such depth. But perhaps, with one piece each year, the meaning and importance of music in our lives will become even more obvious to our students. The experiences of students at Akron Garfield High School certainly reflect the goals in the *Ohio's Model Competency-Based Programs: Comprehensive Arts Education*.

- Goal I: Historical, Cultural, and Social Contexts: Understanding the Role of the Arts in People's Lives
- Goal II: Personal Expression and Production/ Performance: Communicating through the Arts
- Goal III: Arts Criticism: Responding to the Arts
- Goal IV: Nature and Meaning of the Arts: Valuing the Arts

These experiences for the students may be difficult to evaluate in our traditional assessment systems, since often they are carried throughout life and may develop student growth in ways which cannot be measured by present means. All this is certainly not to discourage quality performances, for this is still essential. Yet, perhaps we can also give the students this "extended" musical experience which enhances many areas of student growth through life-centered learning.

Sally Childs is music coordinator for the Akron City Schools in Ohio. James Loach teaches music for the Woodridge Local Schools in Summit County, Ohio. This article originally appeared in the November 1999 issue of Ohio's Triad. *Reprinted by permission.*

A Collaboration Project Bringing Student, Teacher and Composer Together: Music for the Eyes … Art for the Ears

by Lee Shook

Many band directors tend to gauge the degree of their success by the "achievements" of their band programs. That is probably why we so proudly display our festival ratings and contest trophies on our band room walls. Some of us might even allow our level of self-worth to be affected by some of those judges' scores or caption awards. It is the product, after all, that really counts. Isn't it? You know, what we have to show for all of our hard work … our reward. It's that outstanding, award-winning, first-place performance. Or is it?

When I reflect on the 24 years I have spent as a music teacher, there are a few experiences that stand out as most memorable: a trip to the Orange Bowl Parade, performing for the president, students winning the state solo contest, first place at that prestigious jazz festival or marching band show, et cetera. None of these, however, proved to be more rewarding than my middle school band's participation in the process that led to the composition and premier of composer Tom Molter's new piece, *The Valley of the Kings.*

You'd think that in preparing a band to perform at a state conference (ArtsTime '99), the focus of my efforts would have been in producing the highest quality performance possible. My students would have to be motivated to practice harder and made to understand the importance of performing at such an event. What about uniforms, and who's paying for the transportation? Can you feel the stress level rising?

Worry and stress are the result of too much focus on outcome. They will ruin a rehearsal. (They are also tied into that self-worth problem.) I wonder why it took 24 years of teaching for me to figure out that it is really the process that counts the most. Rehearsing is where we spend 95 percent of our time. How can a performance be truly enjoyable and rewarding if our rehearsals are filled with stress? Positive interaction with talented students, learning more about music and making music everyday … and enjoying it! That's where the focus needs to be. Along the way to my band's performance at ArtsTime '99, I learned that very important lesson. Here's how it happened.

After being asked by band curriculum officer Greg Allison to make some type of music/art presentation at ArtsTime '99, I immediately realized that this would be an opportunity to do something very creative with my students.

Upon meeting with our art instructor, Ned Fox, the following goals were set for the project: (1) Commission a new work for middle school band. (2) Composer, conductor and art instructor would collaborate in the selection of thematic material. (3) Both band and art students would be exposed to the creative processes that bring thematic ideas to life in the form of written music and the visual arts. (4) Form a collaborative effort between all participants: composer, teachers and students. All would have input as the project developed. (5) Art students would create visual displays inspired by the musical themes. (6) The project would be completed with a simultaneous presentation of the music and art.

The Process Begins

Teachers met with the composer. Mr. Molter proposed various themes based on an article he'd read in *National Geographic* magazine about the Valley of the Kings, burial site of the pharaohs. We agreed to proceed, and Mr. Fox and his art students began to study Egyptian art and hieroglyphics. I "sold" my students on the idea of commissioning a new work, and we began making plans for a fundraiser to pay for the commission. Subsequent meetings with the composer, Mr. Molter, resulted in a strategy for involving the band students in the compositional process.

Discussion with the composer resulted in determining the number of movements the work would contain, how the art students and their creations would be integrated into the composition process, as well as how the strengths of my band's instrumentation and various soloists could be best utilized.

Mr. Molter visited our rehearsals and worked through the process of selecting the right instrument combinations necessary to achieve the desired tone colors and musical effects necessary to musically convey the thematic moods. Students learned rhythmic themes by rote, and the music began to come alive before it was even down on paper. My students were experiencing the composition processes firsthand! *The Valley of the Kings* began to take shape right in our rehearsals. Needless to say, the students were excited. My focus shifted from teaching notes and rhythms to *making music*. Each rehearsal became a new adventure.

As the band learned each movement of the piece, the music was recorded and sent to the art department where it was replayed as students worked on the art projects. Art students also visited the band room during rehearsals. Working together strengthened the relationship between the art and music departments. The students developed a deeper understanding and appreciation of their roles as musicians and artists as a result of this interaction. As a director, I began to realize just how much more of value can come from a rehearsal besides "just getting it right."

My band students eagerly awaited the arrival of each new section of the music as the composer completed it. Before rehearsing the music, I presented the melodic and rhythmic themes to the students and explained the compositional techniques that Mr. Molter was utilizing. When they realized that he had selected each of them for a specific role in bringing the music to life, they assumed their practice responsibilities with a great sense of pride. They were excited to learn their parts. Rehearsals were fun and creative and had a deepened sense of purpose because the students had become serious about their roles in the production. Imagine that—students just as serious as the director about having a good rehearsal. (More lessons for me about motivation.)

Ready for an Audience

"World Premiere Night," as the students called it, took place on March 19, 1999, in the new auditorium at Mt. Spokane High School in the Mead School District.

The art students presented their sculptures in the lobby prior to the start of the concert. Mr. Fox had prepared a digital projection of all of the students' art projects and synchronized the display to correspond with the performance of the music. It was truly an amazing production—a magical moment, a brilliant piece of new music, one of those performances to remember. But it was so much more! The reward was truly in the process, learning to place the focus on the 95 percent of the time that we really have control over, getting the most out of the rehearsal, enjoying making music with my students every day.

An Overview of *Valley of the Kings,* Tom Moltner, composer

I. Discovery

Enter the ancient burial chamber of an Egyptian pharaoh. Experience the sights and sensations of KV5—the fifth tomb beyond the entrance to KV, the King's Valley, circa 1500 B.C.

Ceremonial percussive effects introduce a haunting melody (solo voice), accompanied by solo oboe, flute and clarinet. The vocal echoes to this theme help sustain a very somber mood, and frequent meter changes (5/4, 2/4, 3/4) will cause an uneasiness to settle over the listener.

II. Temple Dance

Artisans of the Afterlife—musicians and craftsmen dedicate their lives' work to preparing for the burial of a pharaoh—a celebration of sorts, honoring the deceased king as he proceeds along the journey to his afterlife.

Pictographs of drums, tambourines, cymbal-like instruments and hand-clapping musicians appear on the walls of the tomb. Rhymically intense, Temple Dance brings the sounds of ancient Egypt to life.

III. Nile Crossing

Across the river Nile journeys the Pharaoh's procession. Sustainer of life and pathway to the final resting place, the Nile receives the ceremonial boat.

Solo alto saxophone reminds us of a soul on a journey. Flute, clarinet and oboe serve as attendants to the "wandering king." Flowing brass melodies carry us across the river in a royal manner, and the concluding harmonies underscore the seriousness of this journey.

IV. Final Ceremony

The "Opening of the Mouth" ceremony prepares the mummy for its final resting place. The Pharaoh's journey is now complete, and a new journey is about to begin.

Percussive sounds underscore the finality of the events that have taken place. A momentary return of the opening theme accompanies us as we depart KV5, Valley of the Kings.

Lee Shook teaches band at Northwood Middle School and music education classes at Whitworth College in Spokane, Washington. This article originally appeared in the October 1999 issue of Washington's Voice. *Reprinted by permission.*

Section 4

Conducting

Conducting is a fundamental part of being an effective band director. In this section, the authors offer their advice on becoming a better conductor.

 Section 4

Conducting

The Eyes Have It
by Larry MacTaggart

I recently watched a documentary about sheep dogs in New Zealand. It was a truly fascinating program about how a rather ordinary looking Border Collie mustered the rather unordinary task of shepherding over a hundred sheep. The dog, called Shep, relied only on whistle commands from his master which indicated to him where to direct the flock. In one exciting segment, Shep came to a complete stop in front of the herd. A huge ram over twice the size of the small collie emerged and assumed a staunch defensive posture. An intense staring contest ensued—a battle of wills between dog and sheep. At first, neither party moved. Shep made the first move inching ever closer to the seemingly stout young ram. As he moved, he maintained deep, probing, intense eye contact. The ram was no match for Shep and quickly, and without incident, retreated to the holding bin with the rest of the flock in tow. This superb display of focused concentration by Shep the Border Collie brought to mind a parallel comparison to my role as a conductor.

In my experience in music, I have had the privilege to have performed under the leadership of a wide variety of conductors—some terrific, some not so terrific. As I look back at those I enjoyed the most, one trait seems to stand out among those I consider the best—eye contact!

Good eye contact is one of the more difficult things for conductors at various levels of experience to master and rightly so. It is not easy to throw away the crutch that we call the score and really trust our ability to lead the ensemble. Good eye contact requires many things.

Cast All Inhibitions to the Wind …
Don't be afraid to look your flute soloist right in the eye for a measure before, during and after the big solo. How you communicate via eye contact will both reassure, influence, and inspire those sitting in front of you. Stare a hole in the trumpet soloist as he or she plays. Not a mean-spirited hole, a.k.a. "The Hairy Eye." No, a stare of focused concentration, just like Shep the Border Collie. Communicate to the player via eye contact that you believe in him or her, and together you will transform the written notes to beautiful music.

Be Not Afraid …
Let the fear of looking at your players disappear. You are their leader. Your job is to lead them through the piece to achieve the result the composer intended. Insist upon eye contact. It doesn't make any difference whether it is a group of beginners playing "Hot Cross Buns" or an advanced wind ensemble playing Grainger. Look them all right in the eye and insist they look back often. One great director I worked with used to always say, "One eye is yours and the other is mine." This is very profound because although tempi and expressions might be written on the page, players won't find how to transform what they see unless they look up!

Use Your Eyes as a Channel for Your Emotions …
Give them big, wide eyes as a cue for a big entrance; soft eyes during a moving lyric passage. Surprise a soloist or section with a wink after a job well done and even close your eyes at the end of a solemn hymn. You will find good eye contact to be a powerful tool for raising the level of accuracy, musicality, and self-esteem of your ensemble.

Know the Score …
A foregone conclusion right? But to what level? Memorization? That is my goal. But in all fairness to music educators, or part-time community band conductors, there may not be ample time to memorize all your scores. Do not lose heart. Memorization is not a prerequisite for good eye

contact. I believe a more realistic goal is to know a musical score better each time you step on the podium. This is a primary responsibility of all conductors. This will happen not on the podium, but away from the ensemble, in a quiet room, at the piano, or in front of a mirror. Plan your eye contact and practice it by looking at yourself conduct in the mirror. Then, as performance time draws near, relax, get your head up, your eyes open, and look at your players.

How do we improve our eye contact ? I suggest starting with a familiar piece. Maybe a march or a piece you recently performed. Make a concerted effort to not look at the score very often, get your head up and look at your players. Throughout the entire piece, let your eyes move from section to section. Be relentless but kind with your eye contact. Try to obtain the same level of focused concentration as our friend Shep the Border Collie. You'll be surprised at what you hear that you might not have noticed before—and how quickly you will improve as a conductor and musician.

Larry MacTaggart is chief music arranger for the United States Air Force Band in Washington, D.C. This article originally appeared in the August 1996 issue of the Nebraska Music Educator. *Reprinted by permission.*

The Secret of Better Conducting
by Mike Moss

The sins of band conductors are numerous, obvious, and widely reported. We conduct stiffly. We conduct terrible music. We care more about technique than about art. All these heinous crimes are commonly recognized, and many solutions have been offered. I propose an end run around these commonplace complaints. I propose to improve band standards by revealing the true secret of improved conducting.

The secret is study. Study matters more than conducting technique. Study matters more than the maturity of your group. Study improves every aspect of rehearsal. Improved study results in improved performance without fail. So, the question is how to study a piece so as to master it.

The key to meaningful score study is to *make music* while studying. While there is nothing wrong with using recordings in the study process (and there is much to be gained by hearing good performances), recordings rob us of the learning process involved when we have to make the music ourselves. By realizing the score ourselves, whether at the keyboard, on a wind instrument, or by singing, *we develop a feeling for the piece not as sound we listen to but as sound we create.* This experience of calling up our own unique and detailed sound-image of a piece is the ultimate goal of our study. It is a sensation analogous to instrumentalists learning to hear a note before they play it.

We achieve this inner sound-image by developing deep familiarity with the sounds of the piece we are learning. Objective matters as to length, meter, key, and historical provenance are a useful beginning, but they do little to bring us into the actual sounds of a musical piece. For me, discovery of the sensations associated with a piece begins with discovery of the piece's tempos, melodies, and harmonies.

Tempo influences all aspects of performance. Tempo affects character, contrast, articulation, and perception of form. We need to establish tempos in study (though we may change them later), or else we won't really be developing a highly specific image of the piece. Don Schleicher, director of orchestras at the University of Illinois, uses a metronome relentlessly in his early study of a score, striving to lock in his sense of the appropriate tempo. In a piece like the "March" from Holst's *First Suite,* the tempo can be quite brisk, quite reserved, or any place between. Regardless of his specific choice of tempo, the highly prepared conductor will lock in his preferred tempo, adding a degree of interpretive consistency to his work. From that one decision, and his fidelity to it, many other aspects of the piece will take shape. The tempos of other movements may be affected. The tempo will generate certain specific challenges in the trio tune, and in the culmination, when two themes are played at once. Linking a tempo for a piece to a conception of the piece is one crucial goal of score study.

Singing or playing melodies allows us to discern the "attitude" of a piece. Is it a cheerful dance, a sorrowful song, an austere fugue? When we experience these characteristics as sensations, we can convey them as sensations to our players. Playing or singing melodies ourselves until we feel that we have produced their proper character will give us powerful tools for rehearsing these melodies with our groups. Sing the second movement of Hugh Stuart's *Three Ayres from Gloucester* until you've got a strong feel for its ebb and flow, and then get your band to play it with the kind of expression you've developed. We all want bands that play more lyrically, and this will help.

Harmony, I find, has to be played to be appreciated. As soon as we actually put a chord by Hanson or Persichetti under our fingers, we begin to really understand their sound-worlds. I am always surprised by the harmonic impact of pieces once I actually play their chords at the keyboard. (This proves, of course, how limited my aural skills are, but I bet I'm not alone!) Try it with the "conflict" chord in the break strain of a Sousa march. If you play one of those great chords at the keyboard, you'll never rehearse it in the same way again. You'll start to hear every note in the chord. You'll go back to the set of parts to see how the chord is orchestrated. You'll treat the chord as a harmonic entity and begin to care for its tuning and balance as well as for volume or attack. You'll be on the right track!

This sort of study gives us sound images of great utility. The suggestion that we "hear" a piece mentally overlooks a crucial aspect of the conductor's imaginative process. We need to hear the piece, again, not as if we were listening, but as if we were *making* the sounds. What we bring to rehearsal is not a sound-image we remember, but a sound-image we have learned to create. In this active, sensation-oriented mode our impact on the ensemble tends to be direct and musical. We per-

sistently direct the sound being played toward the sound we carry within. Conductors who do this are tangibly different from those who do not. The pace of rehearsing increases. The conductor's voice and actions match the mood of the music. She interrupts the music less often. Her instructions may be nonverbal, sung, gestured, or acted out. Her rehearsal focuses on the sound of the music, not on ideas about it. An observer would be aware of music being made, of an exchange of musical performances and perceptions. If we videotape ourselves in this mode, we will see a more musical demeanor and, most likely, a more successful rehearsal.

All of us are somewhere on the continuum between novice and expert at conducting. Those of you who have gone the furthest may have noticed that conducting doesn't actually get easier, but over time we get better at it. We continue to have to work at it really hard, but (hopefully) the work we put in becomes more effective. And the most effective approach I have yet found, the secret of better conducting, I might even say, is to study a lot and to *hear* the music better every time you sit down to study it.

Mike Moss is director of bands at Southern Connecticut State University in New Haven. This article originally appeared in the Winter 1996 issue of Connecticut's CMEA News. *Reprinted by permission.*

Section 5

Fine-Tuning

The authors featured in this section explore a variety of subjects dealing with band. From providing opportunities for playing chamber music to recognizing student achievement to motivating students to practice, these articles will help improve a band program.

Section 5

Fine-Tuning

Why Band Directors Need Orchestras
by Steven Bird

As Director of Orchestras at the University of Tennessee at Chattanooga, I have had the opportunity to visit with a number of excellent orchestra teachers and programs in east Tennessee. These programs are usually part of a vital, active music department within the high school or middle school and represent some of our very best programs. Many other secondary music programs exist in Tennessee which do not offer any string instrument instruction at any grade level. Some of these programs are also excellent but have not capitalized on the strengths that the full range of music ensembles bring to the music department.

"How Will the Band Benefit?"
If the music department can provide the "orchestra experience," the band program benefits in many ways. The most immediate and apparent impact is on the wind section of the band. The experience of "solo" playing (one on a part); the development of a characteristic, correct tone; learning to play with correct intonation in the sharp keys; and the development of independence as a player has both an immediate and long-term impact on the quality of key wind section leaders. Students with orchestra experience also tend to be more successful in auditions for honors ensembles (both bands and orchestras), because of the confidence gained in solo orchestral performance. They also become more flexible in working with conductors and learn to watch the baton more carefully.

Since Chattanooga lies on the border with Georgia, our local youth orchestra has members from some of the better high school programs in north Georgia. These schools do not offer strings, but their programs benefit greatly from having many of their best wind and percussion players

participate in the Chattanooga Symphony Youth Orchestra. Lakeview-Ft. Oglethorpe and Ringgold High Schools both have substantial participation levels in the youth orchestra; both schools also consistently place many of their students in the Georgia All-State groups.

Most directors like having a string bass or two in their concert band or jazz ensemble. One band director in Chattanooga has even used cello with his group, playing euphonium parts. (The United States Air Force Band, Washington, D.C., also uses cellos and basses as a regular part of their group.) Commonly, a director will find a student who plays bass guitar and "transfer" that student to the upright bass. Problems with this approach include the lack of frets and larger spacing of notes on the upright bass (which results in poor intonation) and the challenge of finding a bass guitarist who can read music! Imagine the advantages to the band director who has access to several bass players who *started* on string bass and can already read bass clef.

"Won't Orchestra Take Time Away from Band Rehearsals?"
School orchestra programs often meet with the string instruments in their own class, adding the woodwinds, brass and percussion instruments in special rehearsals.

If a school can coordinate the rehearsal times of band and orchestra, it is possible to use a "pull-out" approach to some rehearsals, where the wind section of the orchestra is pulled from the band rehearsal on an occasional basis to play with the string section. This approach gives the band director an opportunity to hold a rehearsal with the less advanced members of his group no longer "hiding" behind the lead players of each section. (Imagine having your entire ensemble minus the best two players in each section. You will really be able to focus on the problems!) Most school band/orchestra programs require open communication and planning between the instructors of each group. This is an involved process, but has the advantage of building good collegial relationships.

"What about Scheduling Problems?"
Concerns have arisen in many schools over block scheduling. One beneficial strategy is to schedule both band and orchestra rehearsals during the same class period. Not only does this allow for the occasional "pullout" rehearsal for full orchestra, but it diminishes problems with class conflicts, since the personnel who make up the academic schedule will probably avoid scheduling advanced academic classes during this time slot, due to the sheer number of students in the band and orchestra programs. In this case, the enrollment of each group helps protect the other group from losing membership due to block scheduling.

"But I Don't Know How to Play the Violin!"
Frequently, orchestra teachers in school music programs majored on an instrument other than violin, viola, cello, or bass. In the Chattanooga area, there are four public-school orchestra programs at the high school level—Hixson, Chattanooga School for the Arts and Sciences, Tyner, and Chattanooga Phoenix III. Of these four programs, nonstring majors presently direct two of them, and *three* of the four programs were started by music teachers who are wind instrumentalists! (A fifth program in a private academy, Girls Preparatory School, is directed by a violist.) So, being a violinist or cellist is clearly *not* a prerequisite for leading a school orchestra. In each of these four local cases, a music teacher already on staff at the school who wished to augment his or her music program began programs because of interest.

"My School Is Too Small to Support Two Programs."
Secondary schools with smaller music faculties are not excluded from adding orchestra to their curriculum. Often, music teachers are asked to teach out of their subject area at least one or two periods a day to fill out their teaching loads. Some band directors are asked to supervise study halls and lunches as part of their teaching loads. (Personally, I was required to teach consumer math (!) during my second year of teaching in a small high school in rural Florida.) Orchestra class can provide an educationally viable way for music teachers in this type of situation to complete their teaching loads without resorting to "makework" situations.

"Won't This Hurt My Band Recruiting?"
Band and orchestra members often differ in their expectations about their ensembles, and the student who enrolls in a string program is likely to be a different personality than one who enrolls in band. Band directors concerned about maintaining enrollment in their program may be worried that a string orchestra program will cut into band recruiting. A quick examination of some leading music programs in east Tennessee shows that this fear is unfounded. Hixson, Oak Ridge, and Dobyns-Bennett High Schools all have well-established bands *and* orchestras and are recognized throughout the state of Tennessee as examples of the very best music offerings in our public schools. In other parts of the country, the same results are seen as in Tennessee. For example, in Amherst, N.Y. (a suburb of Buffalo), the entire combined enrollment of the middle school band, orchestra, and choral programs is approximately 800. This is made even more remarkable by their *total* school enrollment of about 600 students! Students are enrolled in multiple music classes and continue to participate throughout their high school experiences. Naturally, the high school in Amherst directly benefits from this wonderful support at the middle school level, and has a superb band orchestra and chorus.

"Will the Community Support an Orchestra Program?" or, The Canary Effect
Most parents of string students start their children at a younger age than with band students (fourth grade is not an unusually early start). The resulting long-term commitment to their children's music education results in very loyal support from the parents involved in orchestra programs. In communities with string education programs, the health of the orchestra program is often a barometer for music support in the community. In other words, a music program with a healthy orchestra is generally in a healthy state; a weak, unsupported string program is often a sign of deeper problems which could ultimately affect the entire school music program. The effect is not altogether unlike coal miners who carried canaries into the mine to warn them of problems with the air—if the canary expires, you're next!

Steven Bird is director of orchestras at the University of Tennessee at Chattanooga. This article originally appeared in the October 1997 issue of the Tennessee Musician. *Reprinted by permission.*

Chamber Music—It's Not Just for Festival Anymore
by Steve Bolstad

With the plethora of demands and expectations placed on Montana band directors, it is easy to understand why creating chamber music experiences for our students often gets put on the back burner. Granted, our programs must be centered around the large concert ensembles; however, our primary goal needs to be teaching the art of music making to our students as individual musicians.

So how do we satisfy the needs of the individual student and still meet the responsibilities of our large ensembles? While it would be desirable for every student to study privately (and we should encourage them to do so), this is probably an unrealistic expectation in most Montana schools. I believe the best way to bridge the gap between teaching the individual musician and the large ensemble is chamber music.

The chamber music experience is an extremely efficient vehicle to nurture the musical growth of the individual. It forces the development of strong independent musicians because, quite frankly, there is no place to hide. And while students are learning to be self-assured players, they must also develop acute ensemble listening skills in order to be sensitive and reactive to the other players. These listening skills are easier to develop in chamber settings because "what to listen for" is more obvious. In a large group, it is often confusing for students to know exactly what to listen for, but in an intimate setting it becomes quite clear. In a large ensemble, players often lose interest in making fine adjustments to each other because it doesn't seem to matter much anyway. But in a small group, the adjustments are clearly heard and the efforts are instantly perceived as meaningful and worthwhile.

As I write this, we are all preparing our students for District Festival and then, hopefully, State Festival. My question for the MBA membership is this: "Does the small ensemble portion of the Festival serve as a vehicle to evaluate and reward long-term efforts in chamber music, or do our students organize small ensembles just in time to enter the Festival?" While there is no doubt that any exposure to chamber music is better than none at all (and I heartily applaud all endeavors in chamber music), it is also important that the tail does not wag the dog.

I understand that everyone's initial response is, "There just isn't enough time to coach small ensembles." In the long run, however, I believe the time spent coaching chamber groups will actually save time. In fact, I believe it will go a long way toward improving your large ensembles.

When establishing a chamber program, start by organizing your principal players: possibly a brass quintet, a woodwind quintet, a saxophone quartet, and a small percussion ensemble. The time you spend with these people is very productive because you develop a nucleus of strong section leaders within your large ensemble. Because they have learned to rehearse on their own, they can, in turn, run better sectionals. Because chamber playing develops better reading skills, this nucleus of players will improve your band's sight-reading abilities, and therefore allow you to work up new music in less time. Because chamber players are used to soloistic and sensitive playing, dangerously scored compositions with exposed playing are no longer works you avoid, but gems you seek out.

Chamber players make great role models for the rest of the band and will inspire younger students to form their own groups. The experienced players could even assume coaching responsibilities of the younger groups. Through leadership opportunities, students develop a sense of ownership and responsibility toward a program, which will only strengthen their commitment to the program. Many of us are frustrated when upperclassman drop out of band. Chamber playing can provide new challenges to older students which will help keep these students motivated and interested in the band program. (After all, we do want to encourage more of our students to seriously consider the music teaching profession.)

Having an established pool of chamber ensembles can also help out with all the requests we get for service gigs. Instead of spending time preparing your entire band for the next store opening, you can send out a chamber group. It gives them a great opportunity to show off their stuff while saving you the time to do more meaningful endeavors with your large ensemble.

The positive influences from a successful chamber music program can go on and on. So this summer, when you are planning for the upcoming year, make chamber music a year-long priority. I guarantee the positive impact on your program will be immediate and long lasting.

Steve Bolstad is director of bands at the University of Montana in Missoula, where he conducts the Symphonic Wind Ensemble, University Concert Band, and University Chamber Winds, and teaches conducting, instrumental methods, and the applied trumpet studio. This article originally appeared in the April 2000 issue of Montana's Cadenza. *Reprinted by permission.*

Promoting the Individual in a Group Activity
by Charles Bolton

There are a number of band directors who are very fine musicians and yet who are not very successful at energizing their students. As directors, they understand intonation, rehearsal and conducting techniques, musical interpretation, etc., but they don't do enough to motivate the members of the group to improve the players' individual skills. We all need to remember that if one individual improves, the group becomes better and everyone benefits.

Through the medium of television and the press, our society has come to glorify athletics and report the results of sporting events at almost all levels, from grade school to professional. This publicity and the attention athletics receives are very strong motivations for students to participate and excel in sports. It is our challenge as believers in music education to find ways to promote and give our students the recognition they deserve, thus making them feel important and motivating them to improve their own individual skills.

Social
We need to provide an open and inviting atmosphere in the band room. The band room should be a gathering place for your students before and after school, and during lunch time. All band students love "hanging out." You can create this atmosphere by having the room open early and locking up late. Students will then know they can always go there for company, a place to study, to use the phone, and so forth. A couch or two is a great attraction. It's good to have music or videos of classical and jazz performances playing in the band room. After all, we are trying to develop an appreciation of serious music. Don't allow the students to listen to *rock,* etc.—they do that on their own time.

We should also take small groups of students to performances or clinics. Another way to have good interaction with and between the students is to participate in special events such as Heavy Metal Marching Band in Portland on the Friday after Thanksgiving, Clarinet Day at PSU, Flute Fair, Tuba Christmas, the Young Audience Concert sponsored by the Portland Community Concert Association, and similar opportunities around the state.

Create ensembles to perform for small community meetings or at retail stores. This is especially easy at Christmas, with sax quartets, flute trios, and many other combinations.

Academic
Promote private lessons. Many directors say they can't get students to take lessons. This doesn't make sense. Most students want to be successful and most students enjoy performing. Therefore, it is our responsibility to create an environment where students want to improve. If students get greater satisfaction out of playing their instrument and recognition from others for their increased ability, they will want to improve. I believe that the better the student plays, the more he or she will enjoy making music.

Talk to the band at length about private lessons and teachers, but don't stop there. Talk to them individually and call their parents. Tell them that if their child is interested in music and they can afford the lessons, it is their responsibility to provide that opportunity. This has to be done in a very careful way. It is then the responsibility of the students to do their part by practicing the lesson material on a regular basis. A few students will have talent and interest but no money. These students could be quietly given scholarships for lessons by your band-parents club or out of your school band account.

Mention private lessons at parent conferences, at performances, in band newsletters, anywhere possible. Above all, keep reminding them that everyone benefits from each individual's improvement. To help promote lessons you also need to provide students and parents with a list of private teachers in your area, complete with phone numbers. The list can be distributed in many ways throughout the school year. Send it out in the fall as part of your mailing of your band newsletter, grading policies, and calendar. Give it to parents at conferences, post it in the band room—share it with everyone.

When possible, bring in clinicians to work with your students. The wide range of knowledge needed to teach the finer points of all instruments is impossible for one person to possess. Some of you are great at encouraging your students to attend concerts or inviting groups to perform at your school. However, the interaction between professional musicians as "people" (not merely music makers) with your students is far more valuable in making impressions and motivating your students to improve.

Performance tests for each grading period are a great way to motivate students. Not only grade the tests, but reassign chairs for each test. Students are very competitive, and many will practice to receive a good grade and to move up in the section. If students know they will have multiple opportunities to move up in the section, they are inclined to practice more. If they want to improve and are practicing, they might take lessons. In your concert programs list the section in order of chair assignment. The student's and parents' pride will help motivate them to sit higher in the section. We would like all of our students to want to excel for the right reasons, but if we can motivate them in other ways, I believe, in this case, the end justifies the means.

Recognition

There are many ways for you to be sure that your students are recognized for their individual achievements. Encourage students to audition for All-State, All-Northwest, WIBC, Music in May, and other honor groups. Write on the board and announce in class and at concerts all of your students who auditioned. Then acknowledge once again all those who made the honor groups.

Be sure the students who are selected are featured in the school and community newspapers. Announce their names in the morning announcements. Write up a summary and give it to the school's counselors and faculty. Put the information in the band's newsletter. Have the accepted students stand at concerts and assemblies.

Encourage students to play at your area's solo contest. Again, publicize all who participate, as well as the ratings and recommendations for the State Solo Contest. Publicize the results of the State Solo Competition. Set up a band Web site listing the students and their individual achievements.

At Sam Barlow High School there is a Wall of Fame where honored students are listed when they graduate. It lists names, instruments, and year graduated. To be eligible, a student must be accepted to the All-State Band or Orchestra, the All-Northwest Band or Orchestra, or compete at the State Solo Contest. When parents and students enter the room they see the names (150+) from the past 30 years. Many students make it their goal to be on "The Wall."

Teach students how to conduct. Select students to choose music, rehearse the band, and conduct in a performance. This is a great learning experience for the student—the band taking direction from a peer—and might even encourage some students to enter our profession. Give the names for your best juniors and seniors to colleges here in the Northwest. We all love to get mail; and when students get recruiting letters from colleges at school, they feel good.

There are many ways to promote individuals in your program, from personal encouragement to public recognition. This short article only begins to touch on ways to recognize your outstanding students, and to motivate others to become outstanding. *Every* school and band has many students who have the potential to excel in music. It is our privilege and obligation to find ways to accomplish this. Each community, school, and band is different. You must decide what is best for your unique situation. I challenge each of you this school year to find new ways to encourage and motivate your students to improve their instrumental skills.

Charles Bolton teaches music at Mt. Hood Community College in Gresham, Oregon. This article originally appeared in the Winter 2000 issue of Oregon Music Educator. *Reprinted by permission.*

Making the Connection

by John Carmichael

The big "IT" of our profession is to teach students to love and value music. To do so, we must provide them with enough literacy skills to pursue music independently. The only way we can effectively measure our success is to note how many of our students continue music participation after they complete our course of instruction. The issue of this article is how a band director can successfully, and with some consistency, enable students to make a strong, life-long connection with music. *You must plan for it because it does not always happen by accident.*

When I was preparing for my junior prom, it was my intention to prompt a positive "feelingful response" from my date. Since I was not yet a licensed driver, I had to double date with a friend who shared my goal for his evening. In careful preparation, we both got haircuts, rented tuxedos, bought corsages, made dinner reservations, splashed on the trendy fragrance of the day, and carefully washed and detailed his vintage model Cadillac. After we finished the car's exterior, my friend and I cleaned and waxed the leather seats—all part of a well-conceived plan.

The route we decided to take to the restaurant and prom location included a number of right turns that would slide the chiffon-clad young ladies toward our side of the car. It was thoroughly devious. Since there were no seatbelt laws at the time, our plan worked quite well. The responses received that evening were indeed positive, but, at least in my case, respectful and conservative.[1]

The point of this story is that we too often leave the musical experience (development of a feelingful connection to music) up to chance as we are mired in the mundane and constantly distracting aspects of our profession, or as we hold other priorities to be more important.[2] As a single young man, I rarely left anything up to chance when planning for a date. Likewise, when I plan a concert program or a single rehearsal, my highest goal is to facilitate a connective musical experience for every student in the ensemble, and I give considerable thought about how I will realize that goal.

Many band directors would define this "feelingful connection" with music as an aesthetic response and would further define aesthetics as having to do with the beautiful in music. A most comprehensive and accurate definition, however, is provided by Willi Apel when he notes that

"Musical aesthetics is the study of the relationship of music to the human senses and intellect."[3] If that definition is accepted, then ugly music can produce an aesthetic response (horror) as can a very ugly performance (revulsion and low ratings).

This article is concerned with the development of connective, feelingful responses to music in a manner envisioned by composers or as possible through responses to sounds correctly produced that are in tune, in balance, blended, and which represent a kind of sonic ear candy which by itself is positively connective. Anyone who has vibrated inside an in-tune B-flat chord knows about the latter experience. What exactly is connective will vary for each student, and when it will happen cannot be predicted. All we can hope for is to constantly control the rehearsal and performance environment to maximize the possibility that such a positive musical experience will happen eventually. Have you ever had the thrill of being told by the 4th chair, 3rd clarinet that, at a particular moment in the music, he or she experienced goose bumps, or have you ever seen your band members cry in response to the effect of a particular composition? These are connective experiences but certainly not the only ones possible.

Proposals for Facilitating a Connective Experience with Music

1. Although this may sound perfunctory, you must first care deeply about the musical experience the students will have under your instruction. Your students more than likely share your musical values, providing that your first priority (the be-all and end-all) is the music itself. It is essential that students see you responding (at least as much as you do to their behavior) enthusiastically to music and utilizing good music as an integral part of your life. If you do not, then it is impossible to expect them to do otherwise. Your emotive responses will elicit emotive responses.

Solution: In rehearsal, speak often of your own musical responses and feelings about what you are preparing. Let them know when you have goose bumps. You might also explain how exceptional music tends to "grow on you" over time, as opposed to making a great first impression before growing dull. Audiotape rehearsals to check the proportion of behavior control comments to those that focus on the music. Videotape yourself to see if your face and gestures reflect appropriate reactions to the music (composer's intent) as well as the performance (what is really happening).

2. The rehearsal environment must be conducive to the occurrence of a connective response. There should be a minimum of distractions, and the room should be orderly and clean. Anything that vies for the musicians' attention other than the music must be eliminated. Good lighting and good temperature control are also important. Public address and physical interruptions must be minimized by agreement with the administration.

Solution: Schedule a meeting with the principal to explain the need for a distraction-free rehearsal environment. Most administrators will respect a teacher who values instructional time so highly. Give the custodial staff seasonal gifts and leftover cheese and sausage whenever possible. Rather than complain to their supervisor about what they have not done, let custodians know directly of your concerns. Thank them often. Have students participate in bandroom maintenance with leadership assigned to supervise in an "officer of the day" program. Student ownership of certain aspects of normal band administration will heighten their sense of responsibility and commitment to the program. The more committed to the program they are, the more chances you will have to touch them musically.

3. It is very difficult to elicit a feelingful response to music when the performance fundamentals are so poor that even good music is unattractive or painful. I have publicly referred to this situation as trying to stage a romantic encounter with another human in the middle of a filthy pigsty.[4] You might be able to accomplish some kind of feelingful reaction, but not the one you would have received if the environment were as pleasant as, say, a candlelight dinner for two in a first-rate restaurant. There has to be a level of correctness before students can perceive the music as the composer intended. Much of daily teaching should be aimed toward making sure that student musicians are capable of performing with a characteristic tone, proper blend and balance, and a correct pitch center. These concerns should be dealt with every day as a part of a progressive warm-up.[5]

Solution: There are many solutions for this area of concern, but there is no substitute for the teacher to know how to produce a characteristic sound on each instrument. Better intonation will necessarily follow, but the only way to play in tune with consistency is for the player to be able to hear the target pitch before they play it. Singing and directed ear training is the best way

to achieve that goal. Three to four minutes every day will accumulate into great skill by the end of the year. Technique and rhythm development are comparatively easy, but must be dealt with on a daily basis. Students will respond to your expectations. If your ears are sufficiently "dirty," or if you do not respect the students' ability to achieve at a high level, then you will be rewarded accordingly.

4. Music programs that affect students for life are those which prepare them for musical independence. In other words, the student must be able to read music competently without the need for aural reference.

Solution: Do not model rhythm by demonstrating it vocally to them, particularly before they have had a chance to solve the musical equations. Instead, teach a system of counting, and reinforce it every day with rhythm exercises that are performed at a steady tempo provided by a metronome. Structure opportunities for individual instruction in and assessment of counting skill. Otherwise, the best you might achieve is only a modest percentage of independent counters. The rest will simply echo to the ones that understand. Precision in performance will never occur when rhythmically-dependent students are in the ensemble. In the absence of convenient aural models in adult life, the dependent instrumentalist will discontinue his or her participation in music.

5. The rehearsal has to be perceived as the place where "it" happens, the "it" being some kind of feelingful, connective response to music making. The process of assimilating a musical composition should be considered more important than the final performance. It is also likely that connective responses will be most powerful when students are less concerned about the many performance variables, including audience response. Many mistakes of approval are given by parents out of love rather than as a knowledgeable response to a worthy performance. How many standing ovations have you received for inferior performances? At some point there must be honesty about the quality of a musical performance in the same manner that a parent would not hang the naive finger painting of a normal eighteen-year-old on the refrigerator.

Solution: Treat each rehearsal as the best part of any day and as a time when something spectacular or moving might happen. Think about what you would like to accomplish on two levels: fundamental improvement and musical connection. Find out what "turns them on." Know what does it for you. As rehearsals improve, so will performances.

6. All materials used must be of the highest quality. For this reason, the less experienced director must refer to selective music lists in some form or solicit the advice of more knowledgeable practitioners.

Solution: Use a selective music list that qualifies the music recommended.[6] Typically, since state music lists tend to be political, they are a bit more inclusive rather than selective. Throughout my career, I have nearly always sought corroboration of my belief in a composition's quality through consultation with a respected colleague. More often than not, a recommendation from an expert has proven to be a good choice.

7. Programmatic music can be a very effective means with which to begin the connective process. Although ultimate connection with music should be generalized to that which elicits a feelingful response, music with specific imagery provides a good starting place.

Solution: Seek out compositions that portray specific stories or which are connected to specific events. There are many good selections available in the genre. Through this process, especially if properly guided, students may learn to connect musical devices to generalized feelings, and thereby develop the ability to respond to music as a type of life-analog rather than as an art that must relate to specific imagery. An important goal of good music teaching would be to teach students to value the sound and structure of the music itself without needing external references. Music without external references is known as absolute music.

8. The more music, the better. It stands to reason that if you present a wide variety of quality literature for the students to assimilate, there will be a heightened chance that at least one of the compositions will affect the individual performer. Too often, we focus for long periods of time on two or three selections (often of inferior quality), and thereby fail to reach a significant portion of the band's membership. In a properly prioritized music program, the subject matter is the reward or payoff. More than ever before, we have a wonderful smorgasbord of music from which to choose. Musical band directors should be like kids in a candy shop whose main problem is what to consume next.

Solution: Increase the number of concert performances while decreasing the number of other after-school demands. Give concerts in the fall. Decrease the amount of preparation time and increase emphasis on individual preparation of parts. Students will generally assume the responsibility to prepare music once it becomes clear that the director will not do it for them. Sight-read different selections on a regular basis—every day, if possible.

9. Choose music that will ensure successful performance in a shorter preparation period. Without due consideration for the students' welfare, or perhaps, because of our own aspirations or musical desires, we often bite off more than they can chew. The students must be ready for what we ask them to perform or the process through which we must teach to survive difficulty will corrupt the musical relationship. Rote drill and constant successive approximations do not foster a loving relationship with music. Save the rote drill for technique development apart from specific music and transfer the learned skills at an appropriate time in an appropriate manner. There is little more connective in life than success, so why not guarantee it for your students?

Solution: The music selected for the band to perform under shorter preparation periods should be readable at about a 75 percent level the first time through. This is a measure used by wise honor band conductors who are given about twelve hours to prepare a twenty-minute program. If you are teaching a good fundamentals program in your warm-up period, technique and reading ability will develop over time, and true ability to perform more difficult, more significant literature will emerge properly.

There is nothing new in these recommendations.[7] We fail too often to think about what we should be doing as we strive from one extraneous job demand to another. And typically, we are the very ones who schedule ourselves into such a dilemma. There is one thing of which we can be assured. Those who do not understand this article will most certainly continue doing what they do without regard to the musical welfare of the students for whom they are responsible. Too many in our profession are busy recreating the competitive thrills of their youth or building careers instead of building connected, independent musicians. The points offered above do not guarantee a connective musical experience for every member of your band. If implemented, however, it is guaranteed that a much larger percentage will experience that sublime moment when the music speaks either to the brain, the heart, or the soul in a way that emotionally bonds the student to the subject matter for life. *Those students whom we have touched with music are the most important trophies anyone in our profession should ever want.*

Notes

1. She later dumped me, thank goodness. My wife proofread this article.

2. Let's see: marching band championships, superior ratings, trophies, medals, membership in selective organizations, any kind of recognition based upon achievement that is awarded publicly. This a tough issue because so many of us need this recognition to corroborate the quality of work we are doing. Unfortunately, all of the above can be achieved through means that are not educationally sound and can produce students who have learned to dislike band and, thereby, dislike band music. If priorities are correct, appropriate recognition will come in time.

3. Willi Apel. *Harvard Dictionary of Music,* 2nd ed. (Cambridge, MA: The Belknap Press of Harvard University Press, 1969), 14.

4. I hope this hits all bases of political correctness. My apologies to those who might enjoy pigsties (and to pigs in general).

5. This is not a rehearsal techniques article. If you do not understand this point, you should consider some kind of remediation in instrumental music teaching.

6. *Music for the Concert Band,* by Joseph Kreines, is a terrific example. Although it is due for a new edition that would incorporate quality works from the past several years, every recommendation made by Mr. Kreines is exceptional literature worthy of performance. It is graded from easy to advanced.

7. A wonderful article that covers much of the same territory in a more scholarly manner was written by Dr. Edwin Kruth entitled "Aesthetics in Rehearsing the Symphonic Band." It is a pamphlet available through the G. Leblanc Corporation, Kenosha, Wisconsin (the code number is E93).

John Carmichael is director of bands and associate professor of music at Western Kentucky University in Bowling Green. This article is taken from an address presented at the Annual Convention of the Kentucky Music Teachers Association held at Campbellsville University from October 31 through November 2, 1999. It originally appeared in the December 1999 issue of Kentucky's Bluegrass Music News. *Reprinted by permission.*

A Curmudgeon's View: Last Chair Third Cornet
by Don Corbett

I have rarely met music teachers who were not able to identify a former teacher who had a profound influence upon their life and may have encouraged them to enter the teaching profession. I had such a teacher. His name is probably not meaningful to any young teacher of this generation, but he was a legend in his time. Clarence Sawhill was the director of bands at UCLA for many years. He was a Kansas farm boy who taught in the public schools before becoming a teacher at a major university.

I met Clarence at a summer band camp and was so impressed with him that I spent every spare moment watching him rehearse the top band. As a young band director, I knew very little about how to rehearse a band. Clarence became my mentor. He saw me regularly in rehearsals and was kind enough to take an interest in me and give me some direction. Clarence was one of the kindest and most gentle men I ever met—

where did we get the idea that you have to be a tyrant on the podium to produce quality musical results?

There are two things that Clarence said to me that greatly influenced my career. I have never forgotten them. The first thing was that you "teach to the last chair third cornet" (or perhaps the last chair second violin or freshman second tenor). His idea was to make the weakest players in your groups become better than they probably believed possible. He believed that great musical groups were outstanding because the players at the "end" of the sections performed to the very best of their potential.

As I reflect on my public school teaching career, I never had a principal flutist in my bands whom I didn't love. How could you not? They were always bright young ladies, studied privately, practiced every day, played solos, went to camps, and were absolute joys to work with. They were the kind of students who gave me such pleasure that I was willing to put up with all of the other nonsense teachers have to deal with and stay in the profession. The last chair third cornet? Who cares! In my view, the great bands that I judge each year are great because conductors have paid attention to these players. These teachers have made their youngest and most inexperienced students feel important and have demanded their best effort. They were not ignored. As my high school bands became stronger, I used two seating arrangements (band "A" and band "B"). That allowed me to rotate young players to the top of the sections and move some of my best performers to lower parts. I didn't have to worry about the third cornet part. It would be well played.

The other thing Clarence said that influenced my career was that "if you are going to teach, you better know what you are teaching." He recommended that I buy some professional quality band instruments and study them privately. I did. I was never interested in going to the teacher's lounge when I had a break—didn't enjoy the smoke or negative comments. I would stay in my office and practice on instruments. How do you teach vibra-to on the flute or saxophone if the students can't "hear" how it sounds? How do you "describe" tone quality? Perhaps even more than that, it became great fun for me to learn other instruments. This old trumpet player learned the chromatic fingerings on the clarinet and the alternate positions on trombone. I think it made me a better teacher to have experienced the same problems my students were having.

I suspect all music teachers have had a Clarence Sawhill in their life. A person who cared and was willing to share. If you had such a "teacher," you were blessed.

Don Corbett, who was MENC president from 1986 to 1988, taught band in the public schools for sixteen years and was on the faculty of Wichita State University for twenty-four years. This article originally appeared in the November 1998 Kansas Music Review. *Reprinted by permission.*

Band Camp ... for Concert Band?
by Frank Hale

The core philosophy of most instrumental music organizations such as NBA encompass the idea that the school instrumental music program should be built around the concert band. In discussions about this philosophy at meetings and conventions, I have never met a band director who stated that he or she disagrees with this concept.

The following questions might give us an evaluation about some of the emphasis of our total band program:

1. Does your band have more marching than concert performances?
2. Do more people see and hear your marching band than concert band?
3. Do you attend more marching band festivals and competitions than concert events?
4. Do you spend more after-school time in marching rehearsals rather than concert rehearsals?
5. How does your instructor budget for marching band compare with that of the concert band?
6. If you hire a marching percussion instructor, do you also hire a clarinet instructor for the same amount of time for the concert band?
7. If you have a flag (aux., rifle, etc.) instructor, do you also have a woodwind teacher?
8. How much money do you spend each year on flags and related equipment as compared to concert band music?
9. How much time do you personally spend planning for marching compared to concert band?

These questions can provoke thought about our actual emphasis in our total band program. Is it really possible to place the greatest emphasis on the concert band in today's traditional high school setting? I believe that most of us want to center our programs around the concert band, but are at a loss to how we can realistically make this work.

I would like to suggest an approach that alters the weight of emphasis without adversely affecting the marching band. Use your imagination. First consider ways to enhance the concert band without implementing any drastic changes in your marching band approach.

The first weekend of January of this year, the first concert band clinic, for our band only, was implemented at our school. This was certainly not a new idea, for other band programs around the country have used this idea and some have used an expanded version, but they are few and far between.

Our schedule for the day was as follows:		
9:00 AM – 10:00 AM		Section rehearsal
10:00 AM – 10:10 AM		Break
10:10 AM – 10:50 AM		Individual practice
10:50 AM – 11:00 AM		Break
11:00 AM – 12:00 PM		Section rehearsal
12:00 PM – 1:30 PM		Lunch
1:30 PM – 2:45 PM		Full band rehearsal
2:45 PM – 3:00 PM		Break
3:00 PM – 4:00 PM		Full band rehearsal

I hired 13 area professionals to serve as clinicians for the day. The instrumental specialists were dominantly members of he Chattanooga Symphony Orchestra and faculty members of the University of Tennessee at Chattanooga. The band clinician was Tony D'Andrea, band director at UTC. Each clinician was given the task of preparing a particular concert selection (the same one for the entire band) and was given the following goal and objectives.

Goal

To create a greater love of and enthusiasm for playing and practice of music by exposing the students to professionals on their instrument individual, section, and full band rehearsals.

Objectives and Techniques

1. Teach a greater awareness of the following fundamentals by demonstration and interaction:
   a. Tone
   b. Intonation
   c. Blowing and Support
   d. Articulation
   e. Finger (slide, stick) Technique
   f. Beat (pulse feel), Counting, Rhythm
   g. Phrasing, Expression, and Style
2. Demonstrate, give to, and stress the importance of a regular and meaningful warm-up routine.
3. Create a greater awareness of the importance of scale and arpeggio practice.
4. Apply all of the above during the rehearsal of "Lochinvar."
5. Be enthusiastic and help the students to enjoy what they are doing.

An informal evaluation of this clinic showed our efforts to be very successful. The students seemed to enjoy themselves very much. I even heard such comments as "Can we do this again?" and " I learned so much from my teacher" and "I didn't realize that my instrument could sound so good until I heard it played by my instructor." All of the instructors gave me positive comments concerning the students' interaction with them. There was a noticeable positive difference in individual, section, and full band sound by the end of the day.

There are certainly many other approaches and implementations to the Band Clinic (Camp) idea. I plan to use other ideas in the future clinics. I would like to suggest to you that if this idea interests you, use your creativity and make it better with other variations.

I have always used area professionals in many capacities: private lessons, section rehearsals, full band rehearsals, and solo and group demonstrations and performances in our extended Concert Band instruction. But, this was the first time that I used such a focused and concentrated all-day approach for the concert band. The students felt as if they were very "special" to be given so much attention during this special clinic day. I will be following up this season with shorter group sessions.

Our marching bands will probably always be the most visible and serve as a heavy promotional and recruitment vehicle of and for our total band program. We also must realize that time and effort devoted to preparing the marching band for its season is directly affected by the strength and emphasis of our concert band approach.

Frank Hale, who is a retired band director from Hixson High School in Chattanooga, Tennessee, is founder and conductor of the Chattanooga Concert Band and serves as executive director of the Tennessee MEA. This article originally appeared in the Fall 1996 issue of The Tennessee Musician. *Reprinted by permission.*

Improve Your Band Program—
By Using Research!
by Dennis J. Hayslett

Much exciting research in the band field has been done recently. In addition to being thought-provoking, some of the findings have the potential to make a major impact upon how we approach the task of teaching our band students. Read on, and you might even find some innovative ways to re-think, re-structure, and promote a positive transformation of your current methods. Examining "how we do what we do" from time to time can be a risky and frightening endeavor, but at the very least, you may find some issues that encourage a healthy thought process about how you administer and teach in *your* program.

Guided Instrument Selection as a Factor in Beginning Band Retention
Are you concerned about beginning band retention and how to deal with the issue of your students' instrument choices? Edward Cannava decided to examine the relationship between guided instrument selection and beginning band retention.

Comparisons were made between three groups of sixth-grade beginning band students in four middle schools using the data obtained from school district records, a questionnaire, and a professionally guided instrument-selection test (hands-on) created by the researcher.

Cannava found that an 11 percent increase in retention occurred as a result of the administration of the professionally guided instrument-selection test. Students who were retained after experiencing the test were more likely to be suited to their instruments and not prone to switch to a different instrument. These students also have more parental support, while the band programs experienced improved instrumentation balance and decreased instrument sex-stereotyping.

Academic Achievement and "Pull-Out" Beginning Programs
Are you being hassled by administrators about pulling students out of regularly scheduled classes in order to teach beginning band or orchestra? Are administrators and parents worried about the effect of the "pull-out" on the academic achievement of the students? In South Bend, Indiana, Pherbia Engdahl examined two groups of 299 sixth-grade students each, an experimental "pull-out" group and a control "non-pull-out" group.

The groups were matched by third-grade total battery NCE scores, and were analyzed by pull-out and non-pull-out status, by race, and by gender.

The findings? The results of the analysis showed that the students who were pulled out of class did not experience a significant loss in achievement and, in many cases, *gained* in achievement when compared to the non-pull-out students. Thus, the findings of these analyses do not support the contention that time spent out of the classroom negatively affects student achievement. In fact, a concurrent teacher survey revealed that the teachers themselves did not feel that the student achievement was harmed by the pull-outs. Although the teachers often felt stressed and annoyed by pull-outs, they still accepted and appreciated the band and orchestra program and saw no other way to implement the instruction except with the pull-out program.

Does Student Attitude toward Band Have a Relationship to the Grade in which Band Instruction Begins?
Now for some real controversy! Linda Hartley from the University of Dayton surveyed 2,249 seventh-grade band students from 45 schools to find an answer to this question. She discovered that in situations where fifth- and sixth-grade students are housed in the same building, the attitudes toward band were similar, regardless of whether the instrumental instruction began in the fifth grade or the sixth grade. However, in "split" school settings (those where fifth and sixth grades were housed in different buildings), the seventh graders who began instruction in sixth grade had a more positive attitude toward band participation than those who began in fifth.

Hartley suggests that band directors and administrators consider these findings when deciding at which grade level to begin instrumental instruction. She points out that the findings of this particular study (coupled with previous research that shows sixth graders can learn at a more rapid rate than fifth graders) may cause educators to question the practice of starting band instruction earlier than the sixth grade, particularly if the students have had a strong general music background and are housed in a "split" school setting.

Based on the results of this and other studies, Hartley concludes that no negative effects will result from starting students in the sixth grade as opposed to earlier grades. These findings will probably please those who have been doing it that way all along, while enraging those who start band in the fourth or fifth grade (or earlier). Read her study in *Contributions to Music Education* and let the arguments and debates begin!

Will Conducting Instruction Improve the Musical Performance of Beginning Band Students?

Have you ever wondered if you could help your beginning band students' phrasing and rhythmic-reading performance by teaching them how to conduct? Steven Kelly from The University of Kansas did, so he examined 151 fifth-grade beginning-band students from eight schools.

After randomly assigning the students to experimental or control groups, both Kelly and an associate (to control for biases) were randomly assigned equal numbers of experimental and control bands. During the instructional period, students in the experimental bands received basic conducting instruction two to three rehearsals per week, for ten weeks, for ten minutes per class. The instruction involved preparatory and cut-off gestures, beat patterns of four and three, and gestures of dynamics, legato, and staccato musical styles. Students in the experimental bands conducted and performed warm-up material provided by the researcher; the control bands received no conducting instruction, but were met and warmed-up by either the author or his associate.

After pre-testing and posttesting all individuals and bands, the researcher found that the students who received conducting instruction showed a significantly greater improvement in their rhythm reading and phrasing abilities than students in the control bands. The conducting instruction was not as effective in improving the ensembles' performances of dynamics, legato and staccato musical styles, or overall general performance, but the results suggest that beginning band students' individual and group rhythmic abilities, and group phrasing abilities, may improve at a greater pace.

Kelly also notes that this improvement was accomplished in ten minutes or less per period and with different instructors. The results further suggest that conducting instruction should be considered a viable teaching technique in an ensemble teaching strategy.

Can Conducting-Gesture Instruction Help Students' Performance Response?

Speaking of conducting instruction, do you ever get frustrated when your young band students

don't seem to understand (or follow) your conducting gestures? You do? Then take a look at how Richard Shayne Cofer investigated the effects of conducting-gesture instruction on seventh-grade band students' recognition of and response to conducting gestures. In addition, he was also interested in discovering which gestures the students recognized as standard conducting signals, which could then be considered "conducting emblems."

Thirty seventh-grade wind instrumentalists received instruction designed to improve their recognition and response to common conducting gestures for five consecutive days. Thirty students in the control group participated in a warm-up designed to review concepts of musical expression without the use of conducting gestures.

After a written multiple-choice test and an individual musical performance test, Cofer found that the group receiving gesture instruction performed as well on the multiple-choice test as the performance test; sixteen gestures reached musical conducting-emblem status for this group. However, while eleven gestures reached musical conducting-emblem status for the control group on the written test, only three reached this status on the performance test.

Results of this study indicate that short-term conducting gesture instruction can be effective in improving the recognition and performance of musical conducting signals.

Now That You've Taught Them What to Watch for, Can "Expressive Conducting" Really Have an Effect on a Band's Performance?

J. Russell Laib from the University of Georgia asked that same question. To find the answer, he examined eight high school concert bands and two college/university bands from Georgia. Each of the ten bands performed two pieces of music twice, once conducted expressively, and once conducted non-expressively. The researcher served as the conductor for both sessions, which were videotaped to document the treatments.

The performances from each treatment session were recorded on audiotape. Tapes were sent to six university band directors who were experienced band adjudicators. They were asked to determine if they perceived a difference between the two performances, and if so, which performance they preferred. The responses of the adjudicators indicated that they preferred the expressively conducted performances in each pair most of the time. In addition, results of a survey indicated that the students responded more positively to the expressive conductor treatment.

Hopefully, the above research findings can give support to methods that you already use, or are considering. Many of these ideas may not affect you directly, but your students and your program may benefit from engaging in the process of analyzing what you do, and then thinking through ways to utilize the results of research to continually improve your efforts.

References

Cannava, E. S. (1994). Professionally guided instrument selection as a factor of beginning band retention (Doctoral Dissertation, University of Colorado at Boulder, 1994). *Dissertation Abstracts International, 55*(10), 3129A. (University Microfilms No. AAI9506315)

Cofer, R. S. (1995). The effects of conducting gesture instruction on seventh-grade band students' recognition of and performance response to musical conducting emblems (Doctoral Dissertation, University of Iowa, 1995). *Dissertation Abstracts International, 56*(10), 3876A. (University Microfilms No. AAI9603017)

Engdahl, P. M. (1994). The effect of pull-out programs on the academic achievements of sixth-grade band students in South Bend, IN (Doctoral Dissertation, Andrews University, 1994). *Dissertation Abstracts International, 55*(05), 1179A. (University Microfilms No. AAI9428809)

Hartley, L. A. (1996). The relationship of student attitude toward instrumental music to beginning instructional grade and grade level organization. *Contributions to Music Education, 23,* 46–61.

Kelly, S. N. (1993). An investigation of the effects of conducting instruction on the musical performance of beginning band students (Doctoral Dissertation, University of Kansas, 1993). *Dissertation Abstracts International, 54*(10), 3876A. (University Microfilms, No. AAI9408990)

Laib, J. R. (1993). The effect of expressive conducting on band performance (Doctoral Dissertation, University of Georgia, 1993). *Dissertation Abstracts International, 54*(09), 3258A. (University Microfilms, No. AAI9404667)

Dennis J. Hayslett is director of bands, director of the instrumental music studies area, and teaches conducting, instrumental methods, and music education courses at Western New Mexico University in Silver City. This article originally appeared in the February/March 1997 issue of Ohio's Triad. *Reprinted by permission.*

Are You Teaching a "Larry"?

Steve Litwiller

"Look at the way those guys are coming in. I don't care for their uniform colors either," Larry says. We're sitting in a concert hall at district contest. Larry has been driving the bus for the past fifteen years and has become a student of band contests and ratings. The band plays a tuning chord and is announced.

"I'm thinking a 'II'" Larry says. Now Larry has had no formal musical training other than being a high school tuba player in the 1960s, past president of the Band Boosters and having two kids in my band program. The band finishes playing.

"Did not change my opinion one bit," he says and writes the rating down on the program to check with the tally at the end of the day.

We've been on the road quite a long time, Larry and I. He knows how the band loads and unloads and where to get the best parking places at all of our festivals. He knows how we want the students to behave and the answers about a thousand questions those freshman band members always ask on trips. Larry is also really good about knowing when the director needs to concentrate on the performance at hand and be left alone or when to badger him and tell him what the truth really is about the band performance. The world is full of yes men. I find it valuable to have someone like Larry around to give me an unvarnished opinion, warts and all.

I started both of Larry's kids in band and they followed the program all the way through graduation while Larry became Band Booster President, Bus Driver, and joined the ranks of the experts by second guessing every judge on concert band performances, solos and small ensembles. His ears have been tuned over the years not only to detect the perfect whine of a good clutch and eight cylinders, but also to take special notice of overbearing trombones, lack of dynamic contrast, or poor balance. And the last bit of training has paid off. Larry has predicted judges' ratings for all concert bands with 100 percent accuracy the last five years straight.

Did Larry's band director know, that besides developing his student's ears for a good concert band sound, what a gift he was giving to music education by teaching someone who 35 years later would be of such help to music? Larry will be the first to tell you that he was not a "hot player." He never played in college or professionally. He never sat first chair in the tuba section. Yet a band director in Boonville, Missouri, named Gerry McCollum still gave him the opportunity to appreciate and enjoy participating in the band. And because Mr. McCollum cared about his students and the quality of his program, the dividends pay off generations to come not only for those of us who teach today, but especially for the students in our programs. Those students are supported and promoted by the adults who had a positive experience in music, regardless of their ability level.

Larry and our other band supporters should be reminders to all of us to guard against showering our attention only on the naturally gifted or the students totally immersed in our programs. Do any of us know that we could be encouraging or discouraging the student who could be a parent, football coach, administrator, board member, politician, or booster-club president? Sometimes people in those positions can make more of a difference in the future of music education than any music performance or education student we send to college because of the negative or positive experience we provide. By teaching and encouraging as many students as possible, we engage and ensure the success of music programs for future generations. Consider that before you deliver that next "my way or the highway" ultimatum to one of your students.

In spite of all of his successes in judging, Larry has had one nemesis the past fifteen years: marching bands. Still, he rises to new challenges. "Well, I think I've got the hang of this corp style judging now," he told me last fall after the buses were loaded and we were on our way home. "I went 100 percent with the judges on eight bands in the first two classes. Now if I can ever figure out what happened to baton twirlers I'll be ready to judge auxiliary."

This year I'm proposing that, as a prerequisite for band-adjudicators certification, the High School Activities Association requires a minimum of fifteen years experience as bus driver.

Steve Litwiller is director of bands for the Boonville Public Schools in Boonville, Missouri, and is active as a clinician, conductor, and adjudicator in Missouri and Iowa. This article originally appeared in the Fall 1998 issue of Missouri School Music. *Reprinted by permission.*

Mr. Mamlok's Opus
by Walter Mamlok

Children are a great deal more apt to follow your lead than the way you point. (Anonymous)

Is there room in your school's instrumental music program for the child who refuses to be auditioned and tells you, "I'm perfectly happy to sit last chair, third part"? And when you ask that child why, he responds, "There's no pressure here. Nobody wants this chair."

Does that tell you something about how your program is going? Or does it tell you something about that child?

Or what about the child who says, "No matter how much I practice I can never be sitting in that first chair because Erin is so good and I'll never be better!" Again, is that telling you something about the program? Or is it providing a peek at what children know?

In both cases, the outcome is the same. The old military model of survival of the fittest is no longer appropriate for today's children. Using competition as a tool to get children to learn or to practice is no longer the most effective tool. In the age of cooperation, synergy, and teamwork, it's difficult to justify competition. How can you encourage children to compete with one another while expecting them to work together? Is it more important to sit first chair or to make music? And in order for one child to be successful, does another child have to experience failure?

In a successful music ensemble, everyone must work toward the same goal. Imagine an ensemble where the clarinets decide the trumpets are too slow, so the clarinets play their passage faster. Or where the flutes decide they don't want to play that piece of music at all, so they decide not to honor any flats or sharps. Or where one section's players race to see who can finish the piece first. You get the picture.

You see, just because you want an outstanding performing group doesn't mean your students want the same thing. If they're not on the same page or even in the same book, you're in for a very difficult time. To today's children, "Because I said so" is not a good enough reason to follow the teacher's lead. Instead, an effective instructor engages the child and helps him or her come up with a goal that the group can work toward. Dr. Stephen R. Covey calls this a mission statement. I call it a godsend.

I first learned about *The Seven Habits of Highly Effective People* with our school's Governance Committee. As part of the ongoing school reform movement which began about 10 years ago, we in Newtown Middle School in Newtown, Connecticut, have embraced the idea of total quality management and continuous improvement. My challenge, as a band director, was to take this concept and apply it to our middle school band program.

I knew it was time to change the way we did things because I saw that we were not on the same page. What good is a teacher with all the knowledge who cannot deliver it to his students? Previous methods left me more and more frustrated; the harder I worked, the less they seemed to work. All I wanted to do was give to my students a love of music and of music-making. The opposite was happening. Then I began to hate the subject I loved.

It was time to be proactive. I realized that as a teacher I needed to be willing to give up some of my authority or "power." I realized that my students truly were there to learn, that they knew what they wanted, and that what they wanted was to be empowered. Students know and can recognize talent and a good performance, but working to achieve them is another issue. I knew I could help them best by showing how they could have fun and improve at the same time. What's interesting about power and authority is that it is the students who can give you strength and it is the students who can take it away. The student-teacher ratio in a large ensemble is 65 students to one teacher. The 65 students will always "win." Unless I could empower the group to come up with a goal, we would never improve.

A Mission

The first thing I do with my ensemble is make it clear to them that this is their band. This band experience creates their memories. I had mine many years ago, and it was so powerful that it was one of the factors that led me to do what I do today. I ask them what they want to get out of band. For example, when they were walking to class, what was it they were thinking about: "Boy, I

hope we do such-and-such in band"? They tell me what direction to go in, and that direction becomes our guide. They make the decisions regarding how we behave, how we organize ourselves, and who should play which parts.

Our discussions typically lead to more questions and answers: What are the characteristics of a good performing ensemble? What characteristics or qualities are necessary for a good rehearsal? Which attributes are needed to play the first part, second part, or third part? Soon the students are no longer viewing this as my rules in my classroom but as their rules in their classroom. I believe this is what principle-centered leadership means.

Applying the habit of beginning with the end in mind requires us to decide what we're going to do with the time, talent, and tools we have to work with. If the band decides to be the best they can (and each group of children I work with decides this together) given the time constraints of the daily schedule as well as each individual's talents, how can the group best use its rehearsal time efficiently? We discover we need a statement of purpose: What do you want and how are we going to get there?

We use a process of consensus to come up with six words to form a single statement of purpose or mission statement. Over the years we've compiled a list of words to choose from or add to, categorized as action words, feeling words, or thought words. Before we choose words for our mission statement, we go over the meaning of each word. The students write down their six choices to describe themselves (not the entire band). Then we vote. The students stand when I call out a word that they chose. I take the two highest vote-getters from each category (action word, feeling word, or thought word) and we write those words on the board. Finally, we come up with a sentence that includes those words and that will become our mission statement. For example, during the 1994–1995 school year, our mission statement was the following: "We will have a band class where humor and self-confidence flourish when we play and create music for everyone's fun end enjoyment." The 1995–1996 group came up with this: "We will enthusiastically create music, with a sense of humor, to make our band powerful, enjoyable, and fun."

Once the statement is created it is then made into a banner and is placed on the wall for everyone to see. But this process is not complete until the students create their own mission statements from their original word choices. They then attach that statement to the same wall, under the band's mission statement. The visual impact this makes becomes a very powerful tool. Each student is committing publicly to their common goal, and each student will be held accountable for it. And this wall becomes a reminder to me as well as to the students to behave in ways that are in alignment with our common objective.

Life-Long Learning

When the students tell me which attributes are needed to play first, second, or third parts for their instruments, they begin to put first things first. That is, if children tell me they want to play the first part and they know the requirements, I ask them if they meet those requirements. If the answer is yes, I give them the part (whether they're ready or not, in my opinion) and hope they enjoy it. Their desire to take the challenge, to work hard, and to overcome their deficiencies is more important than how the part will sound the first time they play it. When it comes time to play, they either play well and meet the challenge or they fall short. If they do fall short, we determine what they could do to improve. And we revisit their mission statement.

Thinking win–win became reality when competition was eliminated from the band. After seeing the results, I will never "chair" my students again. Comparing one student's progress to another's is not effective in a classroom or in an ensemble. Yet, this win–lose method, regardless of its overall ineffectiveness is still used in most bands. The win–win attitude leads to the following types of questions between instructor and student. Do you need me to tell you who the better musicians in this group are? Why should your success create someone else's failure? In order for you to feel good, should someone else feel bad? Then we determine that by year's end each and every band member will have the skills necessary to play the first part. We imagine what that band would sound like, then congratulate those who already can and help those who are working at it.

The response to this win–win approach has been tremendous. It puts all the responsibility of learning where it belongs: on the students. The motivation for learning starts to move from extrinsic to the intrinsic (there are no more contests unless we all win the prize). The instructor's job is to guide back on track those students who've lost sight of their goal. Thinking win–win drives both the teacher and the student to be more creative in solving problems. And that's where we begin to develop life-long learners.

Music Is Synergy

Imagine what a class would be like if students and teachers really listened to one another. The best teachers are those who truly listen. They don't necessarily agree or disagree. This requires restraint and respect.

The process of developing a mission statement begins to prepare students to listen well and carefully. After all, whenever one person pays attention to another's needs, wants, and desires, they are not only gathering information but they're validating worth. Everyone wins. Goals become clear and ways to reach the goals are crystallized. The ensemble shapes its own destiny.

Synergy is what music is all about. When players understand their role in relationship to the whole (that sometimes their instrumental part becomes important to the creation of music while at other times it must serve a supporting role) you start to get music that goes beyond the playing of correct notes. This is where they begin to understand the essence of music. Like an engine with many gears, where each gear must be in sync with the others for that machine to run, each member of the performing ensemble must understand his or her part beyond just pushing down the right key to get the right sound. When should they bring out their part? When should they take over the melody? When do they give up their thread? When you have 120 instrumentalists listening to each other musically, communicating in sound together, responding to what they just heard, and responding to it in a musical way, synergy in all its beauty results.

Practicing

Changing our approach to making music at Newtown Middle School has yielded amazing fruit. We played more music at a higher level of understanding and with a higher level of competence in a shorter period of time than we ever had. We're aware of one another. Everyone working in the same direction adds energy. We understand what it takes to work together to reach common goals. What a concept to teach children! Of course, no musician ever became a good musician without practice, or sharpening the saw. Continuous improvement on an individual level raises the standards of the entire group. Our players, therefore, take lessons, practice, and assess themselves and, in the process, challenge themselves to become better each day.

Interestingly, the mission statements of the bands have never indicated that their objective was to impress the public or to become great musicians. Yet, that is exactly what has happened as a by-product of this synergistic, creative process of owning the band.

We do put on great concerts.

Walter Mamlok is a music teacher at the Metropolitan Learning Center, a Global Studies and Technology magnate school in Bloomfield, Connecticut. This article originally appeared in the Spring 1999 issue of Connecticut's CMEA News. Reprinted by permission.

Want a Really Fine Middle-School Band? … What's Stopping You?
by Mike Pearce

You have recently heard an outstanding middle-school concert band play for the state music teachers' conference or at a band festival. What was your reaction to their accomplished performance?

If it was, "My band plays that well," congratulations! Or if it was, "I'm just getting started, but give us a few years and my band will be up there knocking 'em dead," then you probably will.

But instead, what if your response was, "Must be nice, with all that money and those great kids," or something similar from a sad litany of well-worn excuses like these:

- "Block scheduling is killing me."
- "My instruments are old and cheap."
- "My room's even older."
- "Our school has the lowest test scores in the district (state, region, world, etc.)."
- "I get no administrative support."
- "My parents are too stressed to care what their students do in band."
- "Nobody cares what I do."
- "My students can't afford lessons or good instruments."
- "Students from other schools call us the ghetto school."
- "Our district only cares about academic test scores. They couldn't care less about the arts."
- "I teach six classes each day. Other teachers have four and I'm bummed."
- "When they (the school district) decide to fund it properly, I'll give them a high-quality band program."
- "My feeder program ranges from weak to nonexistent."
- "Kids today just don't care."
- "I have no control over placement of students in band classes."
- "I can't teach 400 students per day."

- "My classes are loaded with chronic bad behaviors."
- "Nobody else cares what I do; why should I?"

These are serious concerns and they should not be trivialized, but rather than let them be the determiners of your teaching style and outcomes, why not relegate them to the role of mere factors or influences or hurdles to be overcome?

Find Out Where You Stand
If you are not satisfied with your band's performance level and the effectiveness of your teaching, how can you get objective evaluation?

Have you attended band festivals in the past two years? Were the results positive or was it a case of "those guys are out of touch" or "they wouldn't know a good band if it ran over them"? Excuses aside, were there criticisms that you need to address—intonation, precision, balance, tone quality, breath support? While competitions, festivals, and other adjudicated events have their share of shortcomings and abuses, they do provide one means of getting feedback and they serve as a yardstick for measuring your work against contemporary standards. If you have glaring weaknesses or blind spots, qualified adjudicators will point them out and suggest remedies. Clinicians at festivals will do the same in a less threatening environment.

Do you ever bring in clinicians to work with your groups in the familiar surroundings of your own band room? High school or college directors will usually clinic your group for modest fees, or you could have another middle school director sit in and give you informal suggestions. Have your school's choir or orchestra director make comments on music you are preparing your group to perform. Do a self-critique of your group's last performance. What did you hear that made you wince or groan? Pick an area and devise a strategy for improving it before the next concert. For example, you might say to yourself, "I guess I could play for the kids more—show them how to use good breath support. Maybe I can get some good high-school or college players to come in and play for us or even play along once in a while." Once you open yourself up to evaluation and feedback, you have begun the process of raising the quality of your work and your group's performance.

Plan for Success

Start thinking about next year's band. Pick the most solvable problem that you are currently facing and begin fixing it. Even if it is a small, seemingly insignificant problem, the fact that you have taken a positive step will have an empowering effect on you.

Plan for success. What event—winter concert, band festival, trip, etc.—would really get you and your kids pumped up? Plan literature and activities that will guarantee success for your group. Save the "unplayable monster piece we played in college" and other "impossible dreams" for the day when you are summoned by the muse of middle-school music to accept the baton and lead the Paradise Middle School *Incredibly Awesome, Divinely Selected Wind Philharmonic* in a concert at Carnegie Hall.

What surefire-winner musical selections can you program that will knock the socks off your kids and parents? What are the building blocks that you need to develop to improve your group? Does your teaching program include a good class method or alternate scheme for building a solid technical base for your band—rhythm, counting, scales, rudiments?

Make it your job to make your kids successful, and they will make you successful.

Get Positive

Let go of the victim mentality—"Of course my groups are bad, look what they (decision makers, external forces) have done to my program"—and adopt a positive, "can-do" mind-set. As your approach becomes more positive, the hopelessness and paralysis caused by feeling controlled by outside forces will diminish, and improvements will happen, probably not in whirlwind fashion at meteoric speed, but at a steady, measured pace. When you find yourself making excuses—"Sure that band's good, but let 'em try to get those results with the slow movers I have," and so on—stop and back up. Try to get on positive footing by completing these sentence starters:

- "Sure, School X has money and good kids, but here's what my school has going for it: …"

- "The thing I know I can be successful at with this situation is …"
- "With a couple of changes, one of the things that great band did that I could use is …"
- "One of the best things about me is … and, the best way I can use that strength is by …"

Taking action to improve your teaching, even in very small ways, can have an empowering effect on you and bring back much of the joy of teaching.

Check Your Vision

When hearing a fine group makes you think, "We're not there yet, but that's where we're headed," you probably are. If you see your mission as being one of becoming an expert at getting results with the kids and resources you have, you are probably going to do exactly that, to some degree or another. If you see yourself as a guide and mentor, capable of leading young players to heights of achievement and musical expression, there is every reason to expect those things to happen.

However, if you are content to check in each day, let the required number of hours slide by, check out on time and collect your paycheck at the end of the month, your groups probably will not be anything to write home about. If you have only a vague idea about what goes into producing a fine band, and little concern about it, you and your students will never experience the thrill of producing great music. If you are devoted to dressing, acting, and speaking like the thirteen-year olds you teach—trying to be the "coolest dude around"—you may find it difficult to achieve the kind of discipline and focus needed for great musical performances. And, if your plan is to wait until you can step in front of the Utopia Middle School Band—well-balanced, loaded with motivated, capable kids playing great instruments—before you decide to get serious and become a great teacher, you may find yourself instead facing a harp band with St. Peter as supervisor of music long before you get the ideal band.

What Next?

If you want to have a great middle-school band, what should you do?

- Start now. Begin working on the easy problems while you look for solutions to the tough ones.
- Check your vision. Are you clear about what you want to accomplish?
- Make the best of what you have. It does not hurt to dream about the ideal situation and work toward it, but you have students facing

you now who need your attention.

- Empower yourself by taking positive steps to improve.
- Do not let external influences dictate how you will teach.
- Open yourself up to evaluation and pay attention to the feedback.
- Avoid victim-mentality thinking.

Take charge. Nobody can make you a weak teacher without your permission. There is immense satisfaction in overcoming obstacles and being good at what you do, and none in having to apologize for the quality of your work.

Get busy. There are fun times ahead.

Mike Pearce is band and orchestra teacher in the Cherry Creek Schools at Prairie Middle School in Aurora, Colorado. This article, which was printed in the Fall 1999 issue of Colorado Music Educator, *originally appeared in the April 1999 issue of* School Band and Orchestra. *Reprinted by permission of* School Band and Orchestra.

Motivation: Some Pieces to the Puzzle
by James South

All of us want to have an excellent ensemble. Fortunately it is a very simple (but not easy!) process. We simply have to know *what* to ask for and *how* to ask it.

In this article I'd like to focus on *how* to ask your students to achieve their potential. The world is full of teachers who know what excellence is, but there are far fewer teachers who are able to ask for it effectively.

At a workshop at the 1995 Oklahoma Bandmasters Association convention, Francis McBeth reminded us to insist that students fix the problems we hear. If a problem isn't corrected immediately, he said, we should keep insisting until the problem is solved.

McBeth's point was to be persistent. Every day, week in and week out, demand excellence. You'll eventually receive it, and the student will be rewarded with a sense of accomplishment as a result. Insist on excellence.

We sometimes forget that students need repetition. Each time you repeat a request, more students will understand the importance of that fundamental. If you are able to state your request in a different way, you will reach even more of your students. Have many ways of explaining the same concept, and use them as appropriate. Remember that when you give up on something and fail to keep insisting, you are sending a message that you don't care anymore whether that something is corrected.

If my clarinets are making an immature sound and I fail to remind them enough times until it is remedied, it won't be fixed, and they will assume I'm no longer concerned with their tone. Be positive, but be persistent.

One of the difficulties young music teachers often face is encouraging excellence in their students without constantly reminding them that they aren't excellent now. It can be hard to strive for constant improvement and at the same time avoid making only negative comments. Many educators try to balance their comments, giving a positive comment for every negative one.

Eddie Green, retired director of bands from the University of Houston, is a master of complimenting in small steps toward excellence. His compliments are frequent and very focused. For example, "Clarinets, you made tremendous improvement in measures 12–13 today—thank you!"

With this kind of praise for small things, it is easier to produce large musical successes.

It is very important that your compliments be sincere. Even very young students see through comments like, "You guys sound *great!*" when it is obvious that they don't sound great. Sincerity is everything when you make a compliment. Likewise, the tone of your negative comments is crucial.

State criticism in behavioral terms. For example: "Trombones, please connect the notes, rather than space them."

This makes the performance the issue. If I say, "Trombones, you never connect notes, you always space them," then I am making the comment more personal and less effective.

Be yourself and be kind, but be persistent! The results are worth the trouble.

James South is director of bands at Southwestern Oklahoma State University in Weatherford. This article originally appeared in the December 1996 issue of Oklahoma Music. *Reprinted by permission.*

Chamber Music Magic for Your Students, Your Program

by Jeffrey L. Traster

Toward Musical Perfection

In high school and much of college, solo and chamber ensemble performance was nerve-racking for me. I knew just how I wanted to hear the music emerge from my tuba, and I prepared well. Even so, in performance I played with knees knocking, giving forth all the musical energy I could focus, striving toward my goal of musical perfection. Even though my recital performances seemed to fall short of my ideals, I received compliments and encouragement from my teachers and friends. Through guidance from my teachers, diligent practice, and numerous performance opportunities, I "magically" got better and better, the nerves dissipated, and performing became much more enjoyable. I began to understand that the real importance of these experiences to my musical development was not the achievement of a "perfect" performance, but the honing of my musicianship, which led me ever closer to the perfect performance.

Solo and chamber music performance forced my playing into the open; there was no place to hide. It provided opportunities to hear myself in ways that are more difficult to perceive in a large ensemble where parts are doubled. I heard what I really sounded like and began to evaluate myself on:

1. Richness of tone ("It's just me out there … Do I sound like Arnold Jacobs?")
2. Note accuracy ("Oops … that should be G-flat.")
3. Flexibility in intonation ("Hmmmm … can't get the piano player to lip up, so I guess I have to come down.")
4. Steadiness of tempo ("I have to think eighth-note pulse through these half notes to fit with the accompaniment/other parts.")
5. Clarity of articulation, style and rhythm ("How *dry* can I make this note? How *smooth* this run? This long note should *resonate* like Pavarotti singing a high C; this passage *dance* like a pixie on pine needles.").

Once I began such self-evaluation, my listening and performance skills took a giant leap forward, and so did the quality of my performance in band.

Solos and Ensembles for Everyone …

Great bands rise from the synergy of great players. Imagine the glorious sound of your band with strong, independent players on every part. With widespread solo and ensemble participation amongst your students, it will happen! In addition, the quality and amount of literature your band performs each year will expand. These are the tangible results of student involvement in solo and ensemble performance.

Initiating or expanding this aspect of your program will require from you dedicated leadership and significant work in organizing groups, helping students select literature, and guiding their progress. Consider this effort a long-term investment. Some positive results will be felt almost immediately; however, the big payoff will come in the next year or two as your students "magically" increase their musicianship, gain new confidence, and the band improves exponentially.

Expect everyone's participation. Literature is readily available to challenge each student—at the right level for them. If you're unsure about a student's ability, stay on the easy side of notes and rhythms; challenge them with dynamic extremes, musical phrasing and contour, and variety of style.

Motivation and Implementation

How do you motivate students to take on the challenge of preparing solos and ensembles? Motivation comes from the promise or achievement of success coupled with recognition for a job well done. Solo and ensemble festival has those elements built in; diligent preparation is rewarded with a superior rating and a medal. Similarly, a successful solo and ensemble program beyond festival has performance outlets, something for which the students prepare. Build in acknowledgment of their accomplishments. Here are some ways to implement the program and motivate students:

- Make solo and ensemble participation part of the requirement for earning a letter in band each year. Students take pride in displaying such marks of achievement.
- Schedule your soloists and ensembles to perform at your band concerts and band booster meetings. They will receive many enthusiastic compliments.
- Encourage your top soloists and ensembles to be ambassadors of their band and school in the community by arranging performances at the local Kiwanis Club or their church. These audiences are always friendly and appreciative.
- Arrange solo and ensemble performances at the middle school or elementary school that feeds your school. Ask one of your administrators to

go along to introduce the group. Students love going back to their old school to play, and your administrator will enjoy the inside view of your program and spending personal time with your students.

- Ask the director of the school's annual staff to include a photo of the band students who received a superior rating at solo and ensemble festival on the page adjacent to the band's group photo. Students will aspire to be pictured in that special group.

- Recognize superior soloists and ensembles at your end-of-year banquet and final concert. Use these festive occasions to applaud strong players in the section, who faithfully play the second and third parts but never receive the accolades given the section leader.

Keep in mind: the more that students perform the solos and ensembles they have prepared, the more they will appreciate the fruits of their labors, enjoy music, and develop their talent. Audiences will express their appreciation at every performance with applause and encouraging comments. Success and recognition then fuel the student's desire to dive into the next musical challenge.

There is one other important element in the motivation equation—enthusiastic leadership from the director. Simply stated, students value the things that we value, from the quality of the music we select for them to play in band to the shine of the shoes on the marching field. So, foremost in motivating students to play solos and ensembles is our placing value on the solo and ensemble experience by talking about it often in the context of rehearsal and incorporating it into our programs through performance experiences, listening to recordings, and guest artist performances.

Once you achieve lift-off into solo and ensemble atmosphere the first year, the second year will be easier. Groundwork will be in place for continuing the activity: students will anticipate that it's part of being in band, and people in the community will be looking forward to more performances by your students. By the third year, solo and ensemble participation will be a tradition!

The fact that the FBA sponsors solo and ensemble festivals throughout the state declares our collective belief and wisdom that this activity is vital to the musical development of our students. Furthermore, solo and ensemble playing is personally rewarding, something students can continue once they graduate, and a bunch of fun! Fully incorporating this experience into our programs is no small undertaking, but it is well worth the effort to make the magic happen, and our students emerge the winners.

Jeffrey L. Traster is director of bands and tuba instructor at the University of Tampa in Florida. This article originally appeared in the October 1999 issue of the Florida Music Director. *Reprinted by permission.*

Section 6

Adjudication and Competition

Like it or not, the issue of competitions is one that every band director must face. The authors in this section explain their philosophies on competitions and festivals and offer tips for participating in adjudicated events.

 Section 6

Adjudication and Competition

Why Our Students Should Audition for Honor Groups—Self-Growth!
by Mark Berntson

For the past few years I've had the privilege of helping coordinate all-state activities in North Dakota as a member of the high school all-state committee and as co-manager of the NDNBA Junior High All-State Band Festival. The experience has given me a unique perspective I'd like to share.

I believe that preparing for a challenge is one of the greatest learning experiences one can have. Preparing a solo for a music festival, preparing for a job interview, or preparing for a music audition causes one to grow immensely as a person. When you get right down to it, self-growth is what keeps us alive, and musical self-growth is one of the most profound, satisfying types of growth one can undergo.

I believe that *all* our students should be given (1) the opportunity, (2) the encouragement, and (3) the help they need to participate fully in the audition experience. Auditions are a way of providing authentic musical challenges for our students which necessitate individual practice and, therefore, result in self-growth. I will not allow any students of mine to audition for All-State or take part in a regional music contest unless they have met with me a certain number of times. They are not permitted to simply show up when the bus leaves and take a vacation from school. They must prepare and, therefore, must grow. It's always very gratifying to see how far they progress because of the experience. Furthermore, I don't believe we should reserve the right to audition for only our most talented musicians. Anyone who is willing to work hard has a place in this process. Should only the best be allowed to grow? I think not.

Another benefit of the audition process is the audition itself. Working up the courage to perform in front of a total stranger or to make an audition tape in front of your hypercritical music teacher is extremely beneficial to our students. It makes them better people and can propel them toward taking even greater risks.

I consider the results of an audition to be almost inconsequential. While I'm always glad when a student of mine is selected for an all-state group, I'm just as happy for the students who grew just as much but who won't be taking part in the festival. The process *makes everyone better,* not just the ones who "make it." While the actual festival is a marvelous experience for those who are selected, it must be remembered that the process is just as, if not more, important because it involves so many more students.

I recently visited with two young teachers whose students were not selected for the junior high all-state band; I was so gratified to hear how they dealt with their students' disappointment. They told their students how difficult it is to be selected (without being bitter about it), how great it was that they tried, and encouraged them to try it again next year. Certainly one can learn as much from a disappointment as from a "victory." The sensible, humble, determined philosophies of these young teachers make me very optimistic about our future. They've got their priorities straight.

In conclusion, please consider these factors when you receive your next mailing regarding an audition opportunity from the ACDA, NDNBA, the NDMEA, or from a collegiate honor festival. If you have the time and energy, I guarantee you will have students eager to participate and to learn. Here's to the self-growth of our students!

Mark Berntson is director of bands at West Fargo High School in West Fargo, North Dakota. This article originally appeared in the May 1998 issue of North Dakota Music Educator. *Reprinted by permission.*

Four Basic Components of Better Bands: Reflections of an Adjudicator
by Richard Clary

Like most of my college and university colleagues around the Commonwealth, I have been honored with numerous opportunities to provide my opinions and value judgments to concert ensembles of all sizes from most of the geographic regions of the United States. I am struck with a couple of thoughts: (1) that there is, inevitably, some very good music teaching going on most everywhere, and (2) I tend to hear some of the same things that could be improved by groups from every range of experience and competency. Given the opportunity to share some thoughts in this forum, I decided to list some of the things I tend to say to most ensembles that I evaluate in hopes that some of these may prove to be useful.

Thoughts on Intonation
Most good groups have a few things going for them that assist them in sounding "in tune" more often than not:

1. They use a standard pitch calibrated at, *or extremely close to,* **A-440.** This is the pitch level at which virtually all wind and percussion instruments are designed to play as well "in the scale" as possible. This standard pitch allows students in the ensemble the chance to literally learn how their instruments vary from equal temperament *on specific notes in specific registers.* Without this "home base," students can be in a position to have to make a *different* set of adjustments *each rehearsal.*

2. They learn to play in tune by *matching pitches in context with other pitches*—not by reconciling a needle (or light) to zero on a tuning meter. This is a critical concept! Players need to learn to tune *by ear, <u>not</u> by eye.*

3. They tend to *blend* **sounds as a general strategy;** this has a way of refining the intonation while also improving beauty and resonance of tone as well—generally desirable goals unto themselves!

4. They understand the acoustical "fingerprints" of the individual instruments — which cause some notes to vary in pitch in generally *predictable* ways. By far the most neglected of these is the way the harmonic series negatively impacts trumpets, trombones, baritones, and tubas, which all must compensate for the two "trouble" modes of response, or partials in the series.

The 5th partial is significantly flat. For the trumpet, we're talking about written E-natural in the fourth space of the staff and the chromatic fingerings *down* (primarily the fourth space E-flat and the fourth line D-natural). Even very fine players will need to be reminded *regularly* of this flat tendency until *they* begin to hear how low it is!

On the other hand, **the 6th partial is** *sharp* **to an even larger degree.** Here we're talking about the written G-natural above the staff for the trumpet (and chromatic fingerings downward: F-sharp and F-natural). Trombones and baritones/euphoniums have these identical problems in the 5th and 6th partials; they merely occur one octave *lower* in sounding pitch to the trumpet (on their concert D and F-natural above the staff). The tuba similarly adjusts the D and F occurring *two* octaves below the trumpet's sounding pitches.

In my experience, given reasonable equipment and training, *no single factor in band performance does as much damage to the tutti sound as uncorrected 5th and 6th partials!* It is well worth finding these notes in your scores and making their correction a high priority in your rehearsal pedagogy!

Thoughts on Dynamics and Balance
I have come to the conclusion that the best way to make virtually any group sound better immediately is to reduce all dynamics by one level from where they are normally played. **Most bands play too loudly too much of the time.** It's really as simple as that. Playing more on the softer end of the dynamic compass will put more of the instruments in their dynamic "sweet spot" where they sound with the most resonance and least distress. Most good choirs scrupulously avoid "shouting," and we band directors would do well to follow our choral colleagues' lead here in striving for sheer beauty of sound. Some other points:

1. The dynamic level of accompaniments is nearly always much too loud, or *thick* in texture. If you set balances to a point where the melodic line is simply heard, you are about halfway there! The melodic line must be accompanied in such a way that not only can the melodic instruments play in their dynamic "sweet spot" where they can sound the best, but they must also be in a position to have room to play with some dynamic contour of their own! Consequently, I recommend in most cases that you balance melody and accompaniment in such a way as to allow for clear projection of the melodic line at its *softest* point in the phrase "arch." *This will change how you hear the band forever!*

2. Try balancing your sections by blending all the sounds in such a way that all section members are playing "into" the sound of the principal player of the moment. I have acquired the term "masking" of sound or "tucking in" consecutive unison sounds *just behind* the principal player's sound in order to give support while not obscuring the character of the "lead." I have since used this notion very successfully in unison textures in any number of musical settings.

3. When playing sections in unison/ octave scoring (march "intros" for example), I recommend that you automatically **reduce the dynamic by one level** and put a premium on blend and intonation. The unison/octave passages, by right of their scoring (the strongest option available to the orchestrator for *projection),* will likely be heard as even *more* pronounced when the sounds are better refined and in tune!

Thoughts on Musical Style and Interpretation

Most groups seem to be taught in such a way that by the time they have solved the myriad technical problems presented by a composition and bring that work to performance, there is often little *gesture* remaining in their music making. Listening to (and performing) music without expressive gesture is, for me, like reading prose without the benefit of punctuation. I believe that *all notes* in a melodic or rhythmic phrase *are not created equal.* **Be sure that from one moment to the next (or from phrase to phrase) the students understand which of the group of notes in question** *you believe* **requires the most dynamic stress, agogic emphasis, or length of duration in order to give this expressive sense of** *gesture* **to the music.** It is well to heed the cliche that "all music is either *going to,* or *coming from* some- place."

Given that most of the phrases which we are called upon to recreate carry some expectation for an "arch" shape (or two!), it makes the most sense to me to approach each phrase with not only a plan for how to build dynamics to the high point(s), but also for a plan to *diminuendo* from this high point to return the "back side" of the phrase to its point of relaxation. Most of our groups play the *crescendo* part of the final few phrases very well but then flatten out dynamics to *forte* because they have not allowed each crescendo to return to its

point of origin. Thus they create a three- or four-tiered continuous crescendo which then runs its course and encourages monodynamic playing for the duration of the piece.

In the immortal words attributed to gravity guru Sir Isaac Newton, "What goes up must come down." I am a firm believer that this concept applies to phrases as well!

Once each phrase has been shaped to your taste, **extra care should be taken so that the "big moments" in the architecture of the musical composition do not go by without a real sense of awareness by the players.** After all, if the players miss the major emotional "arrival points" of the piece (and there are likely to be at least two in the simplest of works), *the audience is certain to miss them.*

One of the most misunderstood musical concepts may be that of the accent. In doing clinics and honor bands, it never fails to amaze me that when students are asked the question, "What is an accent?" there are typically as many answers as there are students responding. Unfortunately, many of these answers tend to reflect the "play louder/tongue harder" notion.

At this point in my musical life, I believe that an accented note is one which is distinguished by its dynamic shape or *taper* **in loudness from attack to release.** The bigger the accent, the faster the taper of the loudness envelope of the note. I often use "bell sounds" as models for this effect ("ding/dong"—"ting/tang" and the like). Some positive yet unanticipated benefits of this approach to the accent include a tendency for there to be more "ring" in the sound of the brass because the taper of the note encourages a more relaxed "sing" to intonation and tonal blend. A pretty good deal, I think!

Thoughts on Programming

For me, the reason for all of this is for our students to perform a *variety* of music with a sense of *stylistic understanding.* I often hear concert and festival programs which feature selections which do not show a range of style, tempo, historical "period," or harmonic or orchestrational "sound worlds." **We should all be aware that even the most beautifully played program lacks some impact if** *all* **of the music comes "from the same place" in its sound.** This is a particular concern when we have generally too few opportunities to play serious musical works in the concert band setting during a given student's career as it is, without having that same student "learning the second clarinet part" to a list of pieces that do not vary substantively from one to the next. We owe our students (and ourselves) the chance to experience music from as many stylistic perspectives as possible so that hopefully some *number* of those styles will resonate within us and encourage *both us and them* to come back throughout our lives for more!

Richard Clary is director of bands and associate professor of conducting at the University of Kentucky in Lexington and enjoys an active schedule as guest conductor and adjudicator in the United States and Canada. This article originally appeared in the May 1997 issue of Kentucky's Bluegrass Music News. *Reprinted by permission.*

When Competition Is Not Healthy
by Ronald E. Kearns

I recently read an article in the *Washington Post* that I found somewhat distressing. It was about two marching band directors in Northern Virginia who threw a trophy they had won in the trash at the end of a competition. They had come in second place out of 19 bands and took issue with the judges' decision.

Over the last 21 years, there have been festivals where I have felt judges could have or should have given my bands higher ratings than they got, but I have never allowed my own ego to get so out of hand that I let students see my frustration in an unprofessional way (not that the child in me didn't want too; the adult in me wouldn't allow me to). The directors involved by all accounts were very responsible individuals up until that moment of impulsive behavior.

There are ways of being able to teach valuable lessons through adversity. Now, I'm in no way attempting to set myself up as being perfect, and I'm sure that my students have always been able to tell when I was disappointed. What I am saying is that they had to guess at how upset I was because I didn't do anything overt to confirm their suspicions. We teach lessons even when we are not trying to. The lesson that the students learned from these directors' actions will last as long as anything they were taught during rehearsals. The bigger issue really is the matter of competition and how we teach our students to deal with losing or coming in lower places than expected. When I was in school there was a saying we were always told: "It doesn't matter whether you win or lose, it's how you play the game." We didn't buy in then, but our coaches and teachers convinced us that they believed it. It may have been naive of us, but we followed our teachers' lead. As long as they held to that belief, we respected them and held it too (even when we knew the child in them was ready to explode).

Parents expect us to be role models even though they sometimes say that they don't want us to be. Their expectation is that we will hold ourselves to a higher standard than most others in the community. This makes an incident like this one take on a much larger meaning and significance. Take, for instance, the behavior of some parents at Little League games. They are sometimes ready to come to blows with a referee or official, but the same parent would get after a coach for being a "bad sport." It may not be fair to us (since we have to give up our humanity from time to time), but it comes with the territory. Beyond anything else, we are teachers and we have to be ever mindful of the great responsibility of that station in life. Anyone who finds it hard to repress their anger while in front of kids should really rethink what they are doing as a professional. We're supposed to teach students how to deal with adversity, and the lessons we sometimes teach are not what we as professionals should teach. This incident is the extreme, but whenever we come back from a festival and diminish the character of judges or challenge the integrity of the festival, we are teaching a lesser extreme of the same lesson these directors taught. If we accept the good evaluations of judges without challenge, then we have to submit to the same standard for those evaluations with which we disagree. Righteous indignation, yes—childlike behavior, no. Do whatever you want behind closed doors when students are not present but keep a stiff upper lip when around kids. Trophies are tangible things, lessons taught and learned are intangible and last a lifetime.

Ronald E. Kearns is director of instrumental music at Walter Johnson High School in Bethesda, Maryland, and adjudicates festivals and conducts clinics and workshops throughout the United States and Canada. This article originally appeared in the November/December 1996 issue of the Maryland Music Educator. *Reprinted by permission.*

Ma, We Got a II at Contest!
by Peter LaRue

A Story

It's late on Saturday evening. Ma has been dozing off as she watches television, waiting up for her son Paul to get home from the band contest.

Ma was never in band, but she is really proud of Paul. Paul is a junior this year and has been moved up to "Percussion Section Leader" for the band. Ma never quite understands Paul when he is talking about band, as she hears him speak a great deal about the virtues of Yamaha *(which she thought was a motorcycle)* versus Pearl *(which she thought would be nice to have on a necklace);* the "battery" *(which she thought you put in flashlights)* and the "pit" *(which she thought was a nasty place for snakes).*

But Ma is a proud parent and tries to support Paul as best she can. Sometimes, she can attend his band contests, but today she had to help serve at the church spaghetti supper and was unable to go—but has been waiting up—eager to hear how the band did at contest.

Ma sometimes has trouble understanding Paul's pronouncements after a contest. Sometimes it seems if the band doesn't receive a I, all hope is lost; but last weekend they seemed giddy to get third place in their class. It puzzles her. The new band director seems to be doing a good job—it is his second year—the kids seem to like him—and the band sounds good—but Ma remains mystified about much of this band contest business.

A car door slams in the drive. Ma wakes up on the couch noticing that it is 11:30. She hears the porch door open and Paul runs in and breathlessly says, "Ma we got a II at contest." Ma, being wise, waits for further information as she wonders *"Is this II good? Is this II bad? Is the band happy with this, or will there be extra practices next week?"*

The Dilemma

This seems to be the dilemma with the contest festival experience: *Perspective.* A II can be the great accomplishment in the season of a band, or it can be a mark as insidious and invidious as the *The Scarlet Letter.* Second Place in a class can be something which causes great rejoicing or the general gnashing of teeth. As Richard Bach says, *"Perspective—use it or lose it."*

The Issue

Contests or festivals in and of themselves are benign entities—they are neither good nor bad. Proponents of the contest experience speak of the many possible advantages which may come as a result of contest participation:

1. Maintenance of standards
2. Motivational device
3. School/community public relations
4. Esprit de corps
5. Expert feedback and advice regarding program accountability
6. Opportunity to see and hear other ensembles
7. "Fun" opportunities for band members.

Antagonists toward contests and festivals, who oft view them as "evil," stalwartly decry every aspect of the activity citing the following possible problems as a result of overemphasis on contest participation:

1. Reduction of the arts to an "athletic contest" mentality
2. A "tail" which currently wags the "dog"
3. Over-commitment of limited financial and time resources to this one end
4. Inexperienced, inadequate or inappropriate adjudication
5. "Burnout" of participants and teachers
6. Limited amount of literature learned or covered
7. Extreme/unnecessary pressure on band members and directors alike.

The Situation

There can be no doubt that there are possible advantages to contest participation and possible disadvantages as well. Whether we prefer it or not, contest and festival participation is an integral part of our band programs of today—a trend which goes back nearly seventy years at this juncture. Starting with the first band festivals of the 1920s and greatly increasing during the late 1950s and early 1960s, we reach today, where on a given Saturday in the fall there might be literally dozens of contests or festivals for high school marching bands in each state. Contests are a fact of life. Today, "success" (or a lack thereof) in contest or festival venues often defines a given band program and establishes or negates the credibility of the band directors or teachers of that program.

The Problem

Too often in our band rooms, the "W" word is used and used often, as in "We must *win* this weekend," or the "B" word is bandied about as in "We must *beat* the other six bands in our class this weekend." Modern society seems to mandate a dumbing down of our program goals and a moving to the lowest common denominator as we immerse ourselves and our bands in this "cutthroat" approach to the contest or festival experience. By definition, this puts our programs in harm's way—when we reduce the overall contest or festival experience to an assessment which is gauged in the pounds and numbers of trophies which we might—or might not—win.

The Solution

As the contest or festival itself is neither good nor evil, it is the way we shape the overall experience for our students which is the key. Participation in any contest or festival, no matter the outcome, may be a great success for our program and our band members if we take the time and effort to "style" and "keep in perspective" the total experience—which includes the "design phase," the "rehearsal phase" and the "performance phase." And from the outset, all members of the school community—students, parents, administrators—must be "onboard" with our overall goals and objectives.

It is we, the teacher and "trained" professional, who have it in our ability to shape the overall school and community's mind-set regarding contest and festival participation. The "W" word (win) must never be used, as, instead of it, we might end up having to use the "L" word (lose). The "B" word (beat) should be avoided at all costs, as another "B" word might come into our lives, as in "beaten."

We must use the contest or festival setting for the growth and improvement of our programs—never allowing our students and ourselves to be used by the system. We should strive to take advantage of the motivation, discipline, accountability and focus which participation in a contest might engender for our programs, without succumbing to the "win-lose" mentality. We must take a leadership role in our school communities, focusing on the great potential advantages which festival participation might foster for our students, while at the same time downplaying the "beat or get beaten" mind-set. We, our students and our programs, need to remind ourselves and be reminded that when honest effort, growth, progress and development are involved, there can be no "losers," only "winners."

No band is going to "win" at every contest if winning is based upon receiving a trophy for "best in class." However, every band can and may win if the performance is a little stronger this week than last, and the overall performance level of the band is a little stronger this year than last. No band is going to "beat" all other bands at every contest if beating is based upon receiving a trophy for "grand champion"; however, every band member can and may beat their performance of last week or last year. No director will achieve personal acclaim and satisfaction at every contest if this is based solely upon receiving a Superior or Distinguished rating, as our best teaching and personal growth might occur during the year when we have a younger band or are "stretching the troops" to a new level of performance and musical responsibilities. Again, "Perspective—use it or lose it."

The Goal

We should strive for excellence in all facets of life pertaining to our bands, remembering a judge's "snapshot" view of our band is necessarily limited. We should strive for musical growth with our programs, knowing that this is "why we draw a paycheck"—for our students and our programs to constantly improve. We should strive for and toward the ongoing learning and understanding of our school communities, helping them to know that though trophies and plaques are nice, of much greater import is the level and degree of participation which our programs represent, and that when our students find true joy, love and happiness with making music, everyone is a winner.

Is this idealistic? Probably. Does this represent some impossible, ivory-tower mind-set which neither can nor could work in a public school? Absolutely not!

When we as teachers shape the contest or festival experience in terms of growth and progress, instead of trophies and plaques, everyone can and will win, and Ma will always know that when her son, Paul, says, "We got a II at contest," it was a great day for everyone involved!

Peter LaRue is director of bands at Georgetown College in Georgetown, Kentucky, and musical director and conductor of the Central Kentucky Concert Band. This article originally appeared in the December 1999 issue of Kentucky's Bluegrass Music News. *Reprinted by permission.*

Helping Parents and Principals Understand Band Contests and Festivals

by Barbara P. McLain

*T*he busses are lined up amid the frantic scurrying of bright-eyed, noisy students and parents in matching t-shirts attempting to pack two tons of equipment and clothing into a space normally reserved for 45 small elementary children. Instruments, duffle bags and coolers now strewn over the sidewalk somehow magically find their place in the yellow caverns, and the school band is off again for an exciting festival. Where are they headed? What happens when they get there? What do they win?

The variety of competitions available to school bands, especially at the senior high level, can be a source of confusion for many parents and administrators. This article may serve as a good primer to help sort out the intricate aspects of this increasingly popular activity.

Looking Back

School band competitions began in the early part of this entry. The first national band contest was sponsored by music instrument manufacturers in 1923. Bands entered a competition in different classifications based on school enrollment. These performances were heard by judges who ranked the bands within each class from best to worst on one or more categories and presented cash awards, trophies, or medals to winners (Burdett, 1985).

From 1923–1932, criticism by school music teachers concerning the eligibility requirements, adjudication procedures, and an increasing emphasis on "winning" forced many changes in the contest format. The most notable of these was the elimination of ranked results found in "contests" in favor of a "festival" system of ratings in 1933. The new festival setting provided that bands within each classification could receive a performance rating of Division I (Superior) through Division V (Poor) providing for the possibility that all bands (or none) within each classification could get the highest (or lowest) award (Burdett, 1985). In most states, further refinements to the concert band festival led to the establishment of a sight-reading requirement to ensure that music teachers were not merely preparing students to play only a few pieces by rote, but were also teaching music-reading fundamentals. This separate sight-reading performance score was added to the concert performance score for a combined overall rating. Historically, bands had to perform a march of the director's choice, a required piece (performed by all bands in that class), and a piece to be selected from a designated list of acceptable and worthy compositions (Burdett, 1985).

The original one judge format was also eliminated in favor of a three or four judge format, three judges for concert performance and a separate judge for sight-reading performance. In addition, many of these early competitions had specific rules concerning the number of players required on each instrument which over the years have standardized the size and make-up of school bands (Burdett, 1985).

Although annual concert band and solo/ensemble festivals have maintained steady support from the music profession, enthusiasm for marching band competitions is a fairly recent phenomenon. This is due, in part, to the success of professional drum and bugle corps, called simply drum corps, who in the 1960s began organizing students ages 12–21 into marching clubs whose only purpose was to travel throughout the summer months competing in contests. These drum corps differed drastically from traditional school bands at the time in several ways. First, following the example of early military bands, they used no woodwind instruments, only brass and percussion. Second, they performed only one musical program and routine for an entire year. School bands before this were regularly preparing a different halftime musical program and drill maneuvers for each football performance. Drum corps, on the other hand, rehearsed throughout to perfect and fine-tune their performance to a level never before experienced by students. Finally, drum corps veered from the traditional high step foot motion in favor of a smoother, parade method called the glide step, enabling the performers to play more difficult music and to perform it while moving. This concept became attractive to school band directors who began adopting this format across the country. Today the corps style of marching is the predominant method used by school bands in the U.S., although most schools don't eliminate woodwind instruments.

What Happens When They Get There?

There are many variations around the country today in how music festivals and contests are organized in terms of format and eligibility requirements. Many states have opted to coordinate eligibility with current music publisher guidelines for music difficulty by using the term grade and a series of Roman numerals one through six, with grade one denoting the easiest music and grade six denoting the most difficult music. For example, if your school band enters a festival in grade III, they are most likely performing grade three music, comparable to the achievement of third year musicians. Other labeling systems are used sporadically and include coordinating music classifications by labels of "AAAA" through "D" based on school or band enrollment similar to athletic events, while others may opt to use labels such as "novice," advanced," or "open," etc.

Planning and managing a music contest can be an enormous challenge, as thousands of students and fans converge at a school or stadium. The primary sponsors of music festivals and competitions continue to be state music professional associations, such as affiliates of MENC: The National Association for Music Education, or state band directors' associations. These organizations administer concert, marching, and solo/ensemble festivals for their members only. If your director or school has not joined your state's association, your groups may not be eligible to participate in these events. Individual schools may also sponsor their own music festival or serve as the host site for a state controlled event. The benefits of hosting a music festival include:

1. Potential revenues from the sale of concessions, cassette or video recordings, programs and program advertising
2. The absence of travel costs for the host school
3. Public relations for the school
4. Control over format and evaluation procedures
5. Control over selection of judges
6. Service to the profession.

Although the benefits usually outweigh the difficulties in scheduling facilities, equipment, parking, and so on—hosting a festival requires that your band director have exceptional organization and communication skills along with tremendous support from parents and other school personnel. It will take massive planning and in excess of 20–30 volunteers to stage a large competition.

Private businesses have capitalized on the increased interest in music festivals by creating a variety of these opportunities, particularly at amusement parks and tourist attractions in the U.S. and abroad. These events offer school music groups the chance for a new audience, travel, different judges and a variety of evaluation formats from which to choose. Many private festivals offer the choice of rankings or ratings and also provide for multiple group entries from each school such as concert band, chorus, and jazz ensemble toward an "overall best program" award.

Marching Bands

Marching bands participate in two types of competitions, field show or parade. Many field show competitions often combine two evaluation formats by providing festival ratings while also offering ranked *caption* awards in various categories. For example, your band participates in another school's marching band invitational festival where they return with a superior rating and second place caption awards in general effect, drum majors, and percussion. This means that in their classification, their overall performance was judged to be the best expected, based on a predetermined standard of quality, and the bands were also ranked within each caption, resulting in your band being judged second best of those groups in these three areas. Judges may watch the groups from the press box or upper level of the bleachers or may actually move around the field with the band for a really close evaluation.

Parade competitions on the other hand, normally involve only one or two musical selections, often marches, performed while the band marches in block formation down a street or track. Judging is similar to that of field shows and takes place during the brief time the band is in view.

Marching band festivals have become increasingly popular in recent years, so much so that several states have had to limit the number of events in which a band may participate. The complexity of movements in corps style marching bands and the increasing popularity of competition requires more in-depth preparation, thus eliminating the opportunity for a school band to learn more than one show per year. This increased emphasis on marching band over concert band is a source of continued controversy among music teachers. In addition, corps style musical arrangements rely heavily on brass and percussion instruments and have created a rather undesirable imbalance in instrumentation (ratio of woodwinds to brass and percussion) in some schools due to this emphasis during the marching season.

Let's Hoist a Flag!

The adoption of the corps style of marching meant the addition of elaborate and detailed routines for colorguard (flags, rifles, dance, pom poms) and intricate skills for percussion instruments.

These groups often rehearse separately and then are combined with the large group of instrumentalists for the actual performance. Colorguard competitions provide a means for these units to continue working on their skills during the winter and spring months. The competitions are generally held in a gymnasium. The results may be listed as rating, but more often are ranked from best to worst.

Who's Got the Best Band?

As the annual "Battle of the Bands" goes on, parents and administrators may often wonder what the results of these events mean in terms of assessing their music program and student progress. Concert bands typically enter festivals in a specified class and must prepare three selections, a march and two numbers which are chosen from a list of required, or suitably difficult pieces for that level. These performances are evaluated in several categories such as tone, ensemble precision, musical expression, intonation, etc., by a panel of three judges. In most cases, following this performance, the students are escorted to a different room and following a brief study period, are asked to sight-read a new selection for a fourth judge.

The scores of the four judges are then combined to produce a final rating. The possible scores from best to worst are similar to: (a) Division I = Superior; (b) Division II = Excellent; (c) Division III = Average/Good; (d) Division IV = Fair; and (e) Division V = Poor. Unfortunately, judges today rarely if ever, confer ratings below Division III, which has resulted in an inflated evaluation system (Olsen, 1975).

The music profession has become dependent to some extent on the results of annual contests as an unwritten definition of success. Ratings below Division II are viewed by the music teacher as disastrous. This places a great deal of stress on the music teacher, whose professional image is at risk during this lone performance.

Three's Company

Individuals and small groups of musicians (duets, trios, etc.) may also have the opportunity to represent your school in a competition/festival. Solo and ensemble festivals require students to prepare one musical selection, usually taken from a list of acceptable pieces, and perform it. Students are then awarded individual medals, ribbons, or certificates based on their final rating in the class in which they entered. Because feedback is determined by only one judge, the results of this type of activity are often viewed with skepticism by music teachers and parents.

What Do the Trophies and Plaques Mean?

I recently overheard parents asking their son's music teacher, "How could the judges think we were a 'Superior' band last week but only a 'Good' band this week?" Unfortunately no national standards or operational guidelines exist for contests and festivals. Each state, professional organization, or private company has its own specific rules for festivals including establishing eligibility and evaluation criteria, training and/or selecting judges, required music lists, and other pertinent guidelines. Although many states have adopted similar formats for music festivals, there still exist wide differences in evaluation criteria, classifications and required music lists. The lack of uniformity in establishing the difficulty level of required music selections creates differing levels of achievement between festivals and is a continuing source of controversy among music teachers. For example, a particular piece of music might be included as Grade IV difficulty on one state's list while appearing on Grade III in another, possibly increasing the skills necessary for a superior performance in Grade III.

Another source of controversy involves the selection of festival judges who will evaluate each band's performance. The judging process is entirely subjective and relies on each judge's idea of what would make a "superior" performance, which could differ depending on the location and the judges for that event.

Band directors complain that although there are no winners or losers in each class, ratings may also hinge on the order in which you perform since the bands that perform first may set the standard for the remainder of that class. This factor makes some privately operated festivals more attractive because there are fewer entries in each classification, and the festival managers and judges may not know anything about your band, thus increasing the chance for success. (McManus, 1984)

For many years, band directors have been accused of teaching and preparing pieces for competition more thoroughly than they prepare their noncompetitive performances. Marching bands have been particularly sensitive to the amount of rehearsal time necessary for successful "corps-style" competition. Some bands' schedules required rehearsals three school nights per week, Friday football halftime performances, and travel

Band Competition Glossary

Captions: The specific criteria used to judge marching festivals and contests; may include (1) music, (2) general effect (G.E.), (3) marching and maneuvering (M & M), and/or individual components of the group such as percussion, colorguard (Silks, Flags, or Dance Team, rifles, twirlers, and drum major/field commanders).

Contest: A performance of soloists, small ensembles, or large groups similar to a festival but with feedback using a system of rankings from best to worst. A contest is designed for one band to compete specifically against other bands. Contests result in only one group receiving "first place," one group receiving "second place," etc., within each class or within all classes.

Drum corps: Taken from the military drum & bugle corps concept; a nonschool-related club of brass and percussion musicians, with colorguards, ages 12–21, who compete in D.C.I. (Drum Corps International) contests around the U.S. during the summer months.

Entry class: Determined by the total school enrollment, size of the group performing, difficulty level of the music to be performed, experience level of the group, or a sophisticated formula combining several of these. Some festivals offer the director no choice in which classification their school must enter while others allow the director to select a classification which represents the achievement level of the particular group.

Festival: A performance of soloists, small ensembles, or large groups where each participant pays a fee to the organizer of the event in order to receive feedback on the quality of that performance; feedback can be oral or written; participants are graded and/ or ranked by quality; trophies, ribbons, certificates, prizes, or medals may be awarded.

Field Show: A marching band performance of several musical selections which are choreographed with marching drills. They are called field shows because they take place on a football field and are often the performances which the band has presented during halftime at football games.

Adjudicator: A judge who is a knowledgeable expert in the field and will provide feedback on the performance through written or taped comments and assign a rating/ranking.

Ranking: Feedback used in contests, which is based on a comparison of performers; results in one 1st place winner, one 2nd place winner, etc.

Rating: Feedback used in festivals, which is based on a set standard quality such as Division I = Superior; Division II = Excellent; Division III =Good; results in the possibility that more than one performer can receive each level.

to competitions every Saturday for four to six weeks. This is generally in addition to a week long marching band camp in August to start the season. With increased demands on student free time, it is important that the band director, parents, and school administration discuss and agree on a unified philosophy on the time allocated to music rehearsals and competitions.

As with any competitive event, the benefits of music contests and festivals are determined to a great extent by how the results are interpreted. Music directors often feel isolated in their individual schools as they are often the only specialist in their area on the faculty. Effective and respected evaluation of their programs and their own abilities often requires outside input from other knowledgeable musicians. A main attraction of music festivals therefore, is the possibility of receiving feedback which will assist in setting future goals and objectives while determining if music personnel are successful in the eyes of fellow musicians. It is important that school administrators encourage their band directors to judge their success on a combination of factors and not merely on the feedback received at music festivals and contests. Also keep in mind that the attitude of the school music teacher is equally important to the success or failure of the music festival. A teacher whose group receives unfavorable ratings or criticism may be tempted to tell their students that the ratings were incorrect and blame the perceived failure on outside influences.

What Does It Cost?

Although most band programs have been forced to become self-supporting through parent and student fund-raising, participation in competitions and festivals requires substantial financial support for entry fees, additional staff, travel, equipment, uniforms, etc. The use of parent clubs for extensive fund-raising also creates a disparity in resources among school districts in what may otherwise be an equal population. It is not unusual for a large and active band program to budget $30,000 or more for a year's activities, while a similar school nearby operates with only $500 (Noble, 1984).

Music ensembles are a unique and valuable portion of the school curriculum. Festivals and competitions for these groups provide a means of motivation and feedback not readily accessible by other means. They offer golden opportunities for administrators to present an image of their school that reflects discipline and quality to a large audience. Beyond the complex skills, knowledge, self-discipline, and appreciation gained from participating in school bands, students also benefit from travel to festivals and the association with other students who share their interest in music and achievement. Once parents and administrators understand school music contests they should use every available means to privately and publicly congratulate their music teachers and students on their achievements where appropriate.

Notes

Burdett, N. (1985). The high school music contest movement in the United States (Doctoral Dissertation, Boston University). p. 18.

Olsen, W. (1975). Parade band adjudication. *The Instrumentalist, 29,* 82.

McManus, J. (1984). How much is too much: Oregon's guidelines for band performance. *Music Educators Journal, 71,* 28–33.

Noble, P. (1984). Choosing a festival. *The Instrumentalist, 39,* 32–33.

Barbara P. McLain is associate professor of music education and director of the Online Graduate Music Education program at the University of Hawaii at Manoa and serves as guest clinician and adjudicator. This article originally appeared in the November 1998 issue of Hawaii's Leka Nu Hou. *Reprinted by permission.*

Section 7

Marching and Pep Bands

Along with preparing the band for concerts each year, many directors must also balance their bands' obligations to support school athletic teams with marching and other pep bands. The articles in this section offer suggestions on developing and maintaining these performing groups.

 Section 7

Marching and Pep Bands

Maneuvering More Effectively
by Bert Creswell

As we begin another marching season, marching and maneuvering consumes a good deal of our time and thoughts. Although marching has been discussed many times in articles and videos, maneuvering has not had as much attention. Marching techniques can be taught on an individual level that allows each marcher to be responsible for his or her own performance. The marcher knows that he or she alone is responsible for getting his or her toes up, stepping off with the left foot, etc. When uniformity is emphasized as the reason to perfect the marching techniques, and if the marcher knows that uniformity is more appealing and impressive to the audience, then he or she cannot blame anyone else for not accomplishing these tasks. You won't hear Johnny blame Susie because he isn't stepping off with the correct foot or holding his horn at the correct angle. Johnny understands that these activities are his responsibility alone. Doing it right just because the director "says so" allows the marcher to put some of the blame for messing up on the director. If the marcher works for this reason alone, then, when he or she makes a mistake, it is not really important to fix it because it wasn't his or her decision to do it right in the first place. The real task is for directors to get the marchers to believe that they are responsible for marching the show correctly.

The emphasis changes when we have to move the band around the field from one set to another. When the goal is to keep the line straight or to keep the form together, the marcher is no longer working on individual tasks. The marcher is working in conjunction with many other people. This gives the marcher a chance to blame others when things do not go right. When a marcher is told that he or she made a mistake, and there is an opportunity to shift the blame to someone else,

many will. Now, combine this tendency with the idea that a marching unit is not assessed by all of the marchers, but by the one or two who are different from the rest. The person who is out of step or out of line is the one who is noticed. As long as there is a way for these few people to shift the blame for their mistakes to others, they will. They may not verbalize their attitude. They may only shrug their shoulders and do it wrong again because, after all, they are not the only ones out there. It can't be all their fault. The director runs into this brick wall over and over again.

Many times I have used the example of running into a door without opening it, then backing up and running into that same door again. Why wasn't there any change? Why didn't I open the door before I tried to go through? If they believe it is someone else's responsibility to open the door, they will wait for someone else to do it. The trick to getting someone to make a change is to make them believe that a change is needed and that they are the only ones who can make it.

I believe that all of the people who are in marching units are there because they want to be there, and that none of them wants to do a bad job. Something causes them to make the same mistake over and over. The marchers who make these mistakes are not always the same people every time. When we have many marchers who make one or two mistakes throughout the show, and they don't make changes, then we have a major problem. As long as we work with the concept of "getting in line," or "keep the line straight," there is the possibility of transferring blame to others. To get around this problem, I suggest the following three steps. They are simple and, more importantly, they put the responsibility on the individual, where it belongs.

First Step
Emphasize that the first step in each maneuver needs to be correct before anything else will

work. Have the marchers concentrate on the direction they will be going, how to get the lead foot going in that direction, and on which beat to begin the maneuver. Notice I said foot, not feet. We need to keep this as simple as possible. Most marchers will have no trouble handling this idea, but they are not the ones that are causing the problem. We generally spend 95 percent of the time going over things because 5 percent of the people are having trouble. If we can adapt our directions at the beginning of the process for that 5 percent, then we can save a lot of aggravation. Once everyone has the first step under control, the rest of the steps will follow more easily.

You can rehearse one step more easily and quickly than the whole maneuver. You can identify and correct the mistake immediately, rather than waiting until the whole maneuver is finished and you have spent a lot more time than was needed. Go over the first step, checking size and direction, and then finish the maneuver when everyone is doing it correctly. If this procedure is emphasized in the beginning and required throughout the learning of the show, the whole show will come together much more quickly and it will be much cleaner. When working on fundamentals with your band, you can have the whole group take just one step forward a few times to practice this concept. This is also the time to work on the timing of the step by everyone making their lead foot hit the ground at the same time.

Equal Steps

Instead of telling the marchers to stay in line while moving, emphasize that each marcher takes equal-size steps between sets. If it is a sixteen step maneuver between sets, ask them to take sixteen equal steps. Do not worry about staying in line at this time. Two things happen. The responsibility is on the individual to perform the maneuver correctly, not a group of people. Straight correct lines will result from the procedure. For example, if the maneuver is a straight diagonal line moving to a straight line on a yard line in sixteen counts, everyone will have a different size step to take. This creates individual responsibility, and as long as each step is one-sixteenth of the total distance

for each marcher, the line will stay straight during the maneuver. The line will gradually change from a diagonal line to a perpendicular line, and all the marchers will arrive at the same time. If someone is ahead of the rest of the marchers, then you tell them they took too large of a step. This is something the marcher can comprehend and correct. Telling them that they were out of line is too vague. We need to remember to tell the marchers the reason we want the lines straight is that it is more appealing and impressive to the audience. During the fundamental practice have the group move up and down the field in straight lines, taking different number of steps between yard lines to get them used to different size "equal" steps.

Correct Path

Before any of this will work, the marchers must follow the "correct path." Most maneuvers require a straight path between sets to be effective. Some maneuvers require the marchers to maintain an equal interval between them and their neighbors during the maneuver. This type of move may require a curved path. If this is the case, then the marcher needs to be instructed specifically so that he or she will know exactly what is expected of them before they begin the maneuver. Another aspect of these maneuvers is that the marchers will need to stay equally between their neighbors.

By emphasizing first step, equal steps, and correct path most of the maneuvering problems will be eliminated. Again, the main reason for using these techniques is to place the responsibility for the execution of the maneuvers on the individual performers. This also gives us a procedure to identify more specifically where our maneuvering problems are. Once we as directors can identify the mistakes and get the marchers to understand them, then and only then can we set about correcting them.

Bert Creswell is director of bands at Orange Park High School in Orange Park, Florida. This article originally appeared in the May 1996 issue of Florida Music Educator. *Reprinted by permission.*

Stump the Jock (a title suggested by our readers)

by Leo Dodd

Question: *Some band members, especially seniors, are expressing frustration at playing for so many ball games, especially since athletes, coaches, and administrators don't show support for music events. Administrators receive calls/complaints when the band is not at a game or does not stay for an entire game. They often ask the band kids why the band wasn't there. I don't want to do the A/B band and double the number of games I do just to pacify the jocks. Has anyone come up with a fair way (to band members) to provide decent instrumentation while not requiring all the band members or the director to be at every game?*

Lesley Moffat, Band Director
Lynnwood High School
Edmonds School District, Washington

Answer: This problem is one that seems to be very prevalent, especially with the rise in popularity of women's sports in the interscholastic activities program. I am not sure there is a concrete solution that will satisfy everyone, but I believe there are things that can be done to help ease the problem. Obviously, the underlying problem involves the different ways that administration, coaches, and directors view the role of the high school band in the activity program. If you have coaches and administrators who believe the primary function of the band program is to act as a service organization for the glorification of the athletic program, you certainly have a problem which needs to be dealt with immediately. The following general suggestions might be helpful in laying groundwork for a system within which everyone can operate.

1. In cooperation with district administration, establish reasonable curricular and extra-curricular expectations for the high school band programs in your school district. (Make use of available information from MENC, WMEA and other school districts who have already established standards.)
2. Use your talents as a conciliator to maintain good relations with coaches and administrators, rather than fostering an "us against them" attitude. Communicate with them and let them be aware of what reasonable expectations are and why.
3. Be positive and sell your program! Work for excellence and do the things that make the band program a positive force in your school. If your program is respected by staff, students, and administration, they will listen to you.
4. Present extracurricular expectations for the band program (preferably arrived at through district negotiations) to coaches and administration and let them be involved in how they are administered. Give them options.
5. Give your band students choices in how they will meet their extracurricular responsibilities. Be fair but flexible and encourage participation.
6. Be willing to meet your own responsibilities as a high school band director. These include outside activities as an integral part of your total program, and you should deal with these in an accepting and positive manner.
7. Sell your students on the importance of band participation in the extracurricular program. Although it should not be viewed as their primary function, it can build a positive image of the band program in your school, build an esprit de corps in the group, and give them a real sense of belonging to something important.

In the Bellevue School District, the first thing we did as a music staff was to establish district-wide expectations (in conjunction with district administration) for extracurricular activities for the high school bands. When this is presented to coaches and principals as district policy, you will find a much higher level of acceptance. In our district, part of these expectations included playing for a maximum of ten games during the winter sports season. We asked the coaches to pick the ten events. This usually ended up being five boys' and five girls' basketball games. We then asked them to select the specific games for which we would play. We excluded games during winter and spring breaks.

At Interlake High School, each band student was responsible for playing for at least five games. (The required number of games would vary by school depending on instrumentation and total number of students in the band program.) The students could pick the games they preferred. We posted sign-up sheets for all ten games with available slots based on proper instrumentation. Usually a number of students will elect to play for more than the minimum number of games. Extra credit was given for this. Students were even allowed to switch an assignment with someone else if a conflict arose.

As band director, I attended all ten games,

although we used student directors on a regular basis. This was a great experience for the students.

Although the system was not foolproof, it worked quite effectively and really allowed the students flexibility in meeting their responsibilities.

Some schools used a select, basketball pep band to play all assigned games. This is a great idea if you can come up with acceptable instrumentation. Bruce Gutgesell at Juanita High School uses this system very effectively.

Remember, it takes work, planning, and dedication to make a system like this work. It won't be easy to change established attitudes, but with perseverance and commitment on your part, it can be done. Good luck!

Leo Dodd, retired
Interlake High School Band Director and
Bellevue Community College

Leo Dodd is a retired band director from Interlake High School and Bellevue Community College in Bellevue, Washington. This article originally appeared in the January 1997 issue of Washington's Voice. Reprinted by permission.

Developing the Marching Band Sound
by Frank Hale

As band directors, we deal with not only the many aspects of teaching, but also those of shaping sound. This article is an excerpt from a soon-to-be published book entitled *Developing The Marching Band Sound*. It represents an expression of my philosophy and techniques that are the result of my training and experiences over the last thirty-odd years.

As with any art form, there is no "one way" to achieve results, and there are few absolutes. But there are some fundamentals that are absolute, such as intonation and precision. Two tones are either in tune, or they are not. Similarly, sounds are either lined up vertically or horizontally in time, or they are not.

There are certainly many directors that have achieved the same, different, or better results than I. This is just simply the way I have done it.

The Mental Concert

A sculptor was once asked, "How do you sculpt the image of an elephant?" He replied, "I just chip away everything that doesn't look like an elephant." This, of course, is a very simplified way of describing the creation process in sculpting, but it is also very accurate. The sculptor has a mental image of his subject and his mind, through much practice, compels him to reproduce that image in his medium.

We, as musicians, follow somewhat the same process when we produce music. We have the sound in mind that we want to produce. Through much practice, we then reproduce that sound through our instrument. If we detect that some characteristic of the sound we produce is not in sync with our aural image, we then work toward refining that sound by "chipping away" that element until we arrive at the desired sound.

It is essential that we do have a "sound image" in our minds in order to produce one that is not "by chance." Otherwise, our resulting sound is chance in characteristic and is inconsistent with each sounding.

How do we develop this "sound concept"? Mostly it is related to our experiences in hearing music over a prolonged period of time, our teacher's sound, our degree of exposure to others with characteristically consistent sounds, and our endeavors to make a conscious effort to craft a sound.

We, as band directors, must also have this "aural concept" of how we want our band to sound, in our "mind's ear," just as performing instrumentalists do.

Unfortunately, many band directors do not have a committed aural image of how they want their band to sound. Therefore, the sound of their band is purely chance and is inconsistent with time and is at the mercy of many other factors. It is also unfortunate that some band directors have a distorted "aural image" and are clearly on the wrong track when it comes to "Band Sound." This does not imply that there is only one acceptable "Band Sound." However, there are fundamental characteristics that are consistent with time and diverse situations.

It is important that we know what these fundamental characteristics are in order to craft our own personal "Band Sound." It is also important to realize that the fine adjustments of these characteristics will determine your own personal "Band Sound." Nevertheless, these characteristics include:

1. A strong and well-supported bass sound
2. A woodwind sound that can be heard even when the full band is playing loudly

Do you have an "aural image" of how you want to sound?

3. A clear presence of all voices of a chord
4. A clear presence of soprano, alto, tenor, and bass voices
5. A percussion sound that enhances without dominating
6. Clear and undistorted brass tone
7. Resonant, and not shrill, woodwind tone
8. Careful attention to intonation for optimum projection
9. An unpinched high register trumpet tone
10. A strong, consistent, fundamental beat and pulse at all volumes and tempos
11. A clear separated style of note spacing for greater definition of rhythms in most situations, except for legato
12. A sensitivity of percussion to wind balance in all situations of field placement and drum head direction
13. A unified accent (or note stress) throughout the full twister of sound
14. Careful attention of pyramid sculpting, not only in sound balance, but also note length (articulation and sound spacing)
15. A use of varied volume levels: Not all loud, and not just loud and soft, but varied, graduated volume levels
16. An overall sound that is clear, balanced, and projecting at all volume levels.

These fundamentals of characteristic "Band Sound" are but "words on a page" until studied, practiced, and understood. It is very important that the band director hear many different bands, not only early in his or her career, but constantly every year until retirement. If a director is careful to analyze why a particular band sounds as it does, that director is then training his or her ear to recreate his or her own sound with that particular group.

Many times, the groups that we hear early in our careers form the basics of the aural image that we have of "Band Sound." If we are fortunate to be in settings where we have the opportunity to hear fine, mature bands, then our aural image of "Band Sound" gets off "on the right foot." Unfortunately, when we are young we do not always know what is characteristic or good when it comes to "Band Sound," and our aural image is in many instances formed by chance circumstances.

I have witnessed numerous instances in which band directors that have had heavy exposure to drum and bugle corps early in their training and career have developed a fondness and sometimes subconscious inclination toward this type of sound.

I would like to again stress that I do not object to how drum and bugle corps should sound, but I feel that this sound clearly should not be emulated by marching bands. Do brass bands try to consistently sound like concert bands? Symphony orchestras like string orchestras? Brass quartets like string quartets? Each of these groups clearly has its own characteristic sound that remains intact even though they emulate a particular nuance of another group in an isolated situation.

It is just that the overall flair and appeal of the drum and bugle corps woos many young, fertile minds to be so captivated with the overall concept that they feel that they must emulate that sound someday with their band. For this reason, it is imperative that university music education departments use mature guidance in this matter.

Developing a mature and fundamentally sound marching "Band Sound" requires both knowing what you want and also knowing an effective process to achieve this goal. You must first know *where* you want to go and then determine how you are going to get there. If you don't have a mental concept of the sound you want, knowing good teaching techniques will only help you achieve the status of a "wandering generality." You can get into a car with a good set of road maps, but if you have no destination in mind, you will be traveling to nowhere.

If you have a clear mental concept of what you want and possess a sincere dedication toward achieving that goal, the chances are great that you will find a way to achieve that result. Techniques are important, but goals are primary.

If you are in the beginning or early years of your career, I would like to encourage you to listen to and analyze as many fine bands as possible regionally, nationally, and internationally in order to develop your mental concept. If you are a veteran director, I would also like to encourage you to do the same, not only in order to maintain your mental concept, but also to further reinforce and refine that image.

"Band Sound" can be a "beautiful thing." Keep that beauty in mind and never be satisfied until you achieve that sound.

Frank Hale, who is a retired band director from Hixson High School in Chattanooga, Tennessee, is founder and conductor of the Chattanooga Concert Band and serves as executive director of the Tennessee MEA. This article originally appeared in the May 1997 issue of The Tennessee Musician. *Reprinted by permission.*

No-Brainer Checklist for Marching Band

by Wayne Pegram

Each year I judge a good variety of marching competitions. These include state contests from South Carolina all the way west to Nevada and from Ohio all the way south to Louisiana. These high-profile events are balanced with a few, less intense regional events. This helps me stay familiar with what bands are presenting in their marching shows. I am sometimes amazed at the flaws in shows which remain unnoticed. Many times these flaws involve units or specialty personnel which typically are not the primary focus for most directors. I am very well aware of what an awesome task it is just to get a show written and on the field. Consequently, it is no wonder that as the creator and teacher of the show you cannot view it from the objective perspective of someone who has not been involved with the process. Here is a list of things to notice and correct in order to avoid some potential pitfalls.

Percussion

1. Multiple Bass Drums that play the same part (usually the beat).
2. Bass Drums (or all percussion) that continually have their instruments projecting sound directly into the audience, regardless of the direction that the winds are facing.
3. Constantly using the "crab step" (an apt term if I've ever heard one) even when it would be more logical to turn and move like a normal person. About ninety percent of those who attempt this step look like they're trying to mount a prostrate camel anyhow.
4. Predominately playing only one dynamic level (typically loud!).
5. Pit equipment that is so extensive that it takes ten minutes to set it up, to say nothing of tearing down (another very apt term), and moving out. I sometimes think percussion equipment manufacturers are the perpetrators of using all the "stuff" that clutters the sidelines. I fondly recall the days when everything was mobile and

gimmicks were limited to cute tricks, rather than bizarre or exotic sounds.

Guard

1. Awkward or impossible equipment changes. These changes interrupt the continuity of the total show, often by lengthy segues, and even after the new equipment is in hand, one cannot help but wonder "what for"? As was mentioned with percussion, I think all this equipment use has been perpetrated by the manufacturers. There are also frequently non-uniformed people running all over the field and taking attention away from the real performers!
2. Feeling like they have to do some routine to every single count of the music, even when in transition.
3. Being so far out of the picture that they really are "out of the picture."

Field Conductors (a more accurate term than "Drum Major")

1. Multiple field conductors for small- or medium-sized bands. Where there are multiple conductors, they typically look at each other instead of the people they are supposed to be conducting anyhow. A forty-member group with multiple conductors looks pretty absurd in my humble opinion.
2. Lengthy segues between musical selections just so field conductors can climb down or mount their towers. These are made even more lengthy when the previously mentioned situation exists, and one conductor has to climb down, followed by the other climbing up. One of our local bands doesn't even use a field conductor, and their sound is much more cohesive than most of the groups that use multiple conductors (granted that they are of moderate size).

Wayne Pegram is professor of music and coordinator of music education at Tennessee Technological University in Cookeville. This article originally appeared in the March 1998 issue of The Tennessee Musician. *Reprinted by permission.*

Section 8

 # Promoting the Music Program

Articles in this section explore outreach efforts for involving the community with the school band program. Strategies for gaining public support for music programs are also presented.

Section 8

Promoting the Music Program

The Band Buddy Program
by Ann Goodwin

Take a minute and think! What is it about music that is essential to your musical being? Is there someone in your life that took the time and energy to make music special for you? What musical events do you remember vividly? Why? Most times as musicians, we remember the good times and the bad. Someone told me once that if music actually makes cold chills go up your spine, it is either very bad or very good. As educators we have the ability to send cold chills down the spines of our students. How would you like their musical experience to be remembered?

Most all musicians are "noted" for their creative ability. We are the "Thinkers" and "Doers." Sometimes it takes extra effort to set programs in place, but if we think it is a good idea we disregard initial hesitations and take the "plunge!"

Four years ago, two musical groups took such a plunge. The goals were simple … to connect two or more generations through *music*. This is the way music has been shared throughout centuries. Music connects people to people and bridges diverse cultures, socioeconomic backgrounds, and generation gaps. We believe that music is meant to be shared. Through sharing, *Band Buddies* was born.

Band Buddies, now in its fifth year, is a mentoring program started by The North Star Community Band and the Volker 5th Grade Concert Band. Band Buddies are assigned according to instrumentation. Adults from the community band are chosen to mentor students who play like instruments (flute to flute, etc.). When this is not possible, we simply assign a buddy. Buddies are required to write to their partners once a week (this helps students write friendly letters), learn a formal introduction (at the "get acquainted pizza party," proper manners dictate that introductions are made), and participate in a rehearsal and concert

(we combined 115 musicians at our first rehearsal!).

The result? Cold introductory letters soon turn into letters about school, hobbies, pets, favorite foods, instruments, jobs, encouraging words, and a few comments about the director … which is when I realize that I am no longer in control! Humor and a love of the *art of music* is essential! Students and adults alike wait impatiently for Band Buddy letters. Treats are boundless. There are faxes, stickers, pencils, note pads, creative technology in the form of cards, posters, book marks, etc. Smiles become the norm for band day. Letters come in at a rate that would make the U.S. Postal Service jealous!

Band Buddies share a sense of unity and purpose. In this way, musicianship is realized and validated. Students and adults alike are motivated to higher learning. Self-esteem increases as students realize that other people really care about them and about their music education. Many students show improved classroom performance and a better attitude about being in school. Parents become more interactive in their children's education. Both local and school communities benefit from the combined efforts and outreach. In my opinion, the results are spectacular!

Buddy systems can be created in many areas; choir to choir, band to band, band to orchestra, community to school. High school students could buddy up with middle school students. Fourth-year players could buddy up with first-year players. How about an e-mail buddy with schools that are networked? The possibilities are endless. Customize your own Buddy program? Take the Plunge! Be prepared for cold chills and dynamite results!!!

Ann Goodwin is director of bands at Park Hill High School in Kansas City, Missouri. This is an excerpt from an article that originally appeared in the Fall 1998 issue of Missouri School Music. *Reprinted with permission.*

Music for a Lifetime: The Elementary Community Band

by Sallie Horner

It was wonderful! Not only did I brush off an old instrument and relive some aspects of my youth, but my son saw that music can be a life-long skill and you're never too old to learn or re-learn!" (Parent of a Rockburn Elementary student).

For four years, the staff, parents, grandparents and older brothers and sisters of the students at Rockburn Elementary School have been joining the band and orchestra. As a result, the Rockburn program features not just a school band but an elementary community band.

During the months of February and March, music teacher Denise Perry sends a questionnaire out to families to assess interest in becoming a part of the spring concert by performing two or three pieces with the advanced band or orchestra. The form assures the respondents that they will be provided with a cassette tape of the music and a copy of the songs to practice, along with the assurance that the music will be easy enough to be prepared in time. The responses vary from, "I am interested in helping with the rehearsal refreshments," to "I am interested in finding out more information (but just thinking about it makes me nervous!)." Those who are interested indicate what instrument they have played and for how many years. There's also a place on the form to indicate that they would need to borrow an instrument to practice and perform in the concert. This past spring, 19 community members joined the band and offered comments like, "This kind of involvement in the community is very important because the people in the community feel like 'insiders' not 'outsiders' and develop an affection for and understanding of the school and faculty."

The idea of an "intergenerational" approach to elementary band began to take shape in her thinking during a graduate class Denise was taking on Trends in Music Education. She also knew someone who included alumni on one particular number in their final concert of each year. These experiences combined with her belief in music for a lifetime and the idea of all those instruments sitting in closets collecting dust brought her to the point of designing a plan to make her instrumental program a community experience.

Five years ago, she first implemented the idea at Worthington Elementary School in Howard County. After receiving comments like, "It keeps people of different ages 'tuned' to each other," she decided to continue with the approach when she transferred to Rockburn Elementary.

Now the ensembles in her spring concert at Rockburn nearly double when the community joins in. Denise says it's really nice to hear the inner and bass parts supported by the adult performers.

In terms of organization, the most difficult task is laying out a rehearsal schedule. In her second contact with homes, Denise collects possible rehearsal times from those who want to participate. Then she lays out possible rehearsal dates for the whole community group that include two evening rehearsals. As a bit of incentive, elementary students who come to evening rehearsals receive a certificate for a twenty-five-cent treat in the cafeteria and also share refreshments after the rehearsal. A schedule of daytime band and orchestra classes is included in the information that goes out to those who responded to the questionnaire, and adults who are free during the day are encouraged to attend rehearsals during regular class times as well.

For instruction, Denise has sequence practice tapes of the material to be learned and includes them with the music she sends home. Occasionally a fingering chart is needed as well. It has proven to be a great boon to student practice time to share the adventure with a parent. "My son and I had something in common! The preteen and teen years are such a transitional time in the child-parent relationship. We really bonded during practice time." And the words of encouragement that pass between family members helps the process along. In evening rehearsals, it's not unusual to hear students tell their parents, "Wow! You did a great job!"

One of the obstacles to be overcome was the need to borrow instruments. Often instruments have been loaned from the teacher's own collection. However, Music and Arts Center, a local music store, has made instruments available without charge for practice and for the performance by community members who want to join the program. One mom who has played in the concerts for three years used her participation to justify buying the wood clarinet she had always wanted. Her children will be in the school for several more years so she knew she would be playing the instrument for years to come.

Each program includes performance of two or three pieces by the community groups at about a grade 1 1/2 or 2 level. One selection is more sustained and difficult but the ending piece is always "jazzy," with the musicians wearing sunglasses for effect. Each program is also followed by special thank-you notes to each member of the community who joined in the event.

Benefits of the elementary community band and orchestra are far reaching. Denise says, "Performing next to Dad or Mom provides a lasting memory and makes the joy of making music that much more personal and rewarding. I've seen it light a fire under some students that previously were just not motivated to do their best." Some parents have indicated that there are not many activities that both parent and child can share—especially mother and son—and they really appreciate this opportunity.

Last year, there were three generations of one family in the orchestra. The grandparents reported, "We were pleased to be asked and our grandchildren were *thrilled!*" Participation also seems to forecast growth in the program. Parents of first graders who are too young to play are volunteering to join the band, looking forward to the day when their student will play beside them. Having a wide variety of ages and occupations also shows students that you don't have to become a profes-

sional musician to keep playing throughout your lifetime. Seeing real people of all ages enjoying making music is valuable to students and adults alike. In addition, adults feel that they are an important part of the program and the audience really enjoys seeing their friends up onstage performing. One parent wrote this comment about the program: "Any time we have multi-generational groups and strengthen the bonds, we strengthen our families, communities and our nation. These experiences help us all to understand and respect each others' interests and abilities. This, we think, is an important part of the socialization of our children."

The elementary community band is an effort that makes the music program very real, visible and valuable to the community.

Sallie Horner teaches vocal/general music in Anne Arundel County, Maryland, and continues music involvement with people of all ages through a large retirement community in the Baltimore area. This article originally appeared in the November/December 1999 issue of the Maryland Music Educator. *Reprinted by permission.*

A POPular Concert
Stephen McGrew

Looking for a different concert concept? Try a Pops Concert in the style of the Boston Pops.

About 25 years ago, in my third year of teaching, I struggled with the dilemma of how to get non-concert goers to attend band concerts. The idea of a Pops Concert in a relaxed setting was intriguing. It would be an extravaganza. Students would take an active role in planning and implementing the event. Both the music and the setting would be more informal than regular season winter and midwinter concerts. Perhaps those who thought of band concerts as stuffy or boring would attend a Pops Concert. This was the rationale.

The experiment resulted in an annual affair now into its 26th year.

The Plan
The first order of business was to find a site. Something less formal than an auditorium was in order. We decided, with the cooperation of the athletic director, to try the gymnasium. Although

an acoustical nightmare, the spaciousness of a 9,000 seat gym was desirable to accommodate our format of patrons seated at tables of 10. Also, the large performance area provided space for other special musical presentations such as dance, vocal, scenes, guest ensembles. Scenery made up of flats, donated greenery, or other objects germane to the theme of the evening can be used in such a large area. One year our theme was "Concert in the Park." The fire department loaned us an antique horse-drawn fire engine for period setting—the turn of the century.

Once the site was determined, logistics came into play. Band location in a gymnasium is critical to the musicality of a performance. We found in a large, rectangular room that bands sound better positioned in a corner rather than on a side. For our most recent concert, we placed each of two concert bands in a corner, and the jazz band in a third corner. In addition to the interest of having music come from every conceivable nook and cranny of the gym, the acoustics were not all that bad for a large barn that was built for roundball.

Tables that seat 10 persons are arranged on the perimeter of the playing floor. A built-up stage

(32" by 12," made up of risers 18" high) is placed on the end of the floor between the two concert bands.

Lighting is accomplished with stand lights for the bands, two to four *follow* spots for dance numbers, and battery-powered candles for the tables. With all lights in the gym switched off, the effect is stunning.

The Pops program will necessarily have a good pace and plenty of variety. Dead spots are death for the new concertgoer. The concert is, of course, built around good music, albeit of a "pop" nature. Also included are cameo appearances by favorite "good spot" faculty members, skits, and guest soloists and ensembles. We once featured good friend Linda Baker, clarinetist with the Chicago Lyric Opera Orchestra, playing the Weber Concertino on bass clarinet. Schools in a metro area would have no trouble rounding up guest soloists or small ensembles.

In our gymnasium venue, we also offer refreshments and provide waiters and waitresses so that the audience does not have to stand in line or leave their seats. Middle school band students love to participate by waiting tables. They also get a firsthand look at what is in store for them in a

year or two. Band parents are also invaluable in helping coordinate and supervise the concession details.

In 26 years of Pops Concerts, we have reached a significant number of people who would normally have not heard our bands except on a parade or at a sporting event. Possibly some of those folks subsequently attended our more formal concerts in the auditorium. If so, our original rationale proves valid.

The Pops Concert also allows us to present good quality music, both dated and current. We can show that some pop music can be entertaining without being angry or violent.

Although a huge undertaking, the possibility for audience building and program sustenance make it clearly an option to consider when planning future concert sessions.

Stephen McGrew is director of bands at Seymour High School in Seymour, Indiana, and is currently editor of the Band Stand column of the Indiana Musicator. *This article originally appeared in the September 1995 issue of the* Indiana Musicator. *Reprinted by permission.*

Other MENC Band Resources

Balance and Pitch in a Band Performance (video) featuring W. Francis McBeth. 1992. VHS. 35 minutes. #3080.

Getting Started with Elementary-Level Band by Marjorie R. Lehr. 1998. 56 pages. #1636.

Getting Started with High School Band by David S. Zerull. 1994. 52 pages. #1627.

Getting Started with Middle Level Band by David G. Reul. 1994. 72 pages. #1631.

Guidelines for Performances of School Music Groups: Expectations and Limitations prepared by the MENC Committee on Standards. 1986. 44 pages. #1016.

Instructional Literature for Middle-Level Band by Edward J. Kvet. 1996. 80 pages. #1641.

Musicality in a Band Performance (video) featuring Vaclav Nelhybel. 1992. VHS. 16 minutes. #3079.

Strategies for Teaching Beginning and Intermediate Band compiled and edited by Edward J. Kvet and Janet M. Tweed. 1996. 80 pages. #1650.

Strategies for Teaching High School Band compiled and edited by Edward J. Kvet and John E. Williamson. 1998. 72 pages. #1651.

Teaching Wind and Percussion Instruments: A Course of Study developed by the MENC Task Force on Band Course of Study. 1991. 72 pages. #1603.

For complete ordering information on these and other publications, contact:

MENC Publications Sales
1806 Robert Fulton Drive
Reston, VA 20191-4348

Credit card holders may call 1-800-828-0229.